THE
MIND
OF THE
SPIRIT

To Jennifer
God Bless!
Twila Wall
07/12/2020

THE MIND OF THE SPIRIT

TWILA WILLIAMS

TATE PUBLISHING & ENTERPRISES

Published by Tate Publishing & Enterprises, LLC
127 E. Trade Center Terrace | Mustang, Oklahoma 73064 USA
1.888.361.9473 | www.tatepublishing.com

Tate Publishing is committed to excellence in the publishing industry. The company reflects the philosophy established by the founders, based on Psalm 68:11,
"The Lord gave the word and great was the company of those who published it."

Book design copyright © 2010 by Tate Publishing, LLC. All rights reserved.
Cover design by Tyler Evans
Interior design by Nathan Harmony

Published in the United States of America
ISBN: 978-1-61566-775-8
Religion: Christian Life: Personal Growth
14.05.13

Acknowledgment

I would like to first give honor to my Lord and Savior Jesus Christ the Messiah and for redeeming my life back to the Father and for giving me the gift of the Holy Spirit. It amazes me to see how the Holy Spirit has counseled me through the gift of writing. I can't thank him enough, but I want to take a moment to say, "Lord, I worship, honor and praise your holy name, for without you this book and all that I am would not hold the power of your substance. You make known to me the path of life, in your presence, there is fullness of joy; at your right hand are pleasures forever more." (Ps. 16:11)

To Tate Publishing & Enterprises, LLC: Stacy Baker, your gift will lead many writers to behold the dream they so desire to fulfill. Thank you for understanding my financial situation and for believing in me, trusting I would hold to my integrity. I also extend a special thanks to Jenn Scott for reading and rereading my manuscript and for your careful time and effort to speak the truth I appreciate your heart felt words, for all your suggestions I did not take them lightly.

To my children: Alishia, Howard, Dwayne, and Isaiah, also my god-daughter, Jihan, without you all encouraging me saying,

"Mommy you have been editing your book it seems like forever, when are you going to get it published?" And at times when I would be working on my book day and night, "One of you would often bring me tea, water, prepared food and whatever I needed around the clock, you all have been the most wonderful children any mother could ever pray and asked the Lord for, thank you from all my heart!" I love you all and pray your dreams, gifts, and talents to achieve all in which our heavenly father have called you into existence for; will be the light in which you walk in for the rest of your days. Never forget to live and love the Lord with all your heart, mind and soul.

To Mr. Larry Donnell Diggs Sr., I love you so much! You are a wonderful man of valor who the Holy Spirit used to counsel me when I had given up on myself. You were there morning, noon, and night, praying me through, comforting me with words of wisdom, knowledge, and directions from above. May God's favor and blessings, with all the miracles He has given to you before the foundation of the earth be poured out upon your life above and beyond what you are able to ask for or even think. I pray for Jesus Christ the Messiah, healing virtue of deliverance to swiftly come upon you and set you free for his glory and for every unspoken prayer request in private you have personally prayed for in your heart to be yours for the asking in the precious name of Jesus Christ the Messiah the only Yahweh! In Jesus name. Amen

To the Reader

This book is written for all who desire to know the truth and can't seem to get a grip on sound doctrine. If you are a new believer in Christ, you will be blessed and your life will be enriched as you learn from one of the simple ways that the Holy Spirit leads one to teach practical skills for ordinary people. I believe after you finish reading *The Mind of the Spirit* you will never be the same again. Reading a book that is based on the Word of God should be simple enough for a child to understand and it has been a blessing to write with practicality for ordinary people which involves an ear to hear what the Spirit is saying to the church. This book will help those who are new to the faith and those who seemed to have lost their way. Also, to those who have been engulfed with the deepest pains of being tricked, conned, and lied to about who they are in Christ, there is much to say to you too. To the atheists, skeptics, and those who have abandoned the truth. To many who disregard or ignore the fact that God is real and at one time in their life desired him, to come into their lives and make his abode, God is calling you to repent and hear his voice. To those who have an emptiness and void in their lives that only God can fill, get ready for the truth to be unveiled like never before.

If your desire is to know God in a deeper way, my desire is to enrich your mind with a practical book by teaching through the Holy Spirit wisdom and knowledge and that through understanding the Word of God will bring the counsel of God to you in a simple way.

To those who never had the opportunity to live in a Christian home. To those who were not brought up with any teaching of who God is through his Word. For those who lived in an environment where the parent(s) or caretaker used the Bible as a weapon of manipulation and control to cause them to never want to hear or go to a church again because of the distortion they experienced as a child and have somewhat hardened their hearts and have become numb to the truth. To all those who have been abused in their pasts, may be in an abusive situation now, and to those who did not have a nurturing mother to protect them but went to church every Sunday, or maybe you had a father that abandoned you because he was not willing to be responsible for you or your other siblings that desired their daddy's love.

This book is also for the husband who lost his wife to a terminal illness and struggled to raise the children alone, or maybe the man whose wife was a drug addict, alcoholic, or a prostitute, and she had a past that he tried to ignore, thinking marriage would make her a good wife. To these many men, I will say, "I dedicate this book to you because even now you may be in search of love but can't seem to get over your past and even now women have taken your kindness for weakness. This book will help heal you where you are wounded because you give your love to the wrong women who seem to have the nature of the Jezebel spirit. Therefore, you have baggage, and even if God sent you someone that was appropriate for your needs, you have a strong tendency to interrogate her to the point of driving her away."

Also, for the women who has been broken, hurt, lied to, misused, and despised through her childhood and into their adult life. This book is for the child molester who was abused himself or herself, for those who have allowed bitterness to set into their hearts through past experiences that damaged their capability to believe in love because they have felt so much pain and never had a chance to see good because evil, horrible things have caused an interruption in their lives to where they don't believe anything good could ever come their way. Things are about to change, and life does get better as you journey with me, taking a deeper look into *The Mind of the Spirit*. Some can't even talk about what happened to them at such a young age for shame, embarrassment, and distrust of people. I want to unveil to you *The Mind of the Spirit* in such a way that your life will never, ever be the same. We will walk on a journey together to uncover what the enemy has blinded many minds to concerning the truth of the Word of God. Even though the enemy has tried to succeed in concealing the Spirit of the Lord from many by using his cunning character to blind many people, God is calling you to live free from anger, doubt, fear, and sleepless nights due to hidden secrets that torment your mind. Down on the inside of your heart in which you may cover with the lies you have been deceived into believing, you will find that there really is a God who loves and cares for you. Come take a journey with me as we explore the deep things of God in a practical book for ordinary people.

Table of Contents

A Dimension into the Mind of the Spirit

The Spirit of God has allowed me to write the truth and make it plain, for many have been mislead, tricked, and deceived by false doctrine. In order for me to walk you into *The Mind of the Spirit*, it's vital that I obey the Holy Spirit. It is God's Spirit who has allowed me to write this book, and by the leading, guidance, and directions of creditable truth, I have enquired into the mysteries of truth to unveil the genuine Word of God. It is yet a journey, and I am committed to its neverending truths. I am not attempting to write with theological wording, per say, or words so difficult that you need a dictionary to define each sentence. This book is simple enough for a child to understand, yet, I have defined many words to help the readers who may not be as literal as others. As I have been moved by the Holy Spirit as to what needs to be written in this book, it has been a long process in the birthing of this book, and through different periods of my spiritual impregnation, this is the book that will change your life. If you hunger and thirst after righteousness, then you will be filled with God's truth. As we know, many other books have been written in Christendom, but all books with biblical principals are derived from the only truth and life-giving word which is the sacred Word of God, the *Holy Bible*.

For over two decades, the Holy Spirit has been pressing these words into my spirit. Through this process, there has been a great compelling of God's will pressing into my spirit. However, in my thirties, my life seemed to be on a downward spiral, and through much pain, suffering, intense processing, and much opposition, I've experienced the true birthing of this book.

You must study the Word for yourself and know that the Word has been tainted in many pulpits, by Satan using many men and woman who shepherd the people of God through false teaching. Not that all pulpits are tainted and teaching false doctrine, but for those who are misleading the children of God, I hope this book will open the eyes of those who are false teachers and to those who are under such leadership and are being mislead, or maybe you know someone in this sort of situation, I speak the words of truth into those crooked places. For the true believer in Christ, must be watchful and pray always, for the enemy has set his false identity in the hearts and minds of those whose belly is full of deceit. The enemy has, since his fall, strategically construed his false teaching into the minds and hearts of those who refuse to take heed to the true doctrine of Christ; therefore, many have heard a voice, but not God's. This voice is the stranger's voice through which Satan has a channel into many men and women's minds, and he has deceived them into starting their own ministry. He gives orders to legions of demons that are assigned to these sort of men and woman to deceive many who are following after false doctrine.

For who hath known the mind of the Lord, that he may instruct him? But we have the mind of Christ.

I Co. 2:16 (kjv)

For the time is coming when people will not endure sound doctrine (teaching), but have itching ears they will accumulate for themselves teachers to suit their own passions, and will turn away from listening to the truth and wander off into myths. As for you, always be sober-minded, endure suffering, do the work of an evangelist, fulfill your ministry.

II Tim. 4:3, 4 (esv)

How often do you take notes at church and go home to look up the scriptures yourself using a Strong's Concordance and a study Bible to compare the lesson taught over the pulpit or in a service? How often do you go into a more in depth understanding of the word when you're by yourself and diligently take the time to search the scriptures making sure through much prayer that you're being taught the truth? If you pray and asked the Holy Spirit to give you the understanding of his word and have a study Bible along with you, after Sunday school, Bible study or church service taking time to be sure you are being fed the correct doctrine of Jesus Christ, you will be one that cannot be mislead. Your sole responsibility for your salvation is that you work it out with God through learning his word for yourself. According to the way in which the Holy Spirit wants you to interpret the word, it's up to you to dig, search and find the truth in the word. Did you know or hasn't someone informed you that, this is a spiritual walk with Christ and you have to be spiritually nourished in order to grow into the things of the Spirit? You have been living for the things that your flesh desires so long that, now you have to grow into the things of the Spirit. Delayed study habits can hinder your growth in Christ and detour you away from the truth which can cause you to be a channel for satanic deception. One important truth to always remember is this; there is the doctrine of God which is from Genesis to Revelation, then there is the doctrine of the devil, then there is the doctrine of men. Which one are you following or patterning yourself after? These findings and many other revelatory truths will be explained and given much attention to, I welcome you to come along with me and take a journey with me into; *The Mind of the Spirit.*

The Plan of
Salvation

How We Are Drawn Nigh to God?

Have you ever wondered how we are drawn to God? It is very imperative for you to know it's by God's Spirit (Holy Spirit) that we are all drawn to him through his love. As we look at one passage of Scripture, we can clearly see that as God told Israel he has drawn them with loving kindness, he also has drawn the whole world through his love (see Jer 31:3 and John 3:3–16). God has preordained a set time and a place for every one that is born upon the face of the earth to hear the gospel of Jesus Christ.

> And this gospel of the kingdom shall be preached in all the world for a witness unto all nations; and then shall the end come.
>
> Matt. 24:14 (kjv)

God loves us so much he even sends the angels in heaven to preach to those who are on the earth.

> And I saw another angel fly in the midst of heaven, having the everlasting gospel to preach unto them that dwell on the earth, and to every nation, and kindred, and tongue, and people.
>
> Re. 14:6 (kjv)

Before God had ever called time by its name and commanded it to come forth, he knew there were many avenues he would have to take to draw us to him and he had a plan already in place to get our attention, giving us many opportunities to receive him into our heart. God knows the times, places, and situations we would get into that he could use to show his love toward us to draw each and every human being to him through his love, yet, he gives us the choice to choose whether or not; if we will hearken to the call of salvation. Even though God knows our beginning and our ending, he does not force anyone to receive Jesus Christ as their Lord and Savior. Yes, he compels all men to come into the knowledge of salvation. He calls men, women and children to come to him throughout a lifetime but gives all the choice to choose freely what he decides on his own. The word *compel* is to constrain someone, in some way, to yield or to do what one wishes. God desires that all would come into the knowledge of Jesus Christ, yet, he knows many will refuse, reject, and turn away from hearing the gospel.

Don't ever think that God, who created the heavens and the earth, wouldn't know the person or thing in which he created. God even knew what resources he would use such as a near death experiences, an angel, death itself, a still small voice, the media, internet, CDs, videos, VHS, DVDs, cassette tapes, word of mouth, coworkers, school, friends, family, and neighbors, etc., to compel man back to himself. Those are just a few ways besides Bible study, Sunday school, and home visits from the local community churches. At times, it may appear as if many will not ever have the opportunity to hear the Word of God to be drawn to him, yet. Always remember that, it is in the plan of God and for his purpose that every individual will hear the gospel of Jesus Christ, before they leave this earth one day. Remember, God sent Jesus Christ to die for the world's sin, to reconcile man back to himself. God did all of this because he loves us that much.

> In the beginning was the Word, and the Word was with God, and the Word was God. He was in the beginning with God. All things were made through him, and without him was not any thing made that was made. In him was life, and the life was the light of men. The light shines in the darkness, and the darkness has not overcome it.
>
> John 1:1–5 (esv)

Notice the scripture which speaks of God being the Word and the Word being God because the Word is who God is. He is the Word and the light, and he lights the way for man, leading all men to the life because his words gives life, which is in Jesus Christ.

> No one can come to me unless the Father who sent me draws him. And I will raise him up on the last day. It is written in the Prophets, And they will all be taught by God. Everyone who has heard and learned from the Father comes to me.
>
> John 6:44, 45 (esv)

God's blessing to the whole world is for all to have eternal life. He gives his eternal plan of salvation to all yet, it's a choice whether one chooses to come into the adoption of salvation through Christ Jesus or choose to ignore his call.

> According as he hath chosen us in him before the foundation of the world, that we should be holy and without blame before him in love: Having predestinated us unto the adoption of

children by Jesus Christ to himself, according to the good pleasure of his will, To the praise of the glory of his grace, wherein he hath made us accepted in the beloved.

Eph. 1:4–6 (kjv)

God has predestined you for a certain time and place to be drawn to him, and it's only through his Spirit that we are compelled to come to him. This presents the argument that maybe not everyone is predestined . . . it might be a good idea to address that issue here.

As we see in Ephesians, God has predestinated many to be drawn to him throughout a person's lifetime and it is a choice whether or not each individual conforms to his calling, we all have a free will. This scripture which says in it that we have been predestinated or foreordained is not to give anyone the impression that God chooses those who will receive salvation and who won't receive salvation. Come go with me to the scripture and let's explore what he predestined all, the world for.

> The Lord is not slack concerning his promise, as some men count slackness; but is longsuffering to us-ward, not willing that any should perish, but that all should come to repentance.
>
> II Pe.3:9 kjv

> For this is good and acceptable in the sight of God our Saviour; Who will have all men to be saved, and to come unto the knowledge of the truth.
>
> I Tim. 2:3, 4 kjv

> For whosoever shall call upon the name of the Lord shall be saved.
>
> Ro. 10:13 kjv

Once a person chooses to adhere to the call of Christ it's at that very moment he or she realized they have been chosen and it's through wisdom and by knowledge of one hearing and receiving the word then believing the word by faith that anyone can be saved from this perishing world. Then once one has received the Lord into their heart, as the scripture lets us know, all believers and unbelievers are predestinated before the foundation of the world that all have been chosen but not all choose to accept the gospel. Therefore, it's the believer who can only experience the truth of the word because; an unbeliever has often turned his or her heart away from the truth and rejected it. This gives God no access to their heart to live because he gives us free will. For all have been called but few come because many choose not to receive the truth of the gospel. Yet, for those who do accept the truth of the gospel, they at one point in time made a choice to hear the word, believe the word and accept the truth of the word and obey his voice, coming into the adoption to be called into his will. Again it is written that, God does not choose this one or that one, all mankind has been given a free will to accept Christ or reject him. Have you heard the call of Christ? Will you accept the truth of the gospel when you have the opportunity to hear what God has already predestined you into? Are you ignoring the truth and rejecting the spirit of God that compelled you to be accepted as one of his children and made you to be accepted as his beloved? If so, then remember it's your choice to do what you choose with your life on this earth and when you die you will be accountable for rejecting and not adhering to the truth of the gospel.

> And many of them that sleep in the dust of the earth shall awake, some to everlasting life, and some to shame and everlasting contempt.
>
> Da. 12:2 kjv

> Marvel not at this: for the hour is coming, in the which all that are in the graves shall hear his voice. And shall come forth; they that have done good, unto the resurrection of life; and they that have done evil, unto the resurrection of damnation.
>
> Jn 5:28, 29 kjv

And have hope toward God, which they themselves also allow, that there shall be a resurrection of the dead, both of the just and unjust.

Ac. 24:15 kjv

Whether you want to believe it or not, God opens a door of divine initiative in which you are compelled throughout your life to be drawn to him. He reaches out to us in many different ways, yet it's still him drawing himself unto us for the purpose in which he has predestined us to. God's part is to draw man unto him because the sin nature that man is born into does not want to obey but would rather rebel; therefore, God constrains man because man's desire is to sin and to resist any one who tries to come in and change the flesh and its desires. The way he draws us to him is through teaching and preaching the gospel of Jesus Christ and this comes through many sources in our life.

To Understand Reconciliation

God was in Jesus Christ, reconciling the world back to himself. Yes, it is God who loved the world so much, that he sent his only begotten son, Jesus Christ and he incarnated himself (in a young virgin woman named Mary) to be born into the world, having the oracle of himself in Jesus Christ.

Therefore the Lord himself shall give you a sign; Behold, a virgin shall conceive, and bear a son, and shall call his name Immanuel.

Is. 7:14 kjv

And the angel came in unto her, and said, Hail, thou that art highly favoured, the Lord is with thee: blessed art thou among women. And when she saw him, she was troubled at his saying, and cast in her mind what manner of salutation this should be. And the angel said unto her, Fear not, Mary:

for thou hast found favour with God. And, behold, thou shalt conceive in thy womb, and bring forth a son, and shalt call his name JESUS.

Lk. 1:28–31 kjv

Jesus Christ was the temple of God, as we are the temple of God, and he also was God in Christ Jesus, who appeared as a man, Christ Jesus. Come walk with me into Corinthians to see this truth:

> And all things are of God, who hath reconciled us to himself by Jesus Christ, and hath given to us the ministry of reconciliation. To wit, that God was in Christ, reconciling the world unto himself, not imputing their trespasses unto them; and hath committed unto us the word of reconciliation.

II Co. 5:18, 19 kjv

Reconciliation means a change from enmity to friendship. It is mutual, i.e., it is a change wrought in both parties who have been at enmity. (1.) In Col. 1:21, 22, the word there used refers to a change wrought in the personal character of the sinner who ceases to be an enemy to God by wicked works, and yields up to him his full confidence and love. In 2 Cor. 5:20 the apostle beseeches the Corinthians to be "reconciled to God", i.e., to lay aside their enmity. (2.) Rom. 5:10 refers not to any change in our disposition toward God, but to God himself, as the party reconciled. Romans 5:11 teaches the same truth.

To change thoroughly, to change from enmity to friendship, to bring together, to restore.

The Savior of the world died the death of flesh, which represents the death of sin. Christ Jesus the Messiah became the propitiation (atonement) for the sins of what flesh causes mankind to do, which is sin, for flesh nature is of sin itself. We have been reconciled back to God through Jesus Christ, who paid the penalty for the sins of mankind. Jesus Christ can only be the Savior, to those who willingly choose to accept his forgiveness. It is necessary for a person to first accept the fact that Jesus Christ is the son of the living God and indeed died, was buried, and resurrected out of the grave, for you and I to be accepted into the reconciliation in which God has made available to all those who choose to believe.

God's grace and truth is the grace of redemption that was paid through Jesus Christ and the truth of God's grace is the Word of God which was from the beginning, that came down from heaven to redeem mankind back to himself.

> "For Christ also suffered once for sins, the righteous for the unrighteous, that he might bring us to God, being put to death in the flesh but made alive in the Spirit."
>
> 1 Peter 3:18, esv

Immediately when Jesus Christ was put to death, giving up the ghost, he was immediately made alive by God. When the believer dies, he is also immediately, like Jesus Christ; like as to a blink of the eye with God. When the day of resurrection comes, the believer that is dead, is immediately changed from mortal into immortality for example: he passes from death into eternal life. It's wonderful to know that God loves the world so much that he gives all the opportunity before they leave this earth to pass from death into life. Yes, the glory for the believer on the day of resurrection is life. We see in the book of Corinthians, Paul the Apostle clearly states how the believer's corruptible body is changed into an incorruptible body. Come go with me to this passage of scriptures and allow me to unveil this truth.

> So also is the resurrection of the dead. It is sown in corruption; it is raised in incorruption: It is sown in dishonour; it is raised in glory: it is sown in weakness; it is raised in power: It is sown a natural body; it is raised a spiritual body, There is a natural body, and there is a spiritual body. And so it is written, The first man Adam was made a living soul; the last Adam was

made a quickening spirit. Howbeit that was not first which is spiritual, but that which is natural; and afterward that which is spiritual. The first man is of the earth, earthy: the second man is the Lord from heaven. As is the earthy, such are they also that are earthy: and as is the heavenly, such are they also that are heavenly. And as we have borne the image of the earthy, we shall also bear the image of the heavenly. Now this I say, brethren, that flesh and blood cannot inherit the kingdom of God; neither doth corruption inherit incorruption. Behold, I shew you a mystery; We shall not all sleep, but we shall all be changed, In a moment, in the twinkling of an eye, at the last trump: for the trumpet shall sound, and the dead shall be raised incorruptible, and we shall be changed. For this corruptible must put on incorruption, and this mortal must put on immortality. So when this corruptible shall have put on incorruption, and this mortal shall have put on immortality, then shall be brought to pass the saying that is written, Death is swallowed up in victory. O death, where is thy sting? O grave, where is thy victory? The sting of death is sin; and the strength of sin is the law. But thanks be to God, which giveth us the victory through our Lord Jesus Christ.

I Co. 15:42–58 kjv

Paul speaks of four different ways our body is now and how our body will be on the day of resurrection. 1. Our earthly body is corruptible. 2. Our resurrected body will be incorruptible. 3. A corruptible body ages, decays, deteriorates, dies and then decomposes. 4. Our heavenly body never ages, and is free from being defiled, depraved, dying and decaying. On resurrection day the believer will transform from death into eternal life and never perish. Our earthly body when we die is buried in dishonor but our resurrected body will be raised in glory with a glorious immortal body. As we know death, the grave and a burial shows that the body is deprived, degraded and cold filled with embalming fluid; and we see that for those who have viewing of an open corpse. After a period of time the body will stink, decay and perish away. Nothing can compare to death and the fact that the beauty of a man's body after death turns into dirt eventually. Yet, the resurrected body, our old human body will be transformed into a body that is full of glory which is a perfect light that is full of splendor, brightness, perfection, luster and majesty for the grace of God will have resurrected the mortal body, changing the image of the earthy body into the image of the heavenly body. We walked together in the scriptures from 42 and 43. Now let's go further to see where 44 through 49 takes us. The fact of the word is that, we live in a natural body and the Bible states that there is also a spiritual body (verse 44). The evidence is in this; In verse 45 we see the man Adam was the first living soul and then the last Adam which was Christ Jesus, he was made a quickening Spirit. These two men's natures, where significantly different from each other. God gave the first Adam a physical or human life and this was to only live upon the earth. This gave Adam the limitation of only being able to pass on a physical or human life to his children or family. Yet, Christ difference was that; he was a quickening Spirit, (verse 45) he is a life giving Spirit. This gave Christ the ability to give a new life to his spiritual family. As the scripture says in (verse 47) the first man is of the earth, earthy, the second man is the Lord from heaven. As in the earthy, such are they also that are earthy. Those who are born first are like Adam of the earth. As is the heavenly, such are they also that are heavenly. All who are born again of the spirit of God, the nature of God, one day when the resurrection comes will bear the image of the heavenly (verses 48 and 49).

Therefore it is imperative for the unbeliever to know and understand that if he or she does not accept Christ Jesus as Lord and Savior, then he lives to die the death of sin which is eternal separation from God. As the scriptures says this also;

> Now this I say, brethren that flesh and blood cannot inherit the kingdom of God; neither doth corruption inherit incorruption.
>
> I Co. 15:50 kjv

Christ is able to transform the earthly body of man who has accepted him through salvation into his heavenly body that is glorious and full of perfect light. If those who are upon the earth refuse, reject and turn away from such a great salvation, once a unbeliever dies; his body is only flesh and blood and was born of the first Adam which is of the earth. Remember, this body goes back to the dust which the Lord giveth it, the spirit of the unrighteous the Bible clearly states, will go to the lake of fire (see: Re. 20:11-15 and 21:7-8, St. Lk. 16: 19-31, II Co. 5:10, Ga. 5:19-21). But, only those who have received the second Adams body through salvation in Christ Jesus will inherit the kingdom of God. For a corrupt body is the old nature of Adam, the flesh and blood earthly body is corrupt and cannot inherit the kingdom of God. For Paul says this; I Co. 15:51–52 kjv

> Behold, I shew you a mystery; We shall not all sleep, but we shall all be changed, In a moment, in the twinkling of an eye, at the last trumpet: for the trumpet shall sound and the dead shall be raised incorruptible, and we shall be changed (verse 51).
>
> So then, the believer will pass from death of the flesh into life in the Spirit with God. The believer is transferred into heaven by the quickening Spirit that he has been given through salvation (the Holy Spirit). Once the believer goes away to be with the Lord, he is perfected in Christ forever. Therefore, mankind can be regenerated through the ministry of reconciliation by being in Christ Jesus, for this is the only way he does not hold us accountable for our sins, but through this process man can become a new creature and the gospel is then committed to man.

> Therefore, if any man be in Christ, he is a new creature: old things are passed away; behold all things are become new. And all things are of God, who hath reconciled us to himself by Jesus Christ, and hath given to us the ministry of reconciliation; To wit, that God was in Christ, reconciling the world unto

himself, not imputing their trespasses unto them; and hath committed unto us the word of reconciliation. Now then we are ambassadors for Christ, as though God did beseech you by us: we pray you in Christ's stead, be ye reconciled to God. For he hath made him to be sin for us, who knew no sin; that we might be made the righteousness of God in him.

II Corinthians 5:17–21 (kjv)

On this earth, it is through man becoming a new creature in Christ that the new creature of man is changed; his whole being, life, nature, and behavior is changed. Yes, this is true, but man also must move forward into the things of the Word in order for Christ Jesus to be formed in him. When man is not reconciled to God, he is dead to God. He has no knowledge of God in his thoughts to even thinking the thoughts of God, for he is dead. For example: When the bank sends a debit card, it will not work until you activate it or if you sit in a car without a key, the car will not go unless you start the car, you must turn the switch on; the Holy Spirit is only activated and will resurrect the immortal body if one has activated the Holy Spirit by calling on the name of the Lord to be saved. Remember, you have a free will and it's your choice to choose death or life, eternal life with God or eternal separation from God. You must confess Christ Jesus as your Lord and Savior or you will be left behind and your mortal body will be placed in eternal separation from God and in eternal damnation you will go due to your choice of rejecting, refusing and turning away from the truth.

Turn with me to this scripture and then we will continue with reconciliation.

And he said unto them, Go ye into all the world, and preach the gospel to every creature. He that believeth and is baptized shall be saved; but he that believeth not shall be damned.

Mk. 16:15, 16

Twila Williams

28

The soul that sinneth, it shall die. The son shall not bear the iniquity of the father, neither shall the father bear the iniquity of the son: the righteousness of the righteous shall be upon him, and the wickedness of the wicked shall be upon him. But if the wicked will turn from all his sins that he hath committed, and keep all my statutes, and do that which is lawful and right, he shall surely live, he shall not die. Eze. 18:20–21 (please take the time to read and study the whole chapter of Ezekiel chapter 18)

Now we can clearly understand reconciliation and the need that mankind has for it. When a man becomes a new creature, he is alive to God and reconciled to God, having knowledge to think like God and receive the Word to continually be regenerated for the relationship he has been given with God. Where there was once doubt in a man's mind about God, through reconciliation there is now assured certainty. As man is dead by way of a sinful nature and has no fellowship with God in the flesh, man can be alive in Christ and have fellowship with God and communion with God, once he becomes a new creature in Jesus Christ, he now can have fellowship and commune with God every day at all times. Before man accepts Jesus Christ, he lives in sin and immoral ways, yet reconciliation brings him into righteousness and holiness through the relationship he now has with Jesus Christ. Before man receives Jesus Christ, he faces death. Now he will never die but live eternally in heaven with God. As we know, death means separation from God eternally. As a new creature, man is given eternal life to live forever and ever with God. A person is a new creature in Christ by God placing him in the position that he has for him in, to live in all that Christ is, through all that Christ is. Man now lives, dies, and arises in Christ by reconciliation. God recognizes him to have identified himself with Christ; therefore, he places and positions the man who believes in Christ by faith in Christ. This is what causes the believer to be with Christ, his faith that he has for and in him.

The songs of Proverbs speak on this wise:

> The Lord possessed me [fathered me] at the beginning of his work, the first of his acts of old. Ages ago I was set up, at the first, before the beginning of the earth. When there were no depth I was brought forth, when there were no springs abounding with water. Before the mountains had been shaped, before the hills, I was brought forth, before he had made the earth with its fields, or the first of the dust of the world, When he established the heavens, I was there; when he drew a circle on the face of the deep, when he assigned to the sea its limit, so that the waters might not transgress his command, when he marked out the foundations of the earth, then I was beside him, like a master workman, and I was daily his delight, rejoicing before him always, rejoicing in his inhabited world and delighting in the children of man.
>
> Proverbs 8:22–31 (esv)

As Proverbs 8 speaks of the Word being first and before the beginning of time, so it was that God had already created a time to compel mankind back to himself. You are to know for yourself what God says about you as a new creature. Your life depends on you as an individual knowing and understanding what God has to say for you and your life first. There are many voices, but there is God's voice in which you are to obey, staying in fellowship and communion with him at all times, as much as you can think of him and think like him. For he is the only invisible God who is present all the time; he is everywhere, for only he is omnipresent. Just because he is not acknowledged as God everywhere in the world does not nullify the fact that he is omnipresent and omnipotent. For God, preeminence is in him who created heaven and the earth.

> He is the image of the invisible God, the firstborn of all creation. For by him all things were created, in heaven and on earth, visible and invisible, whether thrones or dominions or

rulers or authorities—all things were created through him and for him. And he is before all things, and in him all things hold together. And he is the head of the body, the church. He is the beginning, the firstborn from the dead, that in everything he might be preeminent. For in him all the fullness of God was pleased to dwell, and through him to reconcile to himself all things, whether on earth or in heaven, making peace by the blood of his cross. And you, who once were alienated and hostile in mind, doing evil deeds, he has now reconciled in his body of flesh by his death, in order to present you holy and blameless and above reproach before him, if indeed you continue in the faith, stable and steadfast, not shifting from the hope of the gospel that you heard, which has been proclaimed in all creation under heaven, and of which I, Paul become a minister.

Colossians 1:15–23 (esv)

Don't be taken Captive by Empty Words

See to it that no one takes you captive by philosophy and empty deceit, according to human tradition, according to the elemental spirits of the world, and not according to Christ. For in him the whole fullness of deity dwells bodily, and you have been filled in him, who is the head of all rule and authority.

Colossians 2: 8–10 (esv)

Therefore, be very, very careful who you allow to speak into your life, remembering that your beliefs are in God. Yet, it is solely up to you to determine how you will go about the journey with Christ and be learned in the richness of the mysteries which he reveals to those who diligently seek him. You are not to believe what they say unless it lines up with what God says. Know this one thing: God does not show anyone your whole life's journey. He takes you with him into his journey for you to do his will, his way and for his glory. Man can only prophesy to you some parts here and there, but it's up to you to find, seek, ask, and believe by faith that your journey is between you and God. It's up to you to continue with him into the things that are of him.

Unless you are one of those individuals that want to be saved and that's enough, you should want to learn his ways to become more like him. If you don't study the Word, then you don't have a personal relationship with God for yourself through his Word and commune with him daily. It's possible for you to easily be persuaded with every wind of doctrine if you don't know what the Word says and understand it through the Spirit for yourself. Paul put it this way:

> Finally, brothers, whatever is just, whatever is pure, whatever is lovely, whatever is commendable, if there is any excellence, if there is anything worthy of praise, think about these things. What you have learned and received and heard and seen in me—practice these things and the God of peace will be with you.
>
> Philippians 4:8, 9 (esv)

Unless you read and follow the life of Paul, even in this scripture you will misinterpret what he is referring to. You have to study the Scriptures daily and diligently, search for the truth like someone searching diligently for gold, for in the Scriptures you will find the way into the depths of the mind of Christ, which continually leads you from glory to glory into eternal life through Jesus Christ our Lord. Listen, timing is everything because we are living in a time where people are very opinionated (there are many who listen to too many voices, have too many beliefs, and you must know and recognize that we now live in a cultured society with many religious beliefs on top of the ones that were already in us through our parents and those who lived with us and those who we fellowshipped with and allowed into our circle. These sort who have different beliefs you must be careful with and not be persuaded to follow after.) Therefore, we are not to believe or follow after false statements, fables, wise tales, or anyone who speaks contrary to the doctrine of Jesus Christ.

You are responsible for yourself! You are to get into the Word and diligently search the Scriptures for yourself. Don't be complacent, lazy, or dependent on someone else's avid study habits! Get alone as often as you can, and pray to diligently search the Word for yourself, for your sake, to be lead correctly on the journey which Christ has for you in the Holy Spirit. God has saved you and compelled you to come with him, to walk with him, to become a good steward of your own soul by following and patterning yourself after him.

Philosophy and Astrology

The born again believer should therefore live in the reality and truth of the word. False philosophy and astrology is mans' doing and not God's. You cannot search worldly philosophy by taking heed or looking deeply into signs of Astrology and the signs of the Zodiac. For example: Virgos, Pisces, Cancer, etc. The scripture we just looked at tells us to beware of it, or you can easily begin to judge people that you meet by their Zodiac sign, saying you're like this or that because your sign says this about you. Because every culture has its own version of what the day, month, and time when someone was born means in their culture. For example: The Chinese culture has a different belief on who is compatible with who using the years to determine if they are or are not compatible. Therefore, you can get confused and caught up in Astrology and Zodiac signs, putting them before the spirit of discernment which gives us the ability in Christ to know the truth concerning his will for our life and that's not based on any Astrology signs of the Zodiac. Some people are genuinely saved and the zodiac sign has ways of defining someone who God has placed his spirit in. God's spirit (the Holy Spirit) is in a person through salvation so then, we are under the sign of Christ through the blood of Jesus Christ who died, was buried, and rose again for our justification.

There are some people that search for truth and reality but do it by trying to search out the universe through books in Cosmology and Astrology. Yet, this approach causes confusion because this is the same philosophy that man has already tried to follow throughout the ages and is seen throughout the scripture that it is an abomination to God to do witchcraft, black magic, and any such thing. Paul calls this the rudiments or elementary knowledge of this world. The rudiments (elements or material), of the universe is the searching of the stars and planets and God never intended for man to search out these questions like: Who am I? Where did I come from? Is there really a God? Is there really life after death? What is the root of evil? Or where did it come from? Where did the planet originate? The questions to the world do not lie within the world. Worldly philosophy and science can only do two things; give one temporary comfort and make one feel a little more at ease, but not fully because this worldly philosophy offers temporary answers. What's important for man to realize is that this world is fading away at a slow paste and man is going to deteriorate one day therefore, eternal life or eternal separation from this old body is a choice today for man to choose life and not death. Our bodies are mortal that we live in and can never ever transform into the spiritual dimensions and God made it to where no one will ever know everything because it's not his will for us to know everything.

The believer should be more concerned with loving someone enough to share the greatest love than of being concerned to searching out the Astrology, Zodiac signs, Cosmology etc; etc

> Love never ends. As for prophecies, they will pass away; as for tongues, they will cease; as for knowledge, it will pass away. For we know in part and we prophesy in part, but when the perfect comes, the partial will pass away. When I was a child, I spoke like a child, I thought like a child, I reasoned like a child. When I became a man, I gave up childish ways. For now we see in a mirror dimly, but then face to face. Now I know in part; then I shall know fully, even as I have been fully known. So now faith, hope, and love abode, these three; but the greatest of these is love.
>
> I Cor. 13: 8–13 esv

Even though most people use this scripture to argue and debate whether we are to prophecy and speak in an unknown tongue which they refer to in Acts chapter 2; I want you to focus on the fact that knowledge will pass away and to seek for the knowledge through; Cosmology, Astrology, Zodiac signs, witchcraft, black magic, tarot card, palm reading, crystal balls, etc; etc; We have people who claim to be believers of the Bible yet, practice these and other wicked, evil and abominable things.

Paul wants to remind us as believers that God's love is eternal and it will never, ever end. But everything else in this world will one day pass away. This is how we take on other peoples beliefs and become religious. We are to stay in a spirit filled relationship with God through staying free from other erroneous teachings (doctrine) that will only ruin our faith in God. The spirit of pride and arrogance is the spirit of Satan and those who choose to serve this spirit are dooming their souls to eternal separation from God. Even prophesies, tongues and knowledge, will pass away one day. But to rather search for things we will never know, we ought to love God with all of our heart, mind and soul then we can love one another with the never ending love in which Christ loves us.

Remember our bodies are corrupt, for the body is of the earth. The elements in our body will soon decay and deteriorate therefore; it is of the essences to prepare your soul to separate from this old decaying, physical being that is a material substance. Since man is incapable of not being physical and material, then it would behoove man to receive what God has to offer through Christ and allow God to reveal himself to man through his word. Don't ever underestimate God for he only gives man one way to know the spiritual world and that is to know him in his glory which is revealed to us through Christ. The scripture says it this way:

> The Lord is not slow to fulfill his promise as some count
> slowness, but is patient toward you, not wishing that any

should perish, but that all should reach repentance. But the day of the Lord will come like a thief, and then the heavens will pass away with a roar, and the heavenly bodies will be burned up and dissolved, and the earth and the works that are done on it will be exposed. Since all these things are thus to be dissolved, what sort of people ought you to be in lives of holiness and godliness, waiting for and hastening the coming of the day of God, because of which the heavens will be set on fire and dissolved, and the heavenly bodies will melt as they burn! But according to his promise we are waiting for new heavens and a new earth in which righteousness dwells.

2 Pe. 3:9–12 esv

Let's look at verses 9 and 10: Salvation is the message in these verses and we are given forewarning of the earth being destroyed. The reason Christ has not returned is because he is merciful and gracious. He loves man so much that he does not desire for any man to perish. God is being patient with man even though man is sinful and living rebellious. God forewarns us that he is coming as a thief in the night. His coming will appear in the sky quick as lightening; just like you see lightening and you hear it's roar, so shall you hear the entrance of God when he comes back to declare his throne. If we knew when he was coming we would get prepared, we wouldn't be more lazy, complacent and sleep like the disciples to watch and pray while Jesus went up to Gethsemane to pray, Jesus found them sleep twice (Matt. 26:40–43). Just like a thief does not warn us when he is coming and we would also be ready waiting for him or her, at the time and date he was to show up; God does not reveal his coming to us because, this keeps us focused in our minds upon his return. We often look and long for his return. This keeps the believer from getting to careless and tired. This also keeps the believer on guard of his own soul and lifestyle of how he is living on the earth. The believer is on watch looking, waiting, and listening for the trumpet to sound for his return.

And then shall appear the sign of the Son of man in heaven: and then shall all the tribes of the earth mourn, and they shall see the Son of man coming in the clouds of heaven with power and great glory. And he shall send his angels with a great sound of a trumpet, and they shall gather together his elect from the four winds, from one end of heaven to the other.

Matt. 24:30, 31 kjv

(Also, see: 1 Cor 15:51, 52; 1 Th. 4:16–18; Lu. 18:7, 8)

Now let's look at verses 11 and 12: God has power to destroy the earth as he did before. He has the power in his mouth to speak a word into the atmosphere and it will obey him and do exactly what he says. The believer awaits the return of Christ and by faith believes that God is coming back and knows that one day the earth will be destroyed. Most unbelievers think that the earth will not be destroyed and have more faith that man can destroy the earth and dare not believe in God less on him destroying the earth. God destroyed the earth with water in Noah's days (Ge. 7:1–24) and God created the earth in the beginning. And God can speak again and destroy the earth. According to verse 13; God is going to destroy the heavens and the earth, because he is going to create new heavens and earth, where the righteousness will dwell (Re. 21:1-6). The whole earth will be destroyed by a explosion of fire and it will burn so hot that all the elements and everything in it will melt from the fervent heat.

Therefore stay awake-for you do not know when the master of the house will come, in the evening, or at midnight, or when the rooster crows, or in the morning-lest he come suddenly and find you asleep. And what I say to you I say to all: Stay awake."

Mk. 13:35 esv

For as the lightening comes from the east and shines as far as the west, so will be the coming of the Son of Man. Wherever the corpse is, there the vultures will gather.

Mt. 24:27 esv

Some scholars refer to the corpse and the vultures as; the carcass being the Jewish people and the vultures are the Roman armies under Titus that gathered around Jerusalem as to consume the prey. Or the other meaning some scholars believe that the carcass is the world which is the spiritual ones who are dead and the vultures are Christ and with his holy angels and the saints; believing that God and the angels will gather around the earth executing judgment on the world. As we have read here, there is definitely a true meaning and one is that, Christ is coming, quick as lightening to execute judgment on all the earth and shall resurrect the dead first and then the entire world will all be judged.

> For if God did not spare angels when they sinned, but cast them into hell and committed them to chains of gloomy darkness to be kept until the judgment; if he did not spare the ancient world, but preserved Noah, a herald of righteousness, with seven others, when he brought a flood upon the world of the ungodly; If by turning the cities of Sodom and Gomorrah to ashes he condemned them to extinction, making them an example of what is going to happen to the ungodly; and if he rescued righteous Lot, greatly distressed by the sensual conduct of the wicked (for as that righteous man lived among them day after day, he was tormenting his righteous soul over their lawless deeds that he saw and heard); then the Lord knows how to rescue the godly from trials, and to keep the unrighteousness under punishment until the day of judgment, and especially those who indulge in the lust of defiling passion and despise authority.
>
> II Pe. 2:4–10 ESV

> About this we have much to say, and it is hard to explain, since you have become dull of hearing. For though by this time you ought to be teachers, you need someone to teach you again the basic principles of the oracles of God. You need milk, not solid food, for everyone who lives on milk is unskilled in the

Twila Williams

word of righteousness, since he is a child. But solid food is for the mature, for those who have their powers of discernment trained by constant practice to distinguish good from evil.

He. 5:11–14 esv

Wrong Relationships

Some people may be good to you, but not good for you to take advice from. Its okay to effectively communicate with people, but don't take their beliefs and forget who you are as a believer in Christ. It only takes a moment to learn and be convinced about something if you're not aware and alert! Words are easily twisted on the tongue, sounding good, but are not God's words. Be very careful who you let feed your spirit because, just like you can be fed poison by someone fixing you natural food, you can be fed spiritual poison by someone preparing you a false word through false teaching and doctrine of devils. God is who you want to receive. Be thankful, and stay addicted to his words over anyone or anything. It's not about feeling right, thinking are assuming someone is right. It's about an individual knowing what is right that God has spoken, and in time you will continue to know the truth and the truth as you learn to fellowship and commune with Christ daily will set you free. One of the most important things to remember is that if you are born again, you don't walk with God by what you feel. You walk with God on the journey he has for you by what you know about him as he leads and guides you into all truth. Now if you refuse to know the truth and diligently seek for its ways, you will not know the truth, and you will lose your way by being too complacent and lazy, because of your dependence on someone else's study habits.

You are to be a responsible believer, not foolish, gullible, believing anyone and every story or belief. Be protective of the beliefs you should hold dear to your heart because you will find that most people stick to their beliefs and try to persuade you into what they think is right.

For God formed you, created you, and brought you in his time into the faith for such a moment and time to trust him all the way, not half the way. You must stay in the faith by studying, meditating, and praying throughout the day to not let an outsider cause you to fall into a snare of evil for one moment. Who are the outsiders of the Bible? Anyone, whether in the church or out the church, who turns, twists, adds, or subtracts from the Bible, making up their own doctrine with a little Scripture here and a little text there. You are called to live and know who God is for yourself. It's not what they say; it's what God says that matters the most for his Word is precedent over all other words and voices.

> Remind them of these things, and charge them before God not to quarrel about words, which does no good, but only ruins the hearers. Do your best to present yourself to God as one approved, a worker who has no need to be ashamed, rightly handling the word of truth. But avoid irreverent babble, for it will lead people into more and more ungodliness, and their talk will spread like gangrene. [Gangrene is death or decay of blood tissue caused by insufficient blood supply.]
>
> 2 Timothy 2:14–17 (esv)

Listen very carefully to what I'm about to tell you. The Word of God is your blood supply; therefore, the words of those or anyone who quarrels, argues, or babbles on and on about what they don't know nor understand will cause you to have gangrene. (In the spirit your bloodstream or bloodline is in Christ you have a new lineage and you cannot allow death and decay from not receiving the true word of life, which is in Christ Jesus). Those who are not of the faith will suck the life of Christ out of you by poisoning your bloodline through false teaching and false doctrine. This is a scripture we are going to look at that should be memorized and never forgotten. For the life of the flesh is in the blood: and I have given it to you upon the altar to make an atonement for your souls: for it is the blood that maketh an atonement for the soul.

Lev. 17:11 KJV

Twila Williams

We must remember that the blood of Christ is the perfect sacrifice that made atonement for the sins of all mankind. We as believers have the blood of Christ and it is a symbol of the blood of God's Son; and we are not to ever abuse it or allow anyone to contaminate the truth of the word in us by listening to spiritually dead words. Those who eat spiritual food aught not eat the words of death. If you are not careful those who speak of the word without the life which is in the blood, will cause death because, they know not the things which are of God if they haven't received God.

That's like you're with someone and you're with them because they buy you nice things or they give you sexual gratification, and you stay with them for what you can get out of them that is satisfying to you (your flesh) and what you are doing for them it satisfies them (their flesh.) Some people are so confused they often think that love is of the flesh when love is of the spirit first because God is love. And without one understanding the love of God through the death, burial, and resurrection of Jesus Christ, the fulfillment of love cannot ever be fully enjoyed in a relationship without understanding the love in which Christ has offered to all mankind. God's love is greater than what anyone could ever offer you because man will fail you, even those who love you. We serve a God of a quickening spirit and we are to live in the life of his spirit and we do this by staying rooted and grounded in his word. Wow! That's a message the spirit of a quickening love!

Remember this for yourself. It was his love that regenerated you through the Word of life because of the blood that was shed for you. Tell yourself, "I can live and be spiritually gratified and have the blood lineage I need kept clean to flow sufficiently every day, not dying to the gratification of the flesh but living in the gratification of the Spirit. I am to be free from anyone who chooses not to accept the genuine love of Christ to live life through the resurrected words that is found in the lineage of our Lord and our Savior, Jesus Christ."

Let me put it this way. Many times two people are together when they ought not be because each person has something that the other loves, whether material, physical, mental, or emotional—let's not leave out financial. They get attached to one another, yet God is not the center of the relationship, and there really is no future for the two of them to be together. But they stay together in sin and can't seem to understand, nor does it dawn on them why they're together, and time is just ticking. God is not getting any glory out of these sorts of relationships where two people who stay in these kinds of relationships because the flesh is being gratified one way or the other.

God created relationships between people, in many areas of our lives, giving us the ability to multiply what he has placed in us: his power to regenerate others to know him in his love. You are put on this earth to multiply and not demoralize the gift and call of doing his will, his way, for your life. If you are in any sort or kind of relationship that is not benefiting the call, plan, and mission of God, that is on your life, get out of it and leave them alone. You are wasting time, and you are now on God's time! You are responsible for the time you refuse to take to share with the one(s) you love, and if they don't want to receive you, you need to cut them off and go your separate way. We have the love of regeneration to reconcile other people through Jesus Christ to Jesus Christ. We can draw others to him by staying spiritually nourished through the Word. Then we can live healthy lives in Christ and be unto those who are spiritually dead a lifeline to draw men, and we are alive in him to replenish the life to others. In a Godly marriage where two people are both born again believers, God desires for two people to understand that the vows in a marriage are an unconditional love in which two people are to be inseparable—no matter what—and they are to stay together as they spiritually grow in the knowledge of his grace and truth. Now if there is abuse in a relationship, God has no place in this sort of relationship whether marriage, dating, friends, siblings, coworkers, or neighbors. God did not call or create us to be abused because he has designed certain responsibilities to each partner in a marriage and any relationship of any sort (within reason of biblical principles), and vows must be kept by each person continually forgiving one another as Jesus Christ has forgiven us. This does not mean that you abuse someone who is not born again and does not believe, you are to love them but hate the sin that drives them away from knowing the truth. Now don't you be a stumbling block or a hindrance to someone by professing to know him but going with them to sin. Remember, we don't embrace the sin that people choose to live in; we embrace the individual and love them in spite of their sinful nature. If you are born again, you don't have a right to participate with those who run to do evil, wicked, and unrighteous acts. You are to love them but pray against the sins they commit and don't agree with them by letting them tell you all that stuff that they are doing. You are to offer prayer, and if they don't want it and just want to dump the trash they do on you, you are to not allow people to keep coming to you and they refuse to let you pray with them or give them some sort of encouraging word that will rid them of their sin through salvation. Be careful with those who take your time and use it to tell you all their problems but reject the spiritual help you are trying to give them. Some people you have to just, leave alone, when they don't want to talk about anything but garbage (sin). If that means changing your number and moving on without them, God is able to give you what is for you according to his will, not yours. You should be a witness and example in living an upright life in the eyes of anyone who is living in sin and not go together and participate with what they do, in their bodies, but reprove them through the Word of life, and love them but not what they do (see Co. 5:9-13).

Yet, there are times when some relationships are not good because of the evil of man's heart. Some people are just unbearable to live with, fellowship with, be in communion with (conversation daily, getting together). Some people just don't care, and they may have a habitual sin like drugs, alcoholism, verbal abuse, physical abuse, clubbing, sex addiction, lying, playing games in relationships, or any such like, etc. It's people in your life sometimes who wake up using bad language, planning ways to steal, cheat, connive, backbite, constantly murmuring and complaining about this and that yet, have no thought of giving their life to the Lord and just seem to avoid even hearing anyone who tries to share the word of truth with them. If you are following Christ and want to have your life as a true example, then you have to share the word and depart from some people to be in communion with God who wants you to bear fruit of righteousness (Ga. 5:22-26). You cannot live on this earth and not be around these sort of people who do such things but, you don't have to welcome and invite sin into your life; if you know that a person is living any kind of way and refuses to adhere to anything that is righteous and holy; Pray for them, love them but not the things they do and make it known in a godly way how you feel. You must know that, God's love is for us to first understand grace and truth to compel mankind back to himself. You cannot force your beliefs on anyone but, live a life that is upright and find those who desire to do like wise. When we understand our relationship with Christ Jesus—that we have been called into his grace through love—then we can understand the communion through fellowship. We must allow Christ to keep us and we do this by patterning ourselves after him. This is what changes us from glory to glory, and this is the bread of life that we eat daily to grow in the knowledge of Jesus Christ.

The flesh always gets in the way of us growing in the knowledge of Jesus Christ. Yet, we can't allow other's sinful ways to get in the way of us growing into the knowledge of Jesus Christ. Even though this can happen sometimes, is so, we have power to take control over our own bodies through walking in the Spirit and by using self-control. Did you know that the human body was created from the earth and is made of chemicals and substances of the earth? Humans are physical material (animal). Our flesh houses the human soul and spirit. "For we know that if the tent that is our earthly home is destroyed, we have a building from God, a house not made with hands, eternally in the heavens" (2 Cor 5:1, kjv).

We find here that Paul is reminding us that when the born-again believer dies, he goes immediately to the Lord. When we die, we go back to God; yet, while on this earth, we must first learn how to stay in communion with the Lord to live free from our sinful nature by coming under subjection to the Word of God through his grace and truth.

At every moment, we must use our thoughts wisely, make up our minds to stay in communion with God daily, and not choose to go along with our feelings but do what we know is right. Of course, we will have dilemmas such as trials, tribulations, and persecution in different areas of our lives, but we have choices to make, and it's not always based on our feelings. Our feelings are not what we are to live by all the time. There are many choices that we must make based on what the Word of God has to say about our decisions. Most of the time we make wrong decision by saying, "Well, I thought it was the right thing to do at the time," or, "It felt right at that moment to do this or that, and I just knew it was going to work out so I chose to do this or that." We are born again, and we are to effectively go forward in the things of God by letting his Word teach us the truth. Many people can't learn the truth of God because they have not humbled themselves to be taught the truth of the Word. Through the Scriptures and the Holy Spirit, we can be led by faith in God and not by a gut feeling that could be wrong, for it is God's time that we are on and not our own. If the believer is going to stay in communion with the Lord stay in good standing with him, he or she must seek knowledge ask God for wisdom daily in every situation and circumstance, then one will be able to deal with justice, equity with equity. A healthy and good relationship with anyone has to start with the knowledge of God first and one must continually seek and search daily for the knowledge of God through the Holy Spirit and then he can understand truth. Did you know that in order to get knowledge you have to go by the pattern of the bible, to have understanding in order to obtain wisdom and then you will have the spirit of equity?

To know wisdom and instruction, to understand words of

insight, to receive instruction in wise dealing, in righteousness, justice, and equity; to give prudence to the simple, knowledge and discretion to thy youth- Let the wise hear and increase in learning, and the one who understands obtain guidance, to understand a proverb and a saying, the words of the wise and their riddles. The fear of the Lord is the beginning of knowledge; fools despise wisdom and instruction.

Pro.1:2–7 esv

The Greatest Love

When someone hears the Gospel, they must make a choice to hear the Word and listen to what the Word is saying then by faith believe the truth of his Word in their hearts. Then upon believing, they must confess with their mouths that Jesus is Lord, asking him to come into their heart and forgive them of all their sins.

Then God places his Spirit in them, and they are immediately saved, yet they still have a choice to continue in his Word everyday to grow in the knowledge of Jesus Christ or just forget they have to continue moving forward into the things of God to continue drawing closer to him. This is just the beginning of someone's life being changed forever. Once you are compelled to the gospel, you must continue doing the things of the gospel. The gospel is in this:

For God so loved the world, that he gave his only Son, that whoever believes in him should not perish but have eternal life. For God did not send his Son into the world to condemn the world; but, in order that the world might be saved through him. Whoever believes in him is not condemned, but whoever does not believe is condemned already, because he has not believed in the name of the only Son of God. And this is the judgment: the light has come into the world, and people loved the darkness rather than the light because their works were evil. For everyone who does wicked things hates the light and does not come to the light, lest his works should be exposed. But whoever does what is true comes to the light, so that it may be clearly seen that his works have been carried out in God.

John 3:16–21 (esv)

In these verses, we clearly see the demonstration of God's love for the whole world. God expressed to us through Jesus Christ the ultimate degree of love, and that is no greater love than a man laying down his own life for someone. "Greater love hath no man than this that a man lay down his life for his friends" (John 15:13, kjv).

For God so loved the world that he gave. First he gave of himself by sending his son in himself, then he came down from heaven. Before the foundation of the world, he had already prepared for us his son to die for us in himself.

John also wants us to know that we have a choice to be born again and receive eternal life through Jesus Christ. For God made this possible for us way before the world existed. He already had a plan of reconciling the whole world back to himself. Yet, he had already decided to give man a free will just like he gave Adam and Eve and also Satan and the angels. God does not make anyone do anything against his or her will. One chooses to accept him or reject him.

God loves us so much that he had already prepared his son's body to be slain from the foundation of the world. God also chose us in him before the foundation of the world, and this is why he gives us all the opportunity to receive him because it was a done deal that he had already established before time.

According as he hath chosen us in him before the foundation of the world, that we should be holy and without blame before him in love: Having predestinated us unto the adoption of children by Jesus Christ to himself, according to the good pleasure of his will, To the praise of the glory of his grace, wherein he hath made us accepted in the beloved. In whom we have redemption through his blood, the forgiveness of sins, according to the riches of his grace; Wherein he hath abounded toward us in all wisdom and prudence; Having made known unto us the mystery of his will, according to his good pleasure which he hath purposed in himself; That in the dispensation of the fullness of time he might gather together in one all things in Christ, both which are in heaven, and which are on earth; even in him: In whom also we have obtained an inheritance, being predestinated according to the purpose of him who worketh all things after the counsel of his own will: That we should be to the praise of his glory, who first trusted in Christ.

Ephesians 1:4–12 (kjv)

Paul wrote a letter of praise and adoration to our father, claiming the truth of God's will and plan of redemption for man. One of Paul's intentions for writing this letter was to enlighten the believer concerning God's predetermined plan for the world. He clearly states that, God in his sovereignty planned before time through predetermined omnipotent power; had a plan that we should be holy and without blame before him in love. He also predestined us to be adopted as his children by Jesus Christ to himself according to the good pleasure which he purposed in himself. God also planned for a time which he calls the dispensation of the fullness of time that he desires to gather together in one all things in Christ, all things in heaven and in earth and even in him. He also has given the believer an inheritance for what he has predestinated according to the purpose of him and that he works all things after the counsel of his own will. And we are here on this earth for his praise and glory for those who first trusted in Christ. This is why it's so important to seek the wisdom and knowledge of God daily through the counsel of God (through the Holy Spirit). He orchestrated a place and time to bring his word into reality by our Lord Jesus Christ. Without a doubt, Paul tells us that God's purpose for the believer is for us to become like him through living a holy life in him. He goes on to speak of the adoption we have. Through the blood of Jesus Christ we have been redeemed. We can be forgiven of all our sins, and it's because of the grace of God that we have already been forgiven.

As we look at verse five, which tells us that before man even existed, God had already predestinated us to be adopted through his Son, Jesus Christ. In those times that Paul wrote this letter, the adoption of a child was a very familiar practice, which the people of that time where familiar with. The laws under the Greco-Roman world where highly adhered, and it was expected for those who lived under Roman law to abide by them. In the Roman law, those who desired to go through the process of adopting a child had to obtain all the legal rights for the adoption to be legal, and upon the completion of the process, the former family lost all rights to their natural-born child. The child even took on the adopted parent's family name and had full rights as though he was naturally born into his adopted family, just as God promised David a descendent which would be God's very own son, which was the Son of God. An extraordinary promise was given to David by God, and it was the promise of an eternal kingdom. Not only was the promise to David, but God's promise to David is extended to every believer. When David heard of the promise God made, he was taken with awe and excitement, and this caused him to worship God knowing how unworthy he was. As often as we can remember, we should praise, glorify, and worship the Lord for establishing his eternal kingdom within us with a deep awareness of how unworthy we are also. Hear in David's prayer unto the Lord how he acknowledges God as the sovereign, supreme authority over all and for being his Master, a matchless God that none can be compared to.

David's prayer to the Lord was his sense in knowing through his acknowledgment to God in prayer that God also was the supreme authority over all of his affairs. For this, David was so humble before the Lord, he praised and worshipped God the more for raising him up from a little shepherd boy into a great king. David knew it was God all by himself who had brought him to where he was—out of a family in which no one knew into being exalted to the throne of Israel. Just like our thoughts at times, David thought he could not explain the mercies of God and how favored he was in the sight of God. There where no mere words to extol of, to truly express the goodness of God, yet, with as much humility as David could give, we like him ought to give God glory and honor due his name. David did not understand God's goodness to man or how God's blessings seemed to come into existence, knowing that man is so unworthy, yet, David still gave of himself to the Lord in worship through humility for God's incomparable blessings for being the God of everlasting to everlasting.

Even though we live in a world that is filled with wickedness, turmoil, violence, and disorder, God is worthy. And to add to this, man also has to deal with situations that arise from temptation, trials, tribulations, much persecution, and calamities. It is in these times that the goodness of God will forever strengthen us, knowing that our help comes from the Lord. It's in the goodness of God, who forever pours his rich promises out to us, and through his Word that we are reassured daily that we can triumph and remain victorious through living in him by the fruits of his Spirit an undefeated life because of God's awesome, omnipotent promises.

For all of those who will hear the word, it is by faith one must call upon the name of the Lord to be saved, and then Christ Jesus will come into their hearts and be their Lord and Savior. And through our acceptance of this free gift to be born again into the family of God, we have been given all the promises of his Word.

> No man can come to me, except the Father which hath sent me draw him: and I will raise him up at the last day. It is written in the prophets, And they shall be all taught of God. Every man therefore that hath heard, and hath learned of the Father, cometh unto me.
>
> John 6:44, 45 (kjv)

Therefore, we are drawn nigh to God by his Spirit, and without his Spirit, we could not know salvation for it is God's Spirit, the Holy Spirit, that is sent to us to lead, guide, and direct us into all truth!

Jesus Is the Bread of Life

> And Jesus said unto them, I am the bread of life; he that cometh to me shall never hunger; and he that believeth on me shall never thirst.
>
> John 6:35 (kjv)

> Jesus therefore answered and said unto them, Murmur not among yourselves. No man can come to me, except the Father which hath sent me draw him: and I will raise him up at the last day. It is written the prophets, And they shall be all taught of God. Every man therefore that hath heard, and hath learned of the Father, cometh unto me.
>
> John 6:43–45 (kjv)

Jesus is the bread of life, and it's only through him that we can be drawn.

> But what saith it? The word is nigh thee, even in thy mouth, and in thy heart: that is, the word of faith, which we preach; that if thou shalt confess with thy mouth the Lord Jesus, and shalt believe in thine heart that God hath raised him from the dead, thou shalt be saved.
>
> Romans 10:8, 9 (kjv)

There are requirements for man to receive salvation, that if thou shalt confess with thy mouth the Lord Jesus, and shalt believe in thine heart that God hath raised him from the dead, thou shalt be saved.

> For the bread of God is he which cometh down from heaven, and giveth life unto the world.
>
> John 6:33 (kjv)

I am that bread of life. Your fathers did eat manna in the wilderness, and are dead. This is the bread which cometh down from heaven, that a man may eat thereof, and not die. I am the living bread which came down from heaven: if any man eats of this bread, he shall live for ever: and the bread that I will give is my flesh, which I will give for the life of the world.

John 6:48–51 (kjv)

A man must listen and hear what the Word of the Lord is saying. A person has to believe that Christ is the bread of life that nourishes man spiritually and saves man from eternal separation from God by giving him eternal life. Christ gave us an example of the physical food—that it only keeps us alive for a little while and then eventually we will die. But, Christ is clear in teaching us that, he is the bread of life. He says to us through his Word, "I am that bread of life." When a man accepts his salvation and by faith believes in him, he eats of this truth, the bread of life, by being a partaker of Christ. One time is all it takes to confess him by faith, and then you will have eternal life forever with him. Yes, you will still have to live on earth for a season, but you now have more than death to expect. Death no longer has power over you once you receive Jesus as your Lord and Savior, for he is the bread of life. Knowing that before you die one day you shall live forever with God is a wonderful and exciting thought and peace to have within. It is here that the religionists were rebelling against the claim in which Jesus had made to them that he was the bread of life.

They questioned where he came from. They began to murmur amongst themselves because they did not understand his incarnation. They all made a choice to disagree as to who he said he was. They did not believe that he came down from heaven. Because they knew his father, Joseph, his mother, and him personally, they thought there was no way he was the bread of life. To them, he was just a mere man like them. Jesus responded to the crowd by saying that they should stop murmuring and his desire was for them to listen to the truth. He knew as long as they kept murmuring amongst themselves, they could not listen and be taught the truth. This is also the same way the enemy comes in on many of our circumstances. Oftentimes, someone who is knew to the faith gets upset, confused, and disturbed about who Jesus is because there are so many beliefs in the world and different interpretations of books about the Bible. It's often we can begin to complain or find someone to listen to us that is as confused about their life and their beliefs as we are when we're just learning the Word.

Jesus wants us to know that he has predestinated us to know the truth, and it is through the Bible that we have access to know the truth. God does not choose who will go to hell and who will go to heaven; that's not what predestination is all about. Remember, everyone will have an opportunity to choose to except him or reject him one way or the other. As believers, God's reassurance is that our salvation is predestined to happen. It's a choice that we have to make when he comes and draws us as he is, the bread of life, and he will bring himself to us as sure as we are alive upon this earth.

Before every human being dies, they do have the invitation that Christ announces to give all the bread of life. Man's desire is to be selfish and sinful, but God's desire for man is that all will come into the knowledge of Jesus Christ. Therefore, apart from God drawing man to him, he is spiritually dead. Until man is drawn to God, man cannot come to God unless God draws him through his Spirit. Man is rebellious due to the sinful nature within him. Even in this, God's love is more than enough to constrain man at the moment he draws him, and it's upon the act of him hearing and receiving by faith that a man can be saved. When someone is a fugitive, they are on the run. When the authorities put out an all-points bulletin nationwide, once the fugitive is caught, he is constrained into handcuffs as he is read his rights; then the suspect is taken into custody to be placed in jail, waiting for his or her day of sentencing. God is the judge, and he is

The Mind of the Sprit

also the bread of life. He offers you the invitation to receive him to save you from the fallen nature in which you are born with, and it's up to you to choose what your destination will be freely.

Before you ever existed on the earth, God placed an all-points bulletin out for his Word to constrain you throughout your life on the earth. Even as I speak on this subject, you may have seen literature somewhere, like a flyer, magazine, commercial on television, or maybe someone talking to someone else about God. It's at these moments and others that you are given the opportunity to listen and be constrained, yet most people only interrupt a conversation if it's something that interests them. And if your reading a magazine or see a flyer of some sort, most of the time, unless it's something that sounds interesting to you, most likely you will quickly turn the page and totally ignore the flyer; yet these are the times when you are given the opportunity to respond to what you may not know. There are so many times throughout your life that God is keeping an account of and watching, and as he sees a moment that can be presented for you to be constrained, he's right there with his arms open wide to receive you if your listening, observant, and aware that he's waiting on you, striving to give you eternal life freely. It's at those moments throughout your life that you have a choice to partake of the eternal life God is offering you, or, if you choose not to receive him in those times in which he gives you the opportunity to receive him as the bread of life, once you die, you have to face the judgment for the life in which you chose and lived upon the earth.

For those who reject his constraint, his Spirit does not force them to receive him, but once death comes upon you and your time on the earth expires, you go right back to God who created you to take your sentencing. It's all a choice in what you decide to do with your life while you are here upon the face of the earth. Jesus loves you so much he sets up many opportunities in making salvation available for you to receive him as the bread of life daily. His desire is to enlighten your mind and bring you into his kingdom forever. He sent his Son to die for just this cause. How imperative this statement is for us to know that God comes to us through sending his Spirit to constrain us, for he desires that we come to the realization that we need to be born again of his Spirit to have eternal life. Now we know that it's through the quickening of the Holy Spirit that the mind of man is moved in his heart to come to God and receive the bread of life. When you really look at reality and what you desire, you want to be satisfied, rejuvenated, and fed well. These are the desires in which God fulfills as the spiritual food that we need. When you partake of the bread of life in which he has to offer you, you will hunger no more. The desire to live and not die will then be satisfied. One of the beatitudes says,

> "Blessed are those who hunger and thirst for righteousness, for they shall be satisfied"
>
> Matt 5:6. esv

Through the death, burial, and resurrection of Jesus Christ, God was in Jesus Christ reconciling us back to himself. It is only through God drawing mankind unto him that we are able to take of the life he has to offer.

> Therefore, if anyone is in Christ, he is a new creation. The old has passed away; behold, the new has come. All this is from God, who through Christ reconciled us to himself and gave us the ministry of reconciliation; that is, in Christ God was reconciling the world to himself, not counting their trespasses against them, and entrusting to us the message of reconciliation.
>
> 2 Corinthians 5:17–19 (esv)

Paul reminds us that through the death, burial, and resurrection of God reconciling the world back to him through Christ Jesus, this is the new world order through Christ Jesus: 1) Regenerated, 2) reconciled back to God, 3) ambassadors, 4) redeemed, 5) the world has the free choice of accepting or rejecting this new world order. This means if we decide to become born again through this new world order, we are new creatures in Christ Jesus; our whole nature, life, and behavior changes. Only through Christ can we experience the reconciliation. To accept Christ is to continue walking in him and living in him daily. It means for us to walk in the Spirit and not in the flesh.

> There is therefore now no condemnation for those who are in Christ Jesus. For the law of the Spirit of life has set you free in Christ Jesus from the law of sin and death. For God has done what the law, weakened by the flesh, could not do. By sending his own Son in the likeness of sinful flesh and for sin, he condemned sin in the flesh, in order that the righteous requirement of the law might be fulfilled in us, who walk not according to the flesh but according to the Spirit.
>
> Romans 8:1–5 (esv)

The Ways We Are Drawn to God

There are many ways that God's Spirit is sent to many, and he gives all a chance to be drawn to him. Some of the ways that God seeks to save those who are lost are through literature, magazine articles, bill boards, invitations to church, Bible studies, Sunday school, maybe someone invited you to dinner and you left before they started a Bible study, a picnic, a tournament for a game, conversation at a grocery store, a track (a message on a brochure that has Scriptures concerning God's will and plan for salvation—sometimes they are left at businesses), passing by a church—whether you're walking by a church or driving by some sort of business, some way and some how, God gets his message of salvation to you.

It will be no excuse for anyone who chooses to ignore, complain, or murmur, often saying that you did not have the chance to know God. If you're not born again or if you are it's not that you don't ever have the opportunity to known God and have a personal relationship with him you just rejected knowing the truth about God by not taking heed to the truth in the Word to diligently seek after him. Sometimes, some people just want to be left alone out of anger, bitterness, rejection, and things that have happened to them from a bad past church experience, or they have become hard-hearted, stiff-necked, and want to do their own thing. Then there are those who have acknowledged God as their Lord and Savior, yet they wanted to be left alone to live their lives as they please. And because many have seen so much fake, phony, and vain people in the church, they believe everyone is like this. Then they are deceived into thinking that this is just the way it is. Get saved and live any kind of way because no one is living it because God knows we are human first. That's an excuse that the enemy has construed in the minds of those who are weak and refuse to understand the Scriptures.

I've had some people who wanted to befriend me, and they knew I was a born-again believer and witnessed the Word, yet they said, "We can be friends, but I don't want to hear anything about God, church, or the Bible." Or, we can talk about our problems, situations, and boldly feel that it's okay to talk about what they know is wrong but expect me to allow my spirit to be tainted with the mess they know they need to clean up. There are some individuals that I spent time with and still played my gospel music, preaching and teaching DVDs, CDs, teaching tapes on the Lord, and after a year or so, the person now goes to church. Yet, I've heard them say, "I'm still not ready to change and give my life over to God." All I can do is pray for them and keep on moving forward into the call that he has chosen for me to walk in. I must continue to pursue, God and so should you. I did not give up on them. And whether or not they chose to give up their old nature of sin and live for God, I was able to plant a seed into their lives, and I continue to pray that they will give their lives to the Lord.

I have associates that I talk with occasionally, and they seem to go further and further away from serving the Lord because they choose to not surrender their lives to the Lord. I will continue to pray for them, and it does not take me going out with them and doing the things they enjoy doing that are not my lifestyle to know how far to go in a friendship, conversation, or place where my witness to them is null and void. If I have a certain book to write, I have had to experience getting close to someone so that I could write in the Spirit without exposing that person and the kind of lifestyle they live. It's similar to a reporter, we often have to talk to people we normally wouldn't talk to, go places we normally wouldn't, and strike up conversations just to get the story correct. I know my limits because I know God's limit through being sensitive to the Holy Spirit that is down on the inside of my spirit. I never allowed them to turn me away from serving the Lord, and if anyone who serves God comes into this sort of situation with anyone, you are not to start gravitating away from God. If you do, then you will have to give an account to God for being naïve or just stupid for losing time and taking a risk on your relationship with God, who gives you the breath to breathe every day. Be careful, watch, and pray always that you don't fall into the old sinful nature just to be friends, married, or have a relationship with anyone. For it is God who has called you to live born again and to be disciplined in him to do his will. I mentioned that it is God who gives us the breath in our bodies to breathe, for oftentimes we choose to take this for granted and we just go about our day doing whatever with whomever as if this was alright with God. We need to be more mindful of the power in which God has over life and death and choose life in him. Amen.

Turn to Genesis 6:3 (kjv). "And the Lord said, My spirit shall not always strive with man, for that he also is flesh: yet his days shall be an hundred and twenty years." When you die, that is the end of God's Spirit striving, compelling, and pleading with you one way or the other to invite you to be a partaker of the bread of life. Remember, we already discussed the many ways that we are drawn to the Lord; therefore, these are the times somewhere in your life where God is inviting you to be a partaker of the eternal life through the bread of life. Whenever you die, it's over and God's Spirit is finished and done striving with you.

God's Spirit strived with Adam before the fall, yet Adam refused to take heed and he caused himself and all mankind to have to die and face death; therefore, God's Spirit does not always strive with man due to a time called death.

"And all the days that Adam lived were nine hundred and thirty years: and he died" (Gen 5:5, kjv). Adam lived for 930 years. I'm sure he told someone of the story of how he and his wife, Eve, sinned and lost their rights to live in the Garden of Eden. I'm sure he told of God's goodness, mercy, and loving kindness. There is no way he lived that long and did not tell of God's plans of how good he and Eve had it in the Garden of Eden (paradise) and what he had messed up for others before the fall. If you had children and you had sinned against God and somewhere in your life faced the consequences of being put out of the Garden of Eden, wouldn't you tell your children and others about the consequences of disobeying God? Well, just as you would warn your children and others of the punishment of sin, Adam did teach the truth at some point and time in the 930 years in which he was on the face of the earth. He definitely had to proclaim the truth of his fall and how the creation was perfect, for there were people in Adam's day that still rebelled against God.

Enoch also preached and warned the people in those times of the Day of Judgment. "Enoch walked with God: and he was not; for God took him" (Gen 5:24).

Enoch means dedicated. He dedicated his whole life to God. Enoch was so close to the Lord that the Bible says God took him. He was taken back to God from where he came. Since the beginning of time, mankind was warned about the punishment of sin and the death of destruction that will come upon all who disobey the Word of God. Mankind became so wicked and rebellious that in Genesis 6:3, God shortened the days that man would live on the face of the earth tremendously. When God saw that men would not obey him and turn away from their wicked, evil, unrighteous ways, he shortened our days by hundreds of years because of sin. He then said that his Spirit shall not always strive with man because man is flesh. The word *strive* means "contend, try." God's Spirit will not always try to reach mankind to receive salvation by faith. If God has sent his Spirit to anyone over and over and over again, there will come a day when death takes hold of you. When your time comes to die—this day comes at a time when you won't know—you will have met the time that your life expires from off the face of the earth, and then after this, you will be no more upon the face of the earth.

Turn with me to 1 Samuel 16:14 (kjv).

> But the Spirit of the Lord departed from Saul, and an evil spirit from the Lord troubled him.

> And when Saul enquired of the Lord, the Lord answered him, neither by dreams, nor by Urim, nor by prophets.
>
> 1 Samuel 28:6 (kjv)

> If I regard iniquity in my heart, the Lord will not hear me
>
> Psalm 66:18 (kjv)

In this lesson, we see that King Saul chose to ask for advice and counsel from a woman with a familiar spirit (1 Sam 28:7–19). This is someone who is a separatist, sorcerer, psychic, palm-reader, fortune-teller, astrologer, wizard, witch, or any sort of this kind. The Lord would not answer Saul because Saul disobeyed God and did not execute Amalek like he told him to do. In former chapters 13 and 15, Saul was disobedient and rebellious to the Lord, and this time God would not answer Saul when he asked him for guidance and help regarding the invasion of the Philistine army that went up against Israel. God's Word means what it says, and it changes not. When God tells

Twila Williams

mankind to do this or that and many refuse to adhere to the voice of God, there will come a time when God's Spirit will not hear their prayers or answer them because of their disobedient and rebellious spirits. Even in all the many ways God sends his Spirit to many of us pleading, compelling, striving daily with us to turn us away from things that are going to draw us away from serving him, yet, we often still go in the way of disobedience. Therefore, it would behoove you if you are not right with the Lord to, humble yourself to the call of salvation and live for the Lord. I'm not saying if you are not born again because there are many who say they are saved and know the Lord, but they walk backwards and not forward; they have a double tongue and talk holy, yet, behind the scenes, they live a double life. God is speaking to all mankind to get right or get left behind, and it is a choice what you choose to do with the time that God gives you to breathe his life, to breathe again after death and go into eternal life, or take your last breath into the death of eternal damnation. It's your life in God's breathe you breath every day all day; so choose this day, every day, who you will serve, which is God.

Take Notice

There are strategies in which the enemy has used to keep the human race preoccupied. The next time you are out, find a place to sit in a busy business area, and for about thirty minutes to an hour just watch how people respond to life and to what they are doing. You will find that they are busy either text messaging, talking on their cell phones, listening to their iPods, surfing the internet at a cyber coffee shop, reading the news paper, studying for a test of some sort, trying to figure out what they are doing later on that day or evening, reading some love story, talking about what they are going to do for the weekend, vacation, who's dating who, who's getting married, having an affair, and rarely will you hear a conversation concerning Christ. Most people don't realize that we are in the last days. Do you think about the times that we are living in? Are you aware of all the things that are going on in the earth? Has it ever occurred to you that God is on his way back and that he has shortened the days or no man would be saved? We are living in a time when we should be focused on what we can do to save our lives and not focused on material things like houses, land, clothes, cars, jewelry, and money. It's nothing wrong with these things I just talked about, but you must have balance in your life to commune with God and do other things that's all right within reason. The things that we have on this earth are just things that we can't take with us once we die. Therefore, it's imperative for us to be concerned with the times in which we live in, and recognize that things are getting worse, and there is great tribulation which is coming upon the earth that will be unimaginable. God, before time, has shortened the days of tribulation because if he did not have mercy on us; even the elect (those who are born again), we would not even make it. Read Matthew 24, and take some time to study it, and if you have a pastor or someone who you can go to and study this passage with who is born again and an avid reader of the Word, this is a good place to be enlightened on the times we are in and what is to come.

Redemption

Come take a walk with me into the book of Hebrews, and let's see how Christ has paid the full penalty to redeem mankind back from sin.

> For Christ has entered, not into holy places made with hands, which are copies of the true things, but into heaven itself, now to appear in the presence of God on our behalf. Nor was it to offer himself repeatedly, as the high priest enters the holy places every year with blood not his own, for then he would have had to suffer repeatedly since the foundation of the world. But as it is, he has appeared once for all at the end of the ages to put away sin by the sacrifice of himself. And just as it is appointed for man to die once, and after that comes judgment, so Christ, having been offered once to bear the sins

of many, will appear a second time, not to deal with sin but to save those who are eagerly waiting for him.

Hebrews 9:24–28 (esv)

There is no scientific solution, doctor's prescription, medical treatment, plastic surgeon, rejuvenation product, vacation getaway, serum, or antidote of any sort that will alleviate the true fact of the Scripture that tells us man is appointed to die. Let's look at the word *appointed* and what is going to happen that we have been appointed to individually. Don't think or assume that you can escape death by convincing yourself that you are going to die and then it's all over. Let's deal with the facts. 1) Man is appointed one day to die 2) After a human being dies, he has to face judgment. 3) God is the creator of all creation, and he will be the final judge of all mankind. Therefore, we must recognize the true fact of the matter and humble ourselves to these facts, receive Christ as the bread of life, or just live as if the Word of God is just a man-made book and there is no truth to it. It's your choice. Then maybe God will say to you, "That's okay. You thought you could get away with not believing in me and live any kind of way, ignoring that there is a death every second of the day somewhere around the world, and you could be next." Wow! What are you going to do? If you are not saved, are you going to live in the presence of God by making a choice to receive Christ and have the full assurance knowing you have eternal life? Or, would you rather choose to die and be separated from God eternally and be doomed?

Let's define appointed: "predetermined, arranged, set, fixed or established especially by order of command." Okay, now we will determine the fact of the Scripture. Have you ever seen someone live forever? Have you ever seen someone not die that was pronounced dead and come back to live on earth forever? Have you ever wondered if there really was a place of torment? Have you ever thought about what it would be like to see God? Do you avoid, ignore, and just live as if you will never, ever die? Of course, you have thought about these things, especially if you have been to a funeral, but we call them home-goings for those who are born again. Most people, even in the church, are not able to accept when their loved one is gone; they always say, "I lost a loved one." Well, I disagree because when your loved one expires by death and is separated from you, if they are born again, you haven't lost them. They are in heaven, waiting on you to die to come into the new life that was already ours before Adam and Eve made the decision to fall into sin. The body does deteriorate; that's another fact. The body eventually goes back to dust, as the Word teaches us also; therefore, these facts about death are enough to convince me that I need to live in Christ by faith and accept him as the Bread of Life, believing in his Word so that I too can be with him one day. Wouldn't you agree?

Garden of Eden

As we journey back into the Garden of Eden, we will be able to see why mankind has a sinful nature and has to go through the troubles of life. We also will briefly discuss marriage because this is where relationship between man and woman first began and Adam is the only man who ever lived that God created and gave him his wife. Maybe this is why men have so much trouble finding their mates because they meet so many women that are not compatible that they get tired and choose too fast, not searching the Scriptures as to what to look for in a helpmeet. On that note, let's look a little further into the life of Adam and Eve being the first humans to ever live upon the earth and how they made a choice to disobey God and because of this great fall everything that was pure and perfect became a disaster.

Mankind would no longer be pure and perfect because sin immediately marred the perfection within Adam and Eve. Everything was for their use except for one tree, and that was the tree of knowledge of good and evil. God warned Adam, saying, "For in the day that you eat of it, you shall surely die" (Genesis 2:17, esv). What God was saying to Adam was, "You will be completely separated from me, and you will have then given yourself over to the spirit of disobedience and have knowledge of what good and evil taste like." Just like we would tell a child, "Don't touch this," or, "You cannot eat this yet," leave it alone and the child does it anyway. Once they do what you told them not to do, they experience the truth in what you told them would happen. Then they must face the consequences of their actions. Once the child does disobey us, his or her eyes are open, and they have awareness (knowledge) by the experience. For example, there are some movies, relationships, places, and things you do not allow your children to go because they are not ready for that experience and maybe because, as believers, we have to set morals for our children and boundaries. Even though we set rules and regulations, there are times that we're not around and things happen, yet we as believers are to have structure in the home for a basis and a guideline to rear our children for their own good.

Adam and Eve opened the human race to sin through disobedience of God's word. Therefore, we must turn back to God through repentance because we are a born product of the sinful nature in which Adam and Eve placed upon the human race. All humans have desires, and we have a choice to experience and taste the bread of life that gives us eternal life through the knowledge of Jesus Christ. The knowledge of anything new when you physically consume of it or spiritually consume it comes as a result of our desire to consume what we give our attention to. This is why we as believers must be careful what we see, hear, touch, and taste because these are the four ways man can willingly sin.

The penalty that came upon Adam and Eve for disobeying God fell upon the whole human race. Therefore, we are born into sin because our nature is from the earth, and it's our flesh that we are embodied in which desires to please itself. The sinful nature that we have feeds on what our desires are, therefore we must have self-control over our desires by renewing our mind daily in the things that pertain to life and godliness.

And to Adam he said, "Because you have listened to the voice of your wife and have eaten of the tree of which I commanded you, 'You shall not eat of it,' cursed is the ground because of you; in pain you shall eat of it all the days of your life; [this is why mankind has to work to make a living] for you are dust, and to dust you shall return."

Genesis 3:17–19 (esv)

We are made from dust even though we are born out of our mother's womb. We are still dust, and that's another truth that we cannot deny.

Now God said to Eve, "'I will surely multiply your pain in childbearing; in pain you shall bring forth children. Your desire shall be for your husband, and he shall rule over you'" (Genesis 3:16, esv). Do you know or have you ever heard of a woman that has given birth to a child without pain? Only if she was given anesthesia, yet there is still pain that a woman experiences after the medicine wears off from natural birth and C-sections.

The role of a woman coming under subjection to her husband is not controlling, dominating, ruling in a way as to not allow the woman to voice her feelings, her desires, and what she likes or dislikes, but two people must first be born again and come under subjection to the Word of God and be compatible, having a good understanding through effectively communicating. Those who are not born again and married have to live together by their own beliefs, and what they have experienced apart from God is different from two individuals who are saved and should have their lives together, honoring one another according to the Word of God. Once a believer falls away from the faith, they must repent to get back in fellowship with Christ or they tend to go in their own sinful ways and desires, not honoring the marriage vows. Then it leads to all sorts of disorder and mixed roles. That's another message on another day, but when you are born again and forget or fall away into other things, marriage seems to not be honored by the pattern that has been set for the believer by the Bible, and things are not the same in a marriage without God being the center.

For things to work effectively in a marriage, two people must willingly communicate. And to just communicate is not the answer, but two people must effectively communicate to get an understanding for a positive outcome. Many see this curse on the woman as a disadvantage, and many women are offended by the scripture which says the woman is to come under subjection to her husband because they often refuse to spiritually understand what God really meant. Not only that, many woman don't wait on the Lord for a man of God, and they use the excuse, "He claimed to be saved and was active in the church, so it seemed like the right thing to do to get married," then, "Now that we are married, I'm supposed to obey him and come under subjection, and he doesn't even live right or treat me like he should." Well, believe me when I say this: most women marry men that they think they can change and see the signs of incompatibility and expect the man to change because they have passionate love or a child by that man, but that's where most Christian marriages have its first dilemma. Church folks put people together just because they slept together or had a baby, then they want to force marriage on two people that are going in totally different directions. Then you have two people in divorce court that should have never gotten married in the first place. Well, you have to get my book on relationships to hear the rest. Anyway, the Scripture does not work without faith in God. God never intended for the man or the woman to be abused in any kind of way, nor did he plan for married people to neglect each other's duties to their mates. We have to allow the Lord to speak to us concerning some things that we chose to do against his will. Some of us got married and were not saved before we chose a mate. And some have married, and it appeared that you thought you understood what the definition of a saved person was, and you still married someone you found that you just can't seem to come to a common ground with. I will say this: God forgives all sin, except blasphemy against the Holy Ghost. (Mt 12:31; Mk. 3:29) It's your life, and you have to know and understand the Word clearly to hear the truth, and the truth will then set you free. I did not mean to go into this, but I am led to give one Scripture, and, from this, I pray you will find some directions from the Holy Spirit. To those who are having marriage problems or those who are considering marriage with someone and they have seen enough warning signs of incompatibility and folks are pushing them to get married, be wise and don't do something stupid and stop being naive. But if the unbelieving partner separates, let it be so. In such cases the brother or sister is not enslaved. God has called you to peace (1 Cor 7:15). In many cases, you have a spouse that is difficult to reason with. They are beyond any reasonable hope for reconciling the marriage, even living together, even when you are sleeping in the same bedroom still just to avoid the children from knowing. Even though they know, most adults try to make an effort to keep peace in the home because of the children. One thing about humans: when there is sin in the camp (home), two people can't seem to get along for many reasons I won't name. There are moments of breaking down and tears of shame, regret, and remorse of what happened. Well, when a partner or both parties are unrepentant, this is a sin, and God hates sin. Many times the evil and wicked ways of a person not wanting to come off of their prideful spirit and arrogant ways to bring some order back into the marriage by cooperating and being forgiving is what causes most break-ups. Too much sin and too much unforgiveness results, in most people divorcing. The problem is that people normally don't do their research and most people tell you what you want to hear and not what you need to know about them. You normally find out many things after you get married and are supposed to work through your differences, yet some things that were hidden from the other spouse are so unbearable that it's too much to handle mentally, physically emotionally, and spiritually. After praying and doing all that you believe you could do, you must do what's best.

Most people show who they really are; we often ignore them because our desires seem to get the best of us. We want what we

Twila Williams

want, no matter the cost, and then down the line we're living in regret. Or sometimes we are just plain selfish and trying to make someone into something in which they will never be.

How often we are ignorant to the truth that exposed itself through moments in time. The biggest entrapment of marrying someone we're not compatible with is intimacy. We get intertwined with the lust of the flesh, and here comes a baby, and we often believe more babies, a ring, and marriage is going to make what's wrong right. Don't wait until after the "I do," and, "Now, you may kiss the bride," to find out that marriage was not the answer to fixing what should not have been in the first place. Did you know that getting married does not change anyone?

I am not telling you to do anything, but you have to approach the truth as the truth and not live in havoc, hell, and chaos. Remember God has called you to live in peace. If someone is so controlling and possessive and sometimes the other spouse has to get away and settle the differences as best for them and if they have children, it's not good for children to see any kind of abuse that's not fair to their innocent minds. Someone has to be the mature adult and make the right decision. The roles often are reversed when a woman has married a man that wants her, or doesn't want her but doesn't want anyone else to have her, or when a man has married what he thought was his wife and they weren't supposed to take it to this degree; or, she wants him, or doesn't want him but doesn't want anyone else to have him. Some people's love for someone is eros love (passionate love with sensual desire and longing), or it can be a combination philia, which is friendship love. Someone is passionate for you but as friends to enjoy sensual or sexual pleasure. These two are common, and people mix them up together thinking they are in agape love, yet without agape love, relationships are often dissolved because agape love is unconditional, selfless, and you need God's agape love within a marriage to stay strong and not give up with every tide and wind that comes to huff and puff and blow your house down. In Christ, agape love is mandatory, and two people must be willing to stay together no matter the situation, except abuses. Agape love is needed in a relationship for it to last and last forever until death do you part. Not in a bad way should death come, like killing someone, but according to how the Word of God speaks of love—that two people should know and understand the meaning of love first, and then they can make a rational decision and not out of ignorance, thinking because they feel love that they have fallen in love.

Now there also is storge love, which is the love of affection for someone. You can love a friend and not have the desire to be affectionate toward them. It's not wise to become as fools. Understanding the Scriptures and the truth about marriage is a whole other book I am working on. The name of this book that is coming soon again is called *Let's Talk: Relationships God's Way*. In the meantime, get the book, *Redemptive Divorce* by Mark W. Gaither, a biblical process that offers guidance for the suffering partner, healing for the offending spouse, and the best catalyst for restoration

Okay, I hope there was something said about love that helped someone. Now let's go back to the fall and what happened in the Garden of Eden. The serpent was the first to be given his curse, for he is the craftiest one of us all.

According to Genesis 3:1, Satan has been equipped with wisdom and knowledge that most of us will not tap into our entire lives. He is keener than man, and he will use his tools to strategize a divisive scheme to lure you every time he gets the opportunity.

> The Lord God said to the serpent, "Because you have done this, cursed are you above all livestock and above all beast of the field; on your belly you shall go, and dust you shall eat all the days of your life. I will put enmity [hatred] between you and the woman, and between your offspring and her offspring; he shall bruise your head, and you shall bruise his heel."
>
> Genesis 3:14–15 (esv)

Remember, every moment you spend allowing negativity, wicked, evil, and impure thoughts to eat off your mind, you are allowing Satan access to be divisive and scheme his desires into you mind. You're taking time away from God when you allow evil to enter your thoughts; this can be doubt, fear, unbelief, hatred, no trust for anyone due to past experiences you had no business in, and any such thing that is contrary to the nature of God. Many people who say they are born again and ready to meet the Lord cannot even experience true love due to their pasts haunting them. What a shame!

I did not intend to go into all of that, but someone needed to hear it. Was it you?

Therefore, the Garden of Eden was a place that was free from sin, and now we have to be born into sin because of the disobedience of Adam and Eve choosing to be selfish and stepping into the spirit of pride, desiring to know knowledge of good and evil, and they were put out of the Garden never to return again. For God knows they would have tried to partake of the tree of life.

He drove out the man, and at the east of the Garden of Eden, he placed the cherubim and a flaming sword that turned every way to guard the way to the tree of life. Even after God drove Adam and Eve out of the Garden of Eden, he still had a plan to save mankind by drawing him back to himself through redemption. God loves us so much that he had a way of saving man even after that man chooses not to serve him. Yet when a man chooses to allow God into his heart, God puts his nature into man to redeem him back before he dies. How wonderful and marvelous our God is, and we are to be thankful for such greatness to be drawn back to the word of life.

The Two Enemies of Mankind

> Wherefore he saith, When he ascended up on high, he led captivity captive, and gave gifts unto men. (Now that he ascended, what is it but that he also descended first into the lower parts of

the earth? He that descended is the same also that ascended up far above all heavens, that he might fill all things.)

Ephesians 4:8–10 (kjv)

The two enemies of mankind are sin and death. Let's define the two words *sin* and *death*.

Sin: an offense against God, the condition of being guilty of continued offense against God, an offence against any law, standard

Sin is making a choice to do things the way you want to do them. Sin is rebelling against God and refusing to allow him to have control or say in one's life. Sin is to live any kind of way and living to be self-righteous. Sin is being rebellious against God and what the Bible says. When a person does this, he is not God, does not live for God, and in one's natural state is going to eventually be completely separated from God because of sin that brings death.

Death: to die, dying, permanent ending of all life in a person, the state of being dead, any ending resembling dying total destruction. It is because of sin that many die and have to face separation and God's judgment. If you choose to live life apart from God and have nothing to do with God while you are on the earth, you will die, and this is the end of your life: to be separated completely from God.

Just like the devil chose to do his own thing and to have it his way, wanting nothing to do with God, he got what he lived to do. The devil did not want what God had for him to do; he wanted to take all that God was and dethrone God. Yet, it is God who created him. Just like sin entices many people for satisfaction to the lust of the flesh, this same lust is from the devil himself. Satan lives in the flesh and the wicked devices of sin. The devil lusts after the souls of all mankind to fulfill his desires by using their bodies to make them do what he loves the most, and that is sin. Therefore, he goes out sending evil spirits, demons, stronghold demons, all sorts of wicked devices against people for his own purpose. The devil was an angel of light cast down from heaven, and now he is an angel of darkness that can transform himself into an angel of light. If someone is not born again and does not understand who the devil really is and underestimates the thought of him even existing, it's an open door that they give the enemy access to use them because their spirit is dead. They are alive and breathing, but their spirit is not open to knowing the things that are written in the Bible.

> But if our gospel be hid, it is hid to them that are lost: In whom the god of this world hath blinded the minds of them which believe not, lest the light of the glorious gospel of Christ, who is the image of God, should shine unto them.
>
> 2 Corinthians 4:3, 4 (kjv)

In this text, we see that Paul is accused of not handling the gospel correctly but charged with being faint-hearted, shameful, and being disgraceful in his behavior. But, Paul proclaimed that he was not mishandling the gospel but was proclaiming it in a pure manner. He says the gospel, if indeed it was hidden from men, it was because they did not believe and that they were lost due to their own choice of turning away from hearing the Word or wanting to know about it. He felt that men who choose to not hear the Word are perishing, which also means they are lost and are destroying themselves. Because of this, they are corrupt and will soon die for lack of responding to hearing the truth. Those who choose to not hear the gospel are turning away from it willingly on their own. Therefore, they intentionally avoid him and separate themselves from hearing through their ears and eyes they have chosen to close them, looking toward the world which is perishing everyday.

Then people choose to not turn their wicked and sinful heart over to God and choose to reject the Word of God, they give the devil power over them to rule and reign in the lust of the flesh. Remember, the devil is still an (angelic being), that God cursed because of his own lust of pride he believed he could make or persuade God to bow to him and to serve him. It did not happen and now the Devil still has the same gifts, he had in heaven but he uses his gifts and talents as tactics and keen strategies, to work against God and people through using people and things.

Even though "the thief comes only to steal and kill and destroy. I came that they may have life and have it abundantly" (John 10:10, esv). You no long have to live in the lust of the flesh because the devil no longer rules and reigns in your life. If you do sin, you do it by choice and you have access to choose whether you want to do right or wrong in every choice you make. Always remember that you are born to make choices whether right or wrong. You don't have to obey your flesh by the enticements of your desires. It's a choice, and it's yours all by yourself. You don't have to be naïve and allow others that are doing sinful things to influence you to do wrong just to feel you fit in or you may feel you don't want to be left out. You do have a choice to do right or wrong every day of your life. You make your own choices; don't blame someone else. You can stop people from convincing you to do wrong if you learn to control your flesh through obeying the Word. You must choose to do right as much as possible within the boundaries of what the Word has instructed for you to follow every day. If you don't recognize the enemy, believe me when I say this, he knows your old nature and what you like by the description of your fleshly desires of your past, and he will use what he has to strategize against you daily to tempt you and entice you through the lust of your flesh to fall away from the journey that has been set for you.

Now listen closely, my friend. These two enemies I just described are something you should always be thankful to Christ Jesus for destroying by taking them back from the devil. The devil had thought he had sin and death in his hands, but the Bible states that Christ Jesus went down into hell and took these two enemies back! The enemy can only live and rule when we as individuals listen and do what he tries to entice us to do. Also, everything you desire to do is not all the devil. There are many things that we desire of ourselves to do, and it has nothing to do with the devil. He can come into our situation(s) to entice what we have already lusted for in our hearts to do for sinful pleasure, but he is not always the initial instigator all the time. Now you have power in Christ Jesus when you, "submit yourselves therfore to God first. Resist the devil, and he will flee from you (James 4:7, kjv). If you choose to entertain negative thoughts based on an assumption from things that have happened in your past (old nature, sinful nature, the flesh), then you are being bait for Satan to use your mind for negative, ungodly, and unholy activity. You are allowing your thoughts to wander off into areas that have nothing to do with where God is trying to take you, and you are already there, but until you resist the devil and all evil thoughts that come with his wicked, enticing words of fear, then you will embrace fear and love with fear is torment. You have to either embrace love or fear, but both are a chaotic, mind-blowing experience that will cause you to live in doubt of someone who may really love you and has been sent to do you good and not wrong all the days of your life. Therefore, be wise to think on things that are not contrary to the Word—good things, lovely things, pure things and not negative things, doubt, fear, and unbelief. These things will stifle your growth in Christ, and you will be like James said, "A double minded man is unstable in all his ways" (James 1:8, kjv). That is a sin, and you are saved now and have no business living in the mind of double-mindedness. All through the Bible, God requires for man to make the decision to choose righteousness over unrighteousness (sin), and then he will act upon you making the right decisions according to the Word of God.

Turn to James 1:13–16 (kjv).

> Let no one say when he is tempted, I am tempted of God: for God cannot be tempted with evil, neither tempteth he any man: But every man is tempted, when he is drawn away of his own lust, and enticed. Then when lust hath conceived, it bringeth forth sin: and sin, when it is finished, bringeth forth death.

Christ Jesus paid the ultimate price to triumph over the two enemies of mankind, and we no longer have to worry about sin and death if we choose to give our life to God. Now if you need to ever explain to someone why we need Christ Jesus to be the Lord and Savior, then let me tell you. We need Christ Jesus because when he becomes our Lord and Savior, it is through the blood of Jesus that we conquer the two enemies that come against mankind. These two enemies come against us daily to make us feel and think that life has no purpose and that life seems to appear senseless. Because we have a sinful nature, sin comes from within us by what we desire or lust to do, and we are tempted daily. What drives us to do wrong are the things we allow into our ear gates and eye gates; and what we can't see is often what we touch or taste. Sin is all around us daily because our flesh is against the nature of God to drive us to our lust. What is it that you lust for? Do you resist it, or do you just do whatever you desire? Who is it that drives us to sin? Do you find yourself hanging around someone or those who have the same desire? What are you doing to stop, avoid, and get rid of people or not go places that put you in such sinful situations?

You don't have to always see sin to sin. You can feel a thing and desire to sin. You don't always have to hear something wrong to sin. You can imagine or dream about doing something sinful and desire to sin. Haven't you ever dreamed about someone and did everything in your might to get in touch with them? They were just a call away, walk away, drive away, or maybe a plane ticket away, but often you found yourself in sin. That's what sin will do for you—take you where you don't need to go. Then you find yourself where you are deeper and deeper falling into sin because sin brings shame, but if you are in denial and pretending to be something you're not, you will fall even more. Especially if you're with someone or people who don't care and live this way all day, every day. The devil is slick. He knows who to send when you are feeling the way you are through a phone call, text message, e-mail; or, something you may see someone else doing on TV will entice you where you are weak and draw you into dreaming and longing to do whatever it is that your flesh often lusts to do.

Now when you make the choice to sin, you die the death of sin. This means that you lust after whatever your flesh craves to do, then you are enticed (captured at the moment) to do it—whatever that is—then you do it, and then the thrill for that moment is death. You tasted death (separation from God for that moment you gave into that enticement through the lust of your flesh). Did you get it? You sin; you separate yourself from Christ through the flesh because you cannot please God in the flesh. For those who live according to the flesh set their minds on the things of the flesh, but those who live according to the Spirit set their minds on the things of the Spirit.

> For to set the mind on the flesh is death, but to set the mind on the Spirit is life and peace. For the mind that is set on the flesh is hostile to God, for it does not submit to God's law; indeed, it cannot. [The sinful nature that has not received Christ cannot obey the law of the Bible because the flesh is not obedient to the Word of God but desires to lust after what it craves, and that is sin.] Those who are in the flesh cannot please God.
>
> Romans 8:6–8 (esv)

You bring the fleshly desires of your old nature to the front of your thoughts, and then you act upon that desire, and it brings you closer to the death of fleshly consumption. Death of the old nature is what you decided to choose instead of life after the new nature in Christ. You ate from the fleshly pleasures instead of from the Spirit of life, the bread of life. Lustful pleasure is the after-affect of sin. Once lust has conceived and sin has been pleased upon your flesh and upon you, it brings pleasure to the flesh and after that death. The death can be mentally, physically, or even emotionally or intimately. How often we desire to do some things. Maybe one time we sin, and then we find we don't like what comes after the sin, and we don't do it anymore. Or how often have you ever sinned and enjoyed it? Whether you find pleasure in having sex, stealing something, lying, cheating someone, drinking alcohol, or maybe smoking something, these are just a few pleasures. But there are others like shopping too much, eating too much, doubting God (not having faith), worrying about things and what you don't have or what you are about to lose. Sin comes in many ways, and you just need to examine yourself and write down what brings your flesh pleasure and work on having self-control through the fruits of the Spirit and putting on those thoughts that are from above and not on the earth.

We have to control our flesh by keeping it under subjection to the word of God or our flesh will drive us to do what is not Christlike. Make an effort to conquer the flesh daily and stay clear of those who encourage living a reckless life yet say they are serving the Lord, but you find they live any kind of way and do whatever their flesh desires. It's easily done, and you enjoyed it and found pleasure in your fleshly desires, so you kept doing this thing over and over again. Just remember, sin brings death, and it's not just a physical death that we're referring to. It can be something you do once and the desire dies after the taste of sin does not fulfill the lust of your flesh; therefore, the desire of sin is never satisfied. Its pleasures are a bottomless pit that will consume all those who turn to its sinful pleasures. If you're not careful, sin of the old nature will come up strong in your will. If you don't get some self-control over what you enjoy doing, it will get into your mind and take control of your body, causing you to get so deep into sin that you begin to live life as if you are already going to hell. You can be self-destructive through unprotected sex, stealing, cheating, and many other things. You can become reprobate in your thinking by desiring sin for a season of pleasure and then turning away from God to do it. After a while, you convince yourself that it's your life and you can do what you please and deal with the consequences later. It sounds like pride to me!

I will repeat this again just in case you did not get it the first time.

These two enemies come against us daily to make us feel and think that life has no purpose and that life seems to appear senseless. This is another entrance in which the lust of the flesh begins to think of ways to bring excitement to the flesh. Being more promiscuous than you were after you knew right from wrong is worse than when you did not clearly know right from wrong. Adventuring off for one moment into the pleasures of sin for a season brings sickness of the mind, body, and spirit to the forefront, and then you have more things to try and tackle than you had before you went on your adventure, wouldn't you agree? That man or woman you should have just left at a hello and a good-bye, but you decided to go out for a latte or an early morning breakfast. Or you decided to sit down at work and talk out your problems with someone that was not thinking about serving the Lord but serving you in a sexual way. You just gave them an entrance into your life, and oftentimes people will feed off of what you tell them. Many people find a whole lot of pleasure in gossiping. What about the childhood crush that you decided, "Well, nothing new is working for me, so someone from the past may be the answer to fulfill my desire to be married." You got what you bargained for, didn't you? Or, that car you wanted so badly you took your income tax and put it down for the down payment but knew you did not make enough to keep the payments up or the job was already unstable before you spent your income tax on a car when you already had bills.

The flesh will cause you to sin through what you desire in your flesh already convincing you through wickedness, rebellion, and every evil work under the sun, that you have no way out but to eat your way into the pleasures of death, sinful pleasures. Wow! Sin is in you, but you have the ability to say no and take control of your flesh by living a self-controlled life and not an out-of-control life. If you can stop yourself from walking into the traffic when the light is red, if you can train yourself to pass a college course because you are that close to graduating (and so you cut out all the hanging out and late night phone calls to pass a class), if you can save up money for a trip you've been dying to take or a gift to yourself that you can't afford but choose to put money aside to save up for it and see the end results of owning what you so desire, if you can stop drinking or smoking because the person you want to date said they refuse to date you if you don't stop doing this or that, if you can avoid the person that you thought you wanted to be with and now you can't stand them because they weren't the way they appeared to be or the way you imagined them to be, then you can stop yourself from hooking up with other sinful pleasures. Right? These are just a few examples of what self-control we have when we want to. You are to control your flesh, and your flesh is not to control you. If you don't feed yourself spiritual food, you will continue to feed your fleshly desires and be consumed by them.

You die to sinful pleasures. You take control over them and keep them from having an appetite by staying in the Word, meditating on it day and night, letting the Holy Spirit lead you, guide you, and direct you into all truth. No, you're not perfect, and you will fall short sometimes because you are human, but don't just blatantly do it intentionally because, oh, you're just bored or say, "God understands." No more excuses. You need to be an example and a living witness that it can be done. One bored thought can take you on an adventure you wish you never thought of because you never imaged that drifting away or falling away by turning away from the truth could bring to years later of saying to yourself, "I just don't know what happened?" Too much sinful pleasure often brings us too much grief and sorrow that we cause to come into our own lives through refusing to take control through self-control. Not just by spiritual suicide, but living a life of sinful pleasures eventually results in spiritual suicide. You are killing yourself by the lust of your flesh at a rapid pace with time ticking, which waits for no one. Or let me put it this way: Satan often strategically will deceive you into thinking that it's okay to just continue in your old sinful ways because you have no way out but to eventually die and then it's all over. But, the devil is a liar. When Jesus died, he went into hell and took the keys of death and the grave (our two enemies), taking them from Satan and now gives the greatest gifts to all mankind, which is meaning and purpose with eternal life. Upon Jesus' death and resurrection, we can obtain life in him by faith to proclaim the gospel of salvation.

> I am he that liveth, and was dead; and, behold, I am alive for evermore, Amen; and have the keys of hell and of death.
>
> Revelation 1:18 (kjv)

Just remember when the enemy of life tries to oppress you, depress you, or when life seems to try to wear you down by those who you allow into your life or by those who slip themselves cunningly into your life, remember you can control your destiny through living in Christ Jesus and staying free from wrong choices and people who don't desire to have control over their decisions. When you learn to stay free from these things through the truth in the Word of God, you can be an example to others by your lifestyle, teaching other unbelievers how to be born again and teaching those who are believers how to stay free from sin and have the victory over sin and death that you have when you continually walk by faith in Christ Jesus. The most wonderful experience in life is when one is born again of the Spirit, learning daily how to crucify the flesh, putting it to death through the Word of God. Once we die to the old man, then the new man in Christ Jesus can live and fill our lives with power through the Holy Spirit to continue triumphing over our sinful desires and all trials, tribulations, and persecution. When we recognize that we do have power through God's Word and victory over the enemy in knowing how to live in God's Word, that's when we truly experience the gifts that Christ Jesus has freely given to the believer. This is what makes it possible for as many who will believe, they too can have the gifts that Christ Jesus has for all who call on his name to be saved. You must rejoice in the fact that we can now die to the old nature that brought mankind into sin and death and live in the new nature of Christ Jesus that gives us the gift of meaning, purpose, and a promise to live forever.

Hindrances in the Mind

We are living in an era where the Holy Spirit has called the angel armies of God to sound the trumpet on the earth into the ears of the remnant who are spreading truth. God is calling the remnant forth and speaking many words of truth into our spirits to call out demons, commanding them forth and casting out the old tradition, rituals, and ceremonies to bring in the new anointing which is refreshing every day. He is calling those who have surrendered all to him and are willing to humble themselves to the call of the trumpet in heaven's throne. We must come out from among anyone who will not obey the true Spirit, and all who choose to rebel against his Word must be reproved. He has spoken his word into the atmosphere for the remnant to cry loud and spare not against those who have a deaf ear and a mute voice in the pulpit whose purpose is to stop the truth from being told. God has sent the righteous out with a cry from Zion into the wilderness for the righteous to reverse the curse through spiritual warfare. For there has been a spiritual battle upon the earth against the righteousness of God since the fall of the enemy, and it has set on many leaders in clergy, organized religions, and churches who are churchlike, spiritually dysfunctional in their worship, spiritual but have allowed false teaching to hinder their minds. For many people who are working against the true worshippers who come in the name of Jesus Christ, to worship him in spirit and in truth, will come forth to do just what they have been chosen to do. I send a clarion call from the word of truth into the atmosphere calling the true worshippers to come forth and not be hindered in their minds any longer. I declare and decree the mind of the reader to open his or her spirit up to truth and receive it in the name of Jesus Christ.

Listen, my brothers and sisters, if you refuse to come out from among them and be ye separate, than you shall eat of the fruit of damnation unto unrighteousness. The scripture says this: "My sheep know my voice and a stranger's voice they will not hear" (John 10:27, kjv). Open your ears and hear in the name of the Father; hear, my child, in the name of the Son and name of the Holy Ghost. I command you to open your spiritual ears and your spiritual eyes and hear what thus saith the Lord God.

I feel a need to pray before we go any further.

I speak as an ambassador of Jesus Christ to declare, decree the truth by exposing that which is a hindrance to the mind and that through the Holy Spirit you will recognize truth! I speak a word of life into the atmosphere and command your eyes to see and your heart to receive the Word with clarity. In Christ we live, move, and have our being in him to come alive and open the ear gates, and it's God's will for our eyes to be open to the things of God. We sit in heavenly places with Christ Jesus, therefore, I come against every hindrance of the mind and the enemy to take flight away from your ears to hear and your eyes to see the truth as God would have you to see it. I pray against the spirit of control, manipulation, and deception. Father, I pray that the true worshippers will come forth to worship the Lord in Spirit and in truth. It's time to give the true worship that's due to the name above every name! Those who desire to know how to switch from the natural into the Spirit, from the carnal to the Spirit, from the flesh into the supernatural by coming into the divine knowledge of Jesus Christ, I command you to come into alignment with the Word and come up higher into the Spirit. I declare that from now on your flesh will come under subjection to your spirit. You're spirit will have dominion over your flesh, and you will not allow the flesh to lead you, but you will recognize when to make the right choices in your life. I command you to abandon the old nature and to reject its desires to live free from sin. For God has not changed; he is the same yesterday, today, and forever. I command you to be free! In the name of Jesus. Amen.

> Till we all come in the unity of the faith, and of the knowledge of the Son of God, unto the measure of the stature of the fullness of Christ: that we henceforth be no more children, tossed to and fro, and carried about with every wind of doctrine, by the sleight of men, and cunning craftiness, whereby they lie in wait to deceive; But speaking the truth in love, may grow up into him in all things, which is the head, even Christ; From whom the whole body fitly joined together and compacted by that which every joint supplieth, according to the effectual working in the measure of every part, maketh increase of the body unto the edifying of itself in love.
>
> Ephesians 4:14–16 (kjv)

Those who choose to follow man will surely reap damnation. Those who choose to worship the dreams, visions, and mission of a man that is mortal and turn from obeying God will be judged for their rebellious actions. For there will be no excuse when the husbandman comes back for his bride for those who choose to let any man deceive them out of their inheritance.

The call in which God has put on the inside of your spirit you are responsible to carry it out. If you choose to go through life and not get for yourself what God has for you and if you choose to not find out what God has created you to do, you still are held accountable for the work in which he has called you into. If you choose to live a life of being deceived by not being aware of what God has created you to do, it's no ones fault but your own. Don't be deceived, but know what the will of the Lord is and know how to search the Scriptures so you can receive the truth of the Word on the earth in which God has already given to you. There is one appointment that every soul must keep, and that is the time of death.

For we must all appear before the judgment seat of Christ; that every one may receive the things done in his body, according to that he hath done, whether it be good or bad (2 Cor 5:10). Therefore, those who are in leadership have even a greater responsibility because they are required to live by example and teach the truth. For the many that refuse to do right by God's Word and hinder the growth of the weak babes in Christ, they will be held at a higher standard because they know the truth and while they were in leadership chose to hide the truth and teach a lie (false doctrine).

There are many in leadership (all those who are in clergy positions) who say they come in the name of the Lord to do God's will; yet, they have conformed to the teaching of men and the doctrine of Baal and serve a god in the name of a ministry, but it's not God's true doctrine, and it comes to hinder the flow of the Holy Spirit. These false leaders are of the devil, and, for lack of knowledge, those who follow after this sort of leadership, religious organization, and/or denominations are only helping these men and women carry on their false beliefs and teachings, which are far away from what God ever intended for men to do.

When Christ Jesus was upon the face of the earth doing his Father's ministry, he kept on moving and did not settle any particular place. He kept the Word moving down on the inside

Twila Williams

86

of him and taught the doctrine of the Bible as it was written, not adding or subtracting anything from it. If we are going to reach the world, then we as believers must stop filling the pews week after week and Sunday after Sunday and get out of dressing up all the time, saying we are dressing up for Jesus, but teach the truth and hit the streets, the community, cities, states, and go into all the world, giving up everything to follow in the pattern in which Jesus has laid for us. We can sit in church all we want and sing songs of praise and adoration and have all sorts of fellowship; and from one year to the next, the same people are sitting in the same seats and may have been promoted by a man into another position, and that's it. That does not mean God is pleased with those who choose to promote one another in high places to be exalted and honored from one year to the next.

No, we need to go out into the world, forsaking all to follow Jesus, not following a man's agenda, man-made tradition, and rituals. When Christ Jesus chose someone to walk with him in ministry, he told them to leave all and follow him. He did not put them through regiments to form different organizations and groups. The doctrine of the Word of God was in Christ Jesus, and that was enough to draw the people to repent and follow him with an obedient spirit. God does not see the gender of one who is speaking his Word as an oracle for him. What he does see is his doctrine, the Word of God, being lifted up and spoken out of a willing vessel who is not ashamed to speak the truth. For it is God who has preordained, predestinated, called, chosen, sanctified, and anointed who he pleases to do his mission, purpose, and plan. He commands us to worship him in Spirit and in truth. He will use whom he sends his spirit into to get all the glory, honor, and praise out of their lives and for his will to be fulfilled on this earth. It was not Moses that was holy, but God's Word and assignment in which the Spirit was given to him to work for God. God placed his will in Moses' life. He led the children of Israel out of Egypt. Amen.

(see: Ex. 14)

Jesus told Simon, called Peter, and Andrew, his brother, saying, "Follow me and I will make you fishers of men." He also saw two other brethren, James, the son of Zebedee, and John, his brother. They also immediately left the ship and their father and followed him (see: Matt 4:17–25 kjv).

There are many who left all when Jesus called to follow him, and they did not think twice; they immediately did it. A lot of people who say yes to God and say, "Lord, I surrender all," seem to miss it and refuse to immediately leave all to follow him.

The problem with men today is that they choose to turn away from the truth by being hindered through the deception of blindness. Men often choose to not hear the truth because the flesh is being fed more than their spirit man. There are many who choose to follow after other men instead of patterning themselves after God. God's Word speaks against all who walk contrary to his Word. God will ultimately have preeminence in the earth, and his purpose and plan is being fulfilled and made known throughout the earth and will break through the barriers of those who try to hinder it. Our forefathers rejected God's plan and quite often chose to scheme, connive, trick, and deceive people by making their own agendas, missions, and systematic teachings by bringing their selfish ways of teaching the Word into the body of Christ to hinder God's Spirit.

Since the beginning of time, men have chosen to put God in the system of man-made calculus. Men have tried unto their own detriment to collaborate their man-made finite intellect over God's heavenly, delegated government. This has only caused division, dissension, havoc, hell, and chaos to be entertained, and there is nothing but vanity in all of that. People who are misled by false teaching are being detoured, hindered, and set back, and those who teach this foolishness will one day give an account for the many they have misled and hindered from experiencing the outpouring of the spirit of truth. The many man-made agendas that have corrupted the people of God will soon be renounced. Many men, women, and children are still hungry for the Word of God, and there are those who are greedy to profit first, or, after all the Bible says, they still have formed their own governments, but God's Word will prevail before it's all over.

Oftentimes when you go into a church, the stage is set (the pulpit, praise singers are in place, and things look orderly) and it sure looks good and appears right, but you must be well learned in the Word (a seasoned believer) to know how to discern the truth and be ready to beware of this sort of falsehood. Just like in the days of the Old Testament, they had one evil king die and another appointed; so it is in today's churches. One wicked overseer dies and another one has already been trained to conform to that same heresy which the last elder placed his mantle on through a ritual to carry on his form of doctrine. They're not kings, but they are leaders who are raised up in the church and taught how to be corrupt by false leaders of old, and then when one false leader dies, another has already been sworn in to take over and carry out the false agenda of the one who claims he founded the organization. He founded it all right—with the help of the devil and his cohort of demons who teach falsehood with a twist and every evil way. You really must be careful where you are being fed. It does not matter whether the crowd is big or small, you must not sit and feast off of the Word because falsehood is a contamination that is a deadly disease if you catch it. Be careful, watch, and pray that you fall not into this sort of false teaching.

Always remember that we are to worship God in everything that we entertain. If we choose not to scrutinize what those who teach or preach unto us by searching for the truth of the Word so that it lines up right in his sight, it's our responsibility as individuals to search the Scriptures for truth. Whether in our thoughts, desires, or willingness to serve, we must serve God without the spirit of rebellion, which is a form of witchcraft. He says that we have been purposed to do what he has placed in our hearts to do. Yet, if we refuse to search the Scriptures for ourselves, forget the Scriptures, and have lack of knowledge and don't seek the wisdom of God it's to our spiritual detriment. We are to comprehend the Scriptures according to the way that his Spirit gives for us to learn its precepts through his Spirit, or we miss the truth, and the mission of God for our lives is hindered. We are called to serve the Lord in Spirit and in truth, but when the truth of the Word is spoken in corruption—twisted, added, subtracted, and tainted—then it becomes a hindrance to others. We must shift our desires to his, but if we want to keep on being stiff-necked, rebellious, and go in our own ways just because of the masses of people who have fallen away from the faith. We have to know that we are responsible for the choices we make. We will be responsible for allowing the spirit of hindrance to come into our life, which often works its way into our worship when we refuse to preserver into the truth of how to worship God in spirit and in truth.

People are not even convicted of their sins and ashamed to do wrong anymore. Many in the church have allowed right to be wrong and taken on other forms of worship without a thought of the consequences. Many have chosen to be held captive through mere words from mortal men and women who come in the name of a rebellious nature, yet, often-times it seems as though they speak as oracles from God but are oracles from hell itself. Oftentimes, denominations are formed and occults are made without someone forcing anything on us. We often listen to any-thing, and if it sounds good we all say, "Amen." We just allow and accept any kind of man-made sermon and say, "It's God, and that's good." No! It's not God just because someone has prepared a sermon and made it sound good or because someone knows how to use a commentary and a *Strong Concordance* and study for months to prepare false teaching to feed you. That doesn't make it valid and acceptable in God's sight. These are those who distort the truth.

Man can preach this one and that one into heaven all they want by the works of their agendas, yet God is the judge of the heart and the very intent of a man's eternal state. Organized religion is good, but God is not moved, nor do the angels in heaven rejoice if those who are born again are led astray from the truth when they participate and agree with such erroneous doctrine through false agendas. False doctrine is a true hindrance to the body of Christ, individually and collectively. It has been carried on from one decade to the next, destroying billions of people, taking them away from the truth in the knowledge of Jesus Christ.

For those who are born again yet are tricked, deceived, and connived into buying into these man-made systems that come from Satan, who is a liar and the father of lies, it's going to be a sad day when the truth is revealed from heaven. Wow! We have too many educated, self-made clergy who won't bow to God, yet many men and women bow to those who have their own agenda apart from the true and only doctrine, the Bible. Those who teach false doctrines will use the Word to form their points, and they do pray to a god, but not God. There is only one founder of the church: Jesus Christ. There is no other founder. What if you would take the time to read the manuscript and study it for yourself (the Bible) and not allow anyone to insert their own philosophy, which doesn't belong, into the Scriptures? When you go to church to hear someone break open the bread of life and feast with you from the bread of life, if they miss one ingredient from the preparing of making the bread to cooking the bread then breaking the bread, it will not digest correctly and will be sour, bitter, and good for nothing but disposal. You have to know how the bread should be prepared and know what it should taste like before you can rightly digest it in order to get the true revelation of the truth. For the true revelation of truth can only come from the one who is the truth, the way, and the light, and that is Jesus Christ.

Paul said this,

> Wherefore I take you to record this day that I am pure from the blood of all men. For I have not shunned to declare unto you all the counsel of God. Take heed therefore unto yourselves, and to all the flock, over the which the Holy Ghost hath made you overseers, to feed the church of God, which he hath purchased with is own blood. For I know this, that after my departing

shall grievous wolves enter in among you, not sparing the flock. Also of your own selves shall men arise, speaking perverse things, to draw away disciples after them.

Acts 20:26–30 (kjv)

Paul's claim was to the ministers of his day and to all ministers that would come after him. He was confirming that he had done the will of the Lord in preaching and teaching the gospel as Christ would have him to and that if any man was not saved, it was his own fault because he not only spoke and wrote the Word, but he lived it by example. What Paul says here is what every preacher and teacher in any church ought to live up to. These words are the last words that where recorded to the church leaders by Paul. This message is that of a "Woe." A warning to the leaders in the churches then and throughout all ages that they should beware of themselves and guard their lives and that of the church, by watching over the sheep in which God has given to them. They are told to feed the church, which is God's, living only for God and the Word of God. The leaders are warned also not to covet worldly wealth. If one is a leader, Paul warns them to watch their conduct, character, and meet the requirements of God even before they look after or feed God's flock. Leaders must be aware of what they focus on, giving attention to guard their lives and guard their lives against false teaching. A leader should not follow after fables, myths, ideas, genealogies, heritages, and that of his or her ancestry's beliefs. Leaders are to seek the truth by being faithful to the doctrine and the teaching of Scripture. The minister who is true to his call must look after all of God's flock because sheep wander, get lost, and fall weak to sin; therefore, the leader of God's church is to continue in the true doctrine of God to lead his sheep in the way they should go. Sheep can often be a prey to the false teachers of the world and also within the church. Therefore, a true leader of God will be a nurturer and feed the church of God in fear and reverence to the truth of the Word.

Leaders must feed the church of God because it is God's church. He paid the supreme price with his own blood. Jesus is without a doubt God, and he is the one who shed his blood to purchase the church. God owns the church and has the say in everything that goes on with the church. Since he is the purchaser, it is in his Word that the leaders of his church are to not deviate from, the Bible, and God is who dictates what is to be and not to be—not man-made doctrine, not tradition, rituals, ceremonies, and laws of men. The church has been given the truth, and the Word is the truth that leaders are only overseers of the church in which God has already purchased and laid the foundation for man to build on. Leaders are his assistants to what has already been founded by God. This is true, and when man gets in the way and says he founded this and that, this is how false teaching gets into the body of Christ and seducing spirits come in through false teaching to hinder the truth through men who want the glory as if they purchased the church and not God.

The Real Garment

There is a real garment and a fake garment. Which one are you wearing? When you learn of the real garment and learn to recognize the fake garment, you will then be able to distinguish the difference and not be hindered any longer by the enemy who comes to hinder daily.

The garment or attire of someone's clothing and how eloquent they can speak on a subject out of the Bible does not authorize them the delegated heavenly authority to twist, turn, add, and subtract words from the Bible to lure and deceive those who are eating from every word which is spoken. To speak another gospel is to be accursed, and the hindrances it causes to man disrupts the attention of God to call and hold those who teach such corruption accountable to him.

If we are to declare and decree the gospel of Christ Jesus, then we are also to live it in its truth. The garment of our souls is what God is looking into, not the garment of our appearance. It's what you say, how you say it, and when you say it that matters to the Lord, for he sees your heart and knows that if what you are saying is coming from your heart or is it just a form of lip service. Don't be fooled, for he knows your heart. God reads the fine print of your heart. As the scripture declares,

> Either make the tree good and its fruit good, or make the tree bad and its fruit bad, for the tree is known by its fruit. You brood of vipers! How can you speak good, when you are evil? For out of the abundance of the heart the mouth speaks. The good person out of his good treasure brings forth good, and the evil person out of his evil treasure brings forth evil. I tell you, for every careless word they speak, for by your words you will be justified, and by your words you will be condemned.
>
> Matthew 12:33–37 (esv)

I know there are many churches that are doing great things, yet have you ever asked yourself, "Are they doing these great things taking the glory away from the Lord and pulling the wool over the eyes of the masses of people who follow after them?" It's your life, and you have a right to choose to follow the masses of people or to read the fine print for yourself and evaluate it to make sure you're in the right place with God and doing the right thing for God and listening to the right voice. You still need to be sure you are being lead through the ministry you're in by God. Or do you just go along with the crowd? Or do you go and stay in a denomination because your family has been in it from one generation into the next? How are you driven to respond at times if you're among many who think they are in the place that they should be? Do you know how to pray and wait patiently for God to give you an answer as to where you ought to fellowship? What is hindering you from communing with God? If you do find that you have missed his guidance, can you stop and reevaluate the situation and get back on the journey that you may have gotten off of or never began to walk into one way or another?

Do you fall further and further away from God by allowing people to speak what they call a word of wisdom or knowledge into your life, yet you don't know if it's false or true because you refuse to search and seek the truth for yourself? You hinder your own life by being one who refuses to search and seek for truth in taking someone else's word without prayer and communion with the Lord for yourself.

Of course, we are not perfect, and we will make choices that change our lives one way or the other. But, we can regroup to get on track to stay in communion with the Lord, but we must swiftly do it! We must catch ourselves from being fooled by the mere words of someone who may slightly change the Scripture or its root meaning. As individuals we must observe each word or words someone says concerning the Word to discern what is right. The believer has been given the Holy Spirit that can discern the heart and mind of man. If we allow God's heart and his mind to live in us by living in the new nature and not in the old nature, we then will be able to discern the words that a person speaks to see if they line up with the truth in the Word. "Beloved, believe not every spirit, but try the spirits whether they are of God: because many false prophets are gone out into the world" (1 Jn. 4:1. kjv). Even in a church setting, we need not to be so naïve, gullible, and stupid about what we see and hear being careful not to act as if we cannot see when something is not right. We see as believers by the spiritual eye and not the natural. Many times when someone allows something to go on for so long that is wrong, they often become immune to it and begin to conform to wrong and gradually begin to believe the person is right or that the situation they are dealing with is right. Don't allow men's enticing words to lure you away from the Lord, even in a church setting or any relationship, for it's your life and you need to search diligently through the Scriptures every day for the truth. The Word of God should be unto the believer like a feast or a buffet. We are to go back time and time again until we are full and overflowing with the Bread of Life, and it should fill us until the next time we go to feast at its treasures.

Don't Let These Things Hinder You

Don't be hindered by the lights, cameras, and action! There are many people in the church (who love mega churches just to be on television or to impress other's, they want to get the glory for themselves), these are those who are used by the enemy and will play a role in church pretending to be saved when they are just faking it, just to have a part in the scene (just to be in the lime light) and have rehearsed the main characters' role (putting on an act of what a true believer is, they are impostures) and by choice they duplicate the the real genuine worship that belongs to God. Don't be set up by watching a scene that was rehearsed by someone watching every move as to how a believer ought to look, talk, and dress, yet they are pretending and are hypocrites. Many have gotten away from who they have been called to be like and are following the fake, phony, and those who perpetrate the truth. Those who are duplicates of the truth, their words often come off so smooth and sound so good that we often fall for the smooth-talker because we are attracted to someone's voice who is charming. But, it's a set up to deceive you. Don't be taken by the crowds and those who have given in to false ministries that look like they serve Christ, but their hearts are far from serving the Lord (study: 2 Pe. 2:14-17).

How you live your life determines your destination for the journey you're on. Therefore, be careful who you follow. But, you can be taken off of your journey by allowing someone else to mislead you, taking you for a ride you will never forget. Then many years later, you'll find yourself reminiscing on where you could have been and what you should be doing, and now it's too late, and you just have to pick up from where you're at, at that moment.

You have to strategize swiftly and be quick to hear, slow to speak, and slow to wrath, or the enemy will come in through enticing words to lure you away from the truth. You should not even hear or listen to some leaders, for eating the wrong words is like eating poison that gets into your system to taint your blood. Church is like this. You know when you go to school and when you are picking your classes that the first thing that comes to your mind is, *I hope this is a good teacher or instructor*. Often you think when picking classes, *I hope I learn something from this professor*, but you have so many days to see if this is the right professor for you, and you do have time to change classes. Well, when you go into a church service, you need to pray for discernment and make sure it's where God would have you to go. Sometimes some people can put on an act that you don't always catch on the first sermon, but take your time putting your name on a church role. If it's already ten fools following another fool, they are all in the ditch, and you don't need to be the 11th fool. Nor do you need to see 1000 fools following the wrong leadership and become the 1001 fool for following false doctrine. You are warned about false teaching throughout the Bible, just be careful. I know that sounded kind of harsh, but the devil isn't playing, and souls are in the balance that need to not just be saved but led in the truth. Don't come out of the world and think you can be naive and gullible. You need to be on the scene, being your own narrator with the right act, not the narrator of your life being dictated by others and on someone else's scene in the church with the wrong script.

You are what you say, and people's garments are the very essence of what's in their hearts. The nature of your soul lies in what you do with the words you hear that often need to be researched and clearly broken down for your garment to be on right. Many people are not going to heaven because their garment is spotted with false teaching.

When you speak, do you have the authority of the right garment on to be heard and respected, or is your garment (words) a tinkling symbol of broken words with no harmony to heaven's throne (I Co. 13:1, 2 niv)? What garment are you giving your offering in? Is it the garment to be seen or the garment of humility and sincerity? It doesn't matter what men have set up. God already, before the foundation of the world, had a set government in heaven that rules and reigns in the earth. Many churches have already set the scene and they're waiting for a gullible, foolish, naïve person who is willing to play the part for the act in which they have written for someone who is not learned in the Word to play. You have to not take an offer from a church, just like you don't take any offer from a school or a job. If you get a call about a job opening and it's for something you know you have not applied for, do you just go and work somewhere and do a job that someone else wants you to do but you don't even have it in you to do? No, you work in the field you know you can do.

You are called to work in areas that you may not be comfortable with at some point and time in your life, but overall you need to know what the will of the Lord is for your life, for yourself, or people will put you in a scene that you don't belong. Don't let others dictate to you what God has called you to do. Oftentimes it's a position they need filled, and it's not even the will of God, for your life to do it. You are often in a waiting period for what it is that God wants you to do. You need to establish a relationship with God first and then take your time to find out what it is that he has called you to. Sometimes there are some instances where a person goes right into the call of God in which he has called them to, but it's up to you to find the work that you are to do for God before you leave this earth.

Paul said,

> And what I do I will continue to do, in order to undermine the claim of those who would like to claim that in their boasted mission they work on the same terms as we do. For such men are false apostles, deceitful workmen, disguising themselves as apostles of Christ. And no wonder, for even Satan disguises himself as an angel of light. So it is no surprise if his servants also, disguise themselves as servants of righteousness. Their end will correspond to their deeds.
>
> II Cor. 11:12–15 esv

If you have been in sin for decades and now you're in the church and they are hindering the will of God in your life by using the Word to manipulate you into doing the job they want you to do, you have authority through the power of the Holy Spirit to speak a word into the atmosphere according to the Word of God and you can command the spirit of confusion to go. Do not believe what man tells you all the time, not even some of the time. You must believe the Word of God. This means when someone is going to break the Bread of Life, take notes, and go over the Scriptures later to make sure it lines up with the Word, even if they are using the Bible; Remember Satan knows the word too.

Just like you go to court and the judge tells you these are the things you need to take care of before you come back to court, there are directions for your life already printed and spoken to you in the Word of God. You need to get right with God and stay right with God from the first time you get saved, and don't be lazy about your salvation. Read the Word and learn it in the Holy Ghost for yourself! Don't be pretending to live by every Word of the Lord and doubt him yet say you have faith in the Word. For God's Word is his bond, and what his Word says can only come to pass by you believing by faith and living in the garment of praise that it will be done. Many are walking as dead men and women often in many churches by listening to dead words that men wear outwardly but in their hearts the words are not genuine. Too many people refuse to take heed to God's perfect will in the order that it has been established in through the government of heaven. Yes! It's already been written and established. It's time to establish on earth what's already established in heaven! Stop being hindered by mortal men's mere words who speak things about you that they haven't taken the time to pray fervently about to give you the right directions. You will find that people can only take you so far, and you should not let them take you anywhere that can't be completed. That's why you have the Holy Spirit who takes you and is with you all the way until the end to lead, guide, and direct you into all truth.

And God said, "This is the sign of the covenant that I make between me and you and every living creature that is with you, for all future generations: I have set my bow (rainbow) in the cloud, and it shall be a sign of the covenant between me and the earth. When I bring clouds over the earth and the bow is seen in the clouds, I will remember my covenant that is between me and you and every living creature of all flesh. And the waters shall never again become a flood to destroy all flesh. When the bow is in the clouds, I will see it and remember the everlasting covenant between God and every living creature of all flesh that is on the earth." God said to Noah, "This is the sign of the covenant that I have established between me and all flesh that is on the earth.

Genesis 9:12–17 (esv)

Just as God said he places a rainbow in the clouds to remind the future generations of his covenant with Noah to not ever destroy the whole world again with a flood, he has many more covenants that he has established in heaven between every living creature, and it's in his established government that heaven's throne is God's perfect will in which our lives in him can be governed on earth.

Cults and Its Hindrances

Cult: a system or community of religious worship and ritual, a group having a sacred ideology and a set of rites centering around their sacred symbols.

Ideology: a set of doctrines or beliefs that form the basis of a political, economic, or other system.

Ritual: any practice or pattern of behavior regularly performed in a set manner.

Religious: implies adherence to religion in both beliefs and practice.

System: any organized set of interrelated ideas or principles.

There are many people who are sitting under cults, and these cults where formed by the devil himself. Through mere words, Satan himself used his famous, old, ancient nature by being subtle in character. He sent his poisonous hemp into the minds of men and women and changed the doctrine by adding and taking away the words of the Bible by men who twisted the truth of the Bible. He often sends strong delusions into many of men's evil and wicked hearts who are now upon the face of this earth. For there are many men who have died and went on before us yet left other men in charge, who took an oath to carry on the false doctrine and teaching of Satan, the devil himself. Those who are dead and have founded these false denominations that God never intend for his people to submit to have caused more division, dissension, havoc, hell, and chaos than God would ever allow. Just as Christ turned the tables over because of the people selling and buying in the temple, I believe if Christ was on the earth, he would reverse and invalidate a lot of man-made ideas, beliefs, statement of faiths, written and signed oaths, and turn over all the tables that men set up to make merchandise out of the people to get wealthier and wealthier; yet, there are poor, hungry, and homeless people who are going without right in the church. Many are hungry, homeless, and have lost hope living just within a block away from many churches. Okay, I know the Word says that we will always have the poor with us, but that's just the problem. Many denominations are fruitful by the use of other people's labor. They work witchcraft through using the Bible against many who are willing to serve because many people often go into church not knowing anything about the Bible and depend solely on the pulpit to teach them the right way. It's those who are greedy for gain and carry out their desires of deception on innocent believers who are not aware of the games that many play in ministry by deceiving those who refuse to read the Word themselves.

You have pastors and bishops who live in a mansion and don't even use but two rooms and two bathrooms, yet homeless and helpless are right in the neighborhood where their church is built. Watch where you give because you might be giving into a formed cult, and you are responsible for the support you pay into for the garment which speaks into your life.

False denominations and religious people have built their churches on the foundation of these false teachers. God has allowed the spirit of reprobation to come upon them, and devils are entertaining each other through the religious people who have accepted these false teachings. What I mean by this is many people in leadership are so mean-spirited and have no spiritual insight at all that they cannot even pray a demon out of you if you have one because they have too many lesions of demons in their own spirit. Many men have sold their souls out to an oath that they chose to take, and they are to follow their leader, imitating his ways to keep that founder or leader's dream alive. They do just enough to cover up the underground schemes and systematic rituals and rules that keep many under their spell of bondage as they congregate together to devise a church fund in order to house their extravagant luxuries and expensive fixtures instead of building houses and having a fund to help not just the elderly but the single parents, drug addicts, and children who are in the system that have no parents. Using the name of God in vain is like decreeing and declaring war against the righteousness of God. It doesn't matter how many masses of people who come to the church building, God has to be in it, and you will know by the fruit which is being bared. Just because you see masses of people going into a building does not mean God's hand is upon that ministry.

Cults are often not easily detected, but many are conned, connived, tricked, and lured to give up their houses, money, and whatever else these sorts of organizations (which are undercover cults) require. Quite often cults are church buildings that are right in our community. We don't recognize a city or county cult because we have been programmed to believe that a cult is a place far away in no-man's land where a false teacher takes a group of people and leads them astray like Jim Jones. No, a cult is any form of doctrine that is contrary to the Word of truth. A cult does not have to move far out into the desert or into a small community; but in the city, county, state, and wherever there are people, cults are formed and have been in business from one dead bishop, pastor, minister who consecrates his chosen disciples to carry out his plan, dream, and vision, which he has gotten from the devil himself. God has been grieved in the spirit, for his bride has been in travail since the enemy has taken hold of many churches through the leaders he uses to teach false teaching, false religion, and doctrines of devils. In the pulpit, there is more corruption against God than the sinner in the world. These religious people sit in high places and hold leadership positions and use the Bible as a weapon against those who cannot discern the works of the devil himself. Ignorance of the Word has caused masses of people to be lead astray. A good book that will teach you about spiritual warfare is called *Clean House Strong House: A practical Guide to Understanding Spiritual Warfare, Demonic Strongholds and Deliverance* by Kimberly Daniels. There is much deliverance needed to cast out the demons that operate under a cult spirit.

There are so many divorces and single women raising children in the church. There are also men who are raising children, and if you're not careful, you will go into the church thinking you can marry someone just because they're in the church. If only many of us would have taken heed to the warning signs they always show before the initial ceremony. For instance, you can go into a church and see that something is awkward, backwards, twisted, and strange, but since someone invited you or a so-called relative goes there, you feel an obligation to a mere man to satisfy his desire for you to at least stay and see if you can go along with the circus. Wow! You may wonder why I used the word circus, because some church services are on display to provide a performance of acts, then at the end of the service you pay for the entertainment. Don't ever be ashamed to express how you feel in a cordial way and leave right out of the service before you get lured in with enticing words. You are going to church to be fed, and you can't eat at everyone's table. The church service is like a full-course meal, and if any part is tainted, it's all tainted.

Also, if you ever are in a place to be married and see that something is not right, do not ever be ashamed or feel embarrassed to put off, stop, or tell a person you decided not to marry them. It's okay to have a wedding, but not to your detriment!

Remember, you're the one that has to wake up and go to work, lay down, and sleep with someone after the celebration is over. You have to watch and pray, seek the face of God, lay before him and travail, and as you court someone, the signs will show who they really are. If you don't get on your knees and fall prostrate while your getting to know someone, you may find out after your married they where not the one and you should have been more prayerful if this is the case. It's a shame that we are so backwards. Wow!

Many believers must be careful that they are not tricked or hoodwinked into a cult environment, and maybe that's why you cannot find or ever meet the person who you were meant to be with. You cannot get into a false religion and think you're going to have a lifelong partner, mate, and commitment to a person who has been taught erroneous doctrine.

Cults are false doctrine with mere men teaching poison to your very soul. People have slipped into sin and have a way with words to cause many to be lured the same way that they have chosen to go. There are these sorts that have ways to get you entangled through sex, money, or beautiful people who look normal. You watch them act like you think they should act for the moment, but somewhere down the line, you will notice a look of imitation in character that will come out every now and then. Just be careful, pay close attention to chameleon spirits and those who are mimickers of the gospel.

I am talking about people who have professed Jesus as their Lord and Savior, not those who are in the world; therefore, let's go into the deeper secrets of the church leadership. These sorts are those who are in high places yet are homosexuals, lesbians, and bisexuals. I'm talking about church folks who say they are born again. They hide behind the truth by denying the true foundation and doctrine in which Christ Jesus laid before the foundation of the world. You have ministers and bishops who are married with children yet practice homosexuality and you just ignore what the Spirit is showing you and stay faithful to a ministry that is run by these sort of people who twist the Word to fit their fleshly desires. See: Ro. 1:18–32.

I'm still referring to those who go to church and those who preach, teach, and hold the holy Bible so dear to their hearts, yet they live any kind of way and hide it from the public, but what they do in private is a shame.

There are many chosen women who worship God in Spirit and in truth yet are not able to freely do the will of God for the enslavement of false teaching and false religious order. There are many men who are caught up in homosexuality as young men and don't know how to get out because a cult spirit is a strong hold that needs to be cast out, and if wickedness is in the pulpit to the door, then it's going to be a day of judgment that has to fall upon that congregation to bring it to a stop! Innocent children in the church are ruined because they are being molested at home and the parent(s) is so busy dealing with this and that and ignoring what's really going on, not spending quality time and raising their own child or children that there's no relationship connection where the child can feel safe to talk about what's going on. There needs to be order, morals, standards, and a nurturing family as a whole in the home, and a relationship with God must begin and continue in the home before one can live and do the will of God effectively. One must stay in communion and fellowship with God to hear from God. Worship begins at home through being an example and watching fervently, praying with your children, and teaching them the ways of the Lord. It's as if someone wanted to lose weight, but they only stood in one place and did all sorts of movements but didn't do the exercises right. They were working their weight against their purpose by not following the right steps because they went and ate the same way, trying to get different results. If you're born again, you have to change your old, nasty, wicked, and self-righteous ways to get righteous, holy, and live a Christ-like life in order to fulfill the will of the Lord by living in the nature of the Lord. If you profess to know God and do things or associate with these sorts of church people, then there's something wrong with you. You need to reevaluate your life and search yourself. Consider your ways, and stop pretending. Consider your ways, and stop turning a deaf ear to the truth! Open your eyes, and see the salvation of the Lord and stop running after the lust of your flesh. Consider your ways, and be careful how you treat the temple of the Holy Spirit which temple you are? The scripture tell us this, "Train up a child in the way he should go; even when he is old he will not depart from it" (Prov 22:6).

How are we going to teach a child anything when we are fighting over houses, land, cars, jewelry, money in the bank, this one having an affair on that one, a man finding his wife in bed with another woman, and a woman finding her husband in the bed with another man. Let's go deeper. Saved and so-called holy church folks having orgies and threesomes, going on internet sights to find the lust of their passions to fulfill themselves, sneaking and creeping all through the week and then going to church on Sunday, but through the week they have sinned and carried on like some sorts of freaks. What is that? How is it that the born-again believer has gotten so far out of touch with the truth and what family is only to mislead their own children into the pit of hell? That's why when the protestors were out in Washington D.C. to pray against passing the law against same-sex marriages, there were just a handful because church folks, so-called saved folks, those who say they believe, are doing the same as the world, and it's a shame that billions can't band together and come together for what they believe in, but it seems as though those in Christendom have lost their way because they are not standing for

Christ Jesus and are sneaking and creeping, falling prey to any and everything. Wow! What has become of the unity of the faith in the last two decades? (see: Ro. 2:1–16)

Let's take a walk into the book of Deuteronomy for a moment.

> "Hear, O Israel: The Lord our God, the Lord is one. You shall love the Lord your God with all your heart and with all your soul and with all your might. And these words that I command you today shall be on your heart. You shall teach them diligently to your children, and shall talk of them when you sit in your house, and when you walk by the way (when you walk with them) and when you lie down, (bring them in your room and teach them), and when you rise. (In the morning, find time to share a word of truth, pray with your children.) You shall bind them as a sign on your hand, and they shall be as frontlets between your eyes. You shall write them on the doorposts of your house and on your gates. And when the Lord your God brings you into the land that he swore to your fathers, to Abraham, to Isaac, and to Jacob, to give you with great and good cities that you did not build, and houses full of all good things that you did not fill, and cisterns that you did not dig, and vineyards and olive trees that you did not plant and when you eat and are full, then take care lest you forget the Lord, who brought you out of the land of Egypt (bondage) out of the house of slavery. It is the Lord your God you shall fear. Him you shall serve and by his name you shall swear. You shall not go after other gods, the gods of the peoples who are around you for the Lord your God in your midst is a jealous God lest the anger of the Lord your God be kindled against you, and he destroy you from off the face of the earth.

> Deuteronomy 6: 4–15; 16–25 (esv)

> And it will be righteousness for us, if we are careful to do all this commandment before the Lord our God, as he has commanded us.

> Deuteronomy 6:25 (esv)

It's not about the fancy houses, expensive cars, and how much you can strut yourself to the church house every Sunday to play a part in a church scene. That's not what you are called out of darkness into the marvelous light to do. If you have to walk away from things to save your family, then so be it! If you are single and have lost your job, it wasn't God's will for you to have that job, and he is taking you into another direction if you will just listen to him. God is trying to tell you to let it all go for him and he will give it back. If you have been single and can't seem to find the right mate but you are not in a position financially to take care of the things on your own, let go of those things, and God will send you a good thing that has no problem starting over from the ground floor.

If the believer would look into the mind of God and see that it's times when we have to suffer and rejoice in-spite of it. Well anyway. Consider this,

> Now, therefore, thus says the Lord of hosts: Consider your ways. You have sown much, and harvested little. You eat, but you never have enough; you drink, but you never have your fill. You clothe yourselves, but no one is warm, And he who earns wages does so to put them into a bag with holes. Thus says the Lord of host: Consider your ways. Go up to the hills and bring wood and build the house, that I may take pleasure in it and that I may be glorified, says the Lord. You looked for much, and behold, it came to little. And when you brought it home, I blew it away. Why? Declares the Lord of hosts. Because of my house that lies in ruins, while each of you busies himself with his own house. Therefore the heavens above you have withheld the dew, and the earth has withheld its produce. And I have called for a drought on the land and the hills, on the grain, the new wine, the oil, on what the ground brings forth, on man and beast, and on all their labors.
>
> Haggai 1:5–11 (kjv)

If you don't worship and praise God at home, why wait until you get in front of the churchy church folks to fake it and live a lie in church? God is the only order that was, is, and is soon to come, and we must get right to live a life that is pleasing in his sight. Therefore, cults do not and will not be a part of God's glorious kingdom, and if you believe there is something wrong with where you fellowship, you need to seek the Lord and get yourself in a fellowship to be fed the living water that will keep you from unnecessary spiritual diseases that will infest your mind and control your heart! There are some who claim that if the Lord was to come back today, they are ready to leave. Yet, they can't even walk away from a wooden or brick house that they cannot take with them if they died today. If you have to stay in a one-, two-, or three-bedroom with one bath, size it down however it takes to live and afford what you can at the moment and for a short season; keep yourself before the living God who gives living water, and stop complaining and murmuring and serve the Lord with gladness. He said, "In everything give thanks!" Some of you are not that healthy and are bringing more sickness upon yourself worrying about how you are going to pay your mortgage, robbing this one and that one, lying to this one and that one, conning this person and borrowing from that person. We are to be the lenders and not the borrowers. "The rich rule over the poor and the borrower is a slave to the lender" (Proverbs 22:7).

> When the Lord our God brings you into the land that you are entering to take possession of it, and clears away many nations before you, the Hittites, the Girgashites, the Amorites, the Canaanites, the Perizzites, the Hivites, and the Jebusites, seven nations more numerous and mightier than yourselves, and when the Lord your God gives them over to you and you defeat them, then you must devote them to complete destruction, You shall make no covenant with them and show no mercy to them. You shall not intermarry with them, giving your daughters to their sons or taking their daughters for your

sons, for they would turn away your sons from following me, to serve other gods. Then the anger of the Lord would be kindled against you, and he would destroy you quickly. But thus shall you deal with them. You shall break down their altars and dash in pieces their pillars and chop down their Asherim and burn their carved images with fire.

Deuteronomy 7:1–5 (esv)

We are to not even give into other's who live around us that do not believe in what we say we know and believe, and that is the Lord Jesus Christ, the Savior of the world. We are to turn away from those who don't serve the Lord and not be entangled together with them. We are not to treat them badly, but we are to be wise as serpents and harmless as doves. We marry anyone that we feel like and don't try to see if they have chosen to serve the Lord or not. We date anyone who will stroke us the right way. The excuse, "God knows I'm human," is not going to work the day your life expires and you stand before a God who judges the quick and the dead. Don't think I'm not going to get on to the women. Women of God who are single and desire to be married, aught to be more careful of the men they allow around their children. This is why if a single woman has children and a man desire to get to know her, if she is not seasoned in the word, it's good for her to go to her pastor or someone who is seasoned in the word to guide her on how to be lead in waiting on the right mate. Often times, women who are in the church are so excited when a man gives them some attention and they seem so vulnerable to the point of putting a relationship that is not of God before their own children and this is not God's will. What has become of those who profess Jesus as their Lord and their Savior? It's a mess in Christendom, and it doesn't have to be this way. Wishy-washy, double-minded folks are unstable in all of their ways. Watch out and be careful about how you treat one another because one day you will reap what you have sown.

Internal Religion and External Religion

Before we leave this section, I will attempt to describe the internal religion and the external religion to give a biblical principle to tie in with the family and church.

There are two religions in the world: one in which people show on the outside, and the other religion is what people show on the inside. The external religion in which people try to dictate is those who show how they are physically and morally clean. To be internally religious is to be spiritually regenerated and made into a new creature in Christ Jesus. The external-religious people live their lives, to betray keeping the outside clean, and the inside they think will be clean. The internal-religion people live to keep the inside clean, believing then that the outside will also be clean. The external religious develop a system that consists of laws and governed behavior. The internal religious act out of their hearts in love and respect, which they have for God and man. The external religious live to be faithful to religion (the church) and its practices, moral teachings, and say this is the way to be clean. The internal religious believe that to be cleansed within you must do it by Christ Jesus, then you will be faithful to church and live your life justly. The external religion comes from the man-made religion in rituals, ceremonies, laws, works, and tradition. The internal religion is God's religion (foundation, principle) through his son Christ Jesus. Let's go to the Scriptures to see how Christ handled this conflict.

> Then Pharisees and scribes came to Jesus from Jerusalem and said, "Why do your disciples break the tradition of the elders? For they do not wash their hands when they eat." He answered them, "And why do you break the commandment of God for the sake of your tradition? For God commanded, "Honor your father and your mother," and, "Whoever reviles father or mother must surely die." But you say, "If any one tells his father or his mother, "What you would have gained

from me is given to God," he need not honor his father" So for the sake of your tradition you have made void the Word of God. You hypocrites! Well did Isaiah prophesy of you, when he said: "This people honors me with their lips, but their heart is far from me, in vain do they worship, teaching as doctrines the commandments of men."

Matthew 15:1–9 (kjv)

In this day, the Jewish religion over many, many years attempted to make great numbers of rules and regulations trying to govern man's behavior to keep man religious and morally clean. A part of these regulations dealt with rules to keep oneself physically clean. The rule was that a person had to wash their hands before they ate a meal. The disciples failed to wash their hands before eating a meal; therefore, they had broken the tradition of the church, and this was an embarrassment for the religious faithful to the regulations and rules of that day. The Jewish people who were the scribes and Pharisees decided to ask Jesus to respond to the disciples' failing to wash their hands before they ate a meal. Jesus told them that they broke God's law in order to keep the traditions of their religion, giving them this example, "God says, 'Honor thy father and mother.'" But your tradition says that once a person vows to give a gift to the temple, he can never back out of the vow. Jesus let them know that he was not a lawbreaker but told them that they are and that they were hypocrites because they chose to follow after rituals and regulations that were governed by man who thought this was the way to being religious and morally clean. He told them they were putting their own rules before the laws of God.

The religionist's conflict with Jesus was over religious beliefs and rules, and oftentimes, the modern-day people thought this to be of no importance and sometimes too harsh but mostly misunderstood what was going on and what Jesus was trying to teach. Most people have a lack of understanding, and, through rejecting to hear, they often get no understanding by finding fault first. They find fault with what they choose to not take the time to learn. Through the centuries, religious beliefs were what held the Jewish nation together. Even though time and time again they had been conquered by army after army and millions fought them and won. The loss of many wars they never could seem to win, this caused them to be scattered over the world. Even in the days of Jesus, they were enslaved by Rome. Without their religion, they had no binding force to keep them together. There were beliefs that God had called them, calling them to be a distinctive people. They were called to worship the only true and living God. They held strong beliefs that governed the Sabbath and the temple, intermarriage, worship, and cleansing, and what foods they could and could not eat. The rules were the Jews protection from alien or outside beliefs, and they did not want to be overtaken by intermarriage. Holding to their strong beliefs of not marrying out of their race is what they believed would keep them strong. They held their distinctiveness as a nation through their religion. All Jewish leaders held to this and knew this to be the truth that their religion was the only binding force that held them together as a nation, just as we find many religions and cultures that have a binding force that holds them together and sets them apart from others.

We as believers need to have God in us and live as he would have us to live to have his binding force of holiness, righteousness, and Christ-like morals as our first foundation to family and our personal life. We ought not take on other peoples' beliefs and religions and imitate any particular people other than exemplifying the pattern and nature of Christ Jesus. If you are in Christ Jesus and are a new creature, what distinguishes you from the world should be your lifestyle and behavior (attitude, personality). You are to have the heart and mind of God and conform yourself by renewing your mind to the salvation you have taken on in him and have professed. Becoming like him is to stay inside the perimeters of what his Word says and not entangle yourself back into the yoke of bondage to people, places, and things that pull you away from the truth in his Word. You are to live in the profession of your faith with an assuredness that God's Word is the binding force that will concur all things that you will go through for the journey that is set before you.

When you start seeking to please people and choose to follow after things of the world and begin to gravitate away from your communion with God, be careful. These are the behaviors of the world and those who don't know God and have their own beliefs, and if you're not careful, you will find yourself compromising little by little. But, you are not to fall into the old nature and live there anymore. You must choose everyday to follow Jesus and not let your heart and mind be entangled into the rules and rituals and become regulated by what men do. It's God who called you to be liberated out of the bondage of sin and man-made truths that are contrary to the Word of truth.

The Jewish nation had something they believed in, and they stood strong in their beliefs. You too have something that you should stand strong in and believe in as you carry out its truths, and that is the Word of God. He is your leader, dictator, and you are to imitate him as often as you think, and know in yourself that you are his and he is yours. For he has come to give you life more abundantly, but you can only experience his abundance when you walk in him, live in him, and know that through him you can do all things through Christ that strengthens you. He can only strengthen you when you walk in him through acknowledging him through humility of the heart, allowing his nature to lead, guide, and direct you into all truth by his Spirit.

Just as the religionist of any religion has their strong beliefs and they hold to them, and even though they are contrary to the Word of God, they still hold to them as their truth. We as believers are not to stray, sway, and be double-minded, going back and forth in what we say we believe when many don't know what to believe because they refuse to learn the nature of God to walk in him. One minute we want to be saved for a season, and then all of a sudden out of nowhere we find ourselves heartbroken over this situation and that person or that thing that we wanted, and we did not pray and seek God to be led in the right direction; therefore, we miss the way in which Christ would have us to deal with ourselves and then our family and those who we desire to be in our lives. We choose all of this over God and find ourselves down and out and left for dead. Then those who we thought we could depend on let us down, and we are feeling brokenhearted because we chose to not adhere and take notice of God's will and his ways first. God told us to guard our hearts with all diligence. But, instead, we give our hearts to those who don't know how to keep their own hearts, and they drag us right down to the bottomless pit of sin where they live.

Most of the time we are in the predicaments we are in because we're often choosing not to humble ourselves to the Lord, by following his nature. To stay in him is to worship him through prayer and fellowship at all times. Just as the Jewish leaders had a deep conviction of their doctrine and religion. They stuck with the rules (their traditions or beliefs) they had made for their people which regulated them and this is what held them together, they stuck to what they believed. You as a believer are to hold true to the Word of God and allow its precepts and commandments to hold you together with or without anyone. You are to live Christ-like at all times, putting him first, and then you will not be entangled in illogical and unreasonable actions that come from walking in the flesh and not in the Spirit. If you won't be regulated by the Word of God, you will be regulated by someone or something that will cause you to walk contrary to the Word of God.

The religionists were men that had professions, positions, and were recognized and esteemed highly. Yet, anyone who went contrary to what they believed and taught, they held as a threat to all they had, and that was their belief. If they lost the war, they still had their belief. If they had to bury a loved one, they still had their belief. If they had nowhere to live, they still had their belief. If they felt threatened by God sending Christ Jesus, they held on to their beliefs, and they were so strong in what they believed and what their religion meant to them and their nation, they crucified Christ because they felt he was a threat to their nation and its beliefs. They felt that he broke their laws and he undermined their position and security.

There was a fourfold error in the religionist beliefs. 1) They misinterpreted God's Word 2) and corrupted it. 3) They committed all sorts of sin in the eyes of God (crucified Christ, 1Thes 2:15; they refused to embrace the gospel, Rom 2:17–29; 4), They chose to preach against God's law and enforced their own laws' rules and regulations that were of no effect to the new life that Christ came to give all through the Spirit of truth. (study the book of Romans)

The religionist in that day allowed their religion, tradition, and rituals to become more important than meeting the basic needs of human life. There is the need for God and the need for spiritual, mental, and physical health, yet they refused to teach about Christ, the true Messiah, yet he came and exposed their error. This is where the battle line was drawn. Christ came to liberate people from this sort of enslavement of teachings that caused this sort of behavior. He came to save them so they could worship God through his free Spirit. Those who where religionists felt they needed to put an end to Christ because to them he was a threat to their nation and to their position, and what they held as security was their belief, so they chose to oppose him at whatever means, even if it called for putting him to death.

We cannot choose to be ourselves and follow after other cultures and beliefs and live a self-righteous life, not helping others and playing religion and not living godly lives by not being conformed to the true Word of God and say we know the Lord. We cannot feel threatened by the truth and run from it, living day-to-day contrary to the salvation we have been given to live in him and have been given the true gospel; yet, to walk in it is to expose our sin, and we cannot turn away from it and expect to get God's spiritual richness that comes only through the Spirit of truth. We have to teach and model his Word through a self-controlled position and not waver in our faith. Even in today's economy and all that it's worth, we are not to depend on what the news and media says; we are to depend on the Lord.

We are definitely living in a time when God is holding people accountable for not being willing to humble themselves and walk away from things like houses and cars—even some family members can sometimes hinder you—and all sorts of things that have no position or place in kingdom business. There is a time and a season to let go and forget about how hard we worked for things and live as though Christ is coming at any moment. Until we can let go of things and stop preying on other's yet say we are believers in Christ, we are choosing to love the world and the things in the world first over our salvation, and we will be held accountable for not helping one another because we choose often to look at the past in what people have done to us and refuse to help others who God has sent to walk side by side with us into our future. Therefore, we often have rejected the true help that God is sending because it does not look or appear the way we think it should.

Yes, Living Water

The woman of Samaria asked Jesus for living water, and she had to first face the truth. She had to be convicted of her sin and, upon her conviction, renounce it (John 4:1–26, esv). There are many believers in Christ who need to be convicted of their sin(s) and go back to living a clean, godly, and moral life. There are so many who need to admit to their sinful living, rededicate their lives back to the Lord, and be cleansed by the living water of Christ Jesus. If it's you, you must go back to the place where you lost your faith, and whatever sin which is driving you away from the Lord, you need to repent, turn away from that sin(s), let go of that person or thing that's holding you captive or enslaving you to them or it, and ask God for forgiveness for not adhering to the Word. David prayed to God after Nathan the prophet went to him, after he had slept with, Bathsheba. (see: II Sam. 11:1–17, 26, 27)

Just like David's prayer in Psalms 51, was for repentance for the wrong he had done, we need to know how to pray the prayer of repentance when we have done wrong and sinned against God. Living water from Christ Jesus will heal your broken heart, and he will give you a new heart by engrafting his heart into yours, and you have the choice everyday to walk in his heart or your own. Remember, Jesus died of a broken heart so that you do not have to die with one from all the different situations, circumstances, and obstacles that come through life and its ups and downs. The living water from Christ Jesus will draw you closer to him so that you can learn how to worship him through fellowship and communing with him as you journey with him, putting him first above all things. Worshiping God can only be done by not representing him with unsafe, false, fake, and phony worship. You taint yourself by being false, fake, and phony (a hypocrite), and the living water in which Jesus has for you will not flow in you because you have clogged up your own streams. You stop the flow of living water when you allow sin to be your god and not God to be your stream of living water. Yes, you will sin, but you can allow sin to go on too long repeatedly, and the living does not communicate with the dead. You kill your flow in the spirit of living water by sin that separates you from life in Christ Jesus.

Living water will refresh your life, and, if you have children or a child, they too will be set free as you call on the name of the Lord to deliver you from allowing foolishness to lure you away from spending quality time with God. The times you lived in sin, you had death evading you and eternal damnation. When you repent and turn away from sin, you can draw from the living water and no longer from the fountain of poison hemp that caused your living fountain to dry up. It's never a time to say God left your side or turned away from you. He turns away from the sin that separates us from him. Not that God left you. He's right here right now, waiting with his arms open wide. God's Spirit does not live in fleshly desires, that's anything impure and against the Spirit of truth. It's time to pray, repent, to start now being sensitive to the Holy Spirit, and allow him to have free course in your life to cleanse you from all unrighteousness and deliver you like you are right now, so that you can get in fellowship with God to do his will. You have a journey you need to go on with God. You once were on this journey and lost your way, yet Christ was always there, watching you, making intersession for you, calling you to repentance even in the midst of your mess. God still allowed you to live, and you're truly blessed! Yet, there's something or someone who hindered you that you would not obey the truth. Paul said it this way:

> Ye did run well; who did hinder you that ye should not obey the truth?
>
> Gal. 5:7 kjv

Whatever it is in your life that is hindering you from serving the Lord, get rid of whatever it is and serve the Lord with gladness! Whatever it is could be material, physical, mental, emotional or financial. For example: If you are overwhelmed by something like a car note and you have no job to pay the car note, let the car go and take the bus for a while, it's hard to serve the Lord if you are worrying all the time and may be your 3 or 4 notes behind on your car note. You can't hide a car that you know you're too behind on the note to catch up on. If you can't seem to pay the rent, gas and electric or buy food; something has to go, your credit score is not where your faith should be, God will make provision when you learn to let go of things that are causing you to take from your necessities to pay for something that your financial situation does not allow you to afford anymore. If you are physically working two jobs and exhausted and find yourself sick more often than you know you should be, reevaluate your bills and see what you can get rid of as far as liquid assets and tell your family things are too overwhelming for you physically it's better to let go of things than to be laid up in the hospital stressed out and unable to work one job less on two. You are wearing yourself down. Find a smaller place to live and you can get rid of the stress, pressure and material gain that is weighing you down to the point that you could be hospitalized if you don't let go of some things. God gives us peace, but we make war in our own physical body when we try to do too much, if your saved then use wisdom (common sense, see Jas. 1:5), your family needs you alive and well not physically worn down and sick from trying to do what you weren't designed to do, work 12 or 18 hours a day is just too much for any human being with a wife or husband with children. Just know that season's came in fours, spring, summer, fall and winter. You spiritually have them and you may be in your winter but spring is on the way.

In time if you just wait on the Lord and let him direct you in knowledge and wisdom; it might be rough now but, release some things and you will not be so physically worn down. There's mental stress that you can often bring upon yourself, remember, you control your emotions by what you allow to get to you mentally. It's not what's going on around you it's how you deal with what's going on around you. How you are going to do this and make that work is all up to you and how you live your life. There are things I just walked away from many of times and I often choose to not let things stress me, overwhelm me and mentally I give it all to God. I am feeling so much better because, I learned to not hold on to things that I can't take with me when I leave this earth anyway. I tell myself, they were just things and I can think clearer because, the mental stress of how to hold on to this and that is over. I am at peace with myself because I know who I am and who's I am. I can wake up in worship the Lord for life, health and strength to do the best that I can do for me and my family, for the season in which I am in. Emotionally, I am not going through the struggle of saying to myself, if I let go of the house and the car and all the overhead that goes with it, how will my family and I make it? Well, I learned like Paul to be content with whatever state in which I am in. Yes, we are eating, have a roof over our head, clothes and transportation. It's not anything on this earth worth holding on to that will separate me from worshipping God, because we will have trials, tribulation, persecution and turmoil throughout a life time and you can live by faith and not choose to adhere to what you see but trust in God for what you know in him and through him. For his grace is sufficient!

> Let your conversation be without covetousness; and be content with such things as you have: for he hath said, I will never leave thee, nor forsake thee. So that we may boldly say, The Lord is my helper, and I will not fear what man shall do unto me.
>
> He. 13: 5, 6 kjv

As believers we are not to be greedy and covet our money or possessions. Our thoughts are not to entertain covetousness (loving money or possessions too much) we are to focus on Christ and the hope of the glory we will one day posses through eternal life we have in Jesus Christ. We are not to love the world and the things that are in the world. God knows the very intent of the heart and you may hide the desire to hunger for wealth from people but, God knows the way that you think. A believer is called to be content with what he or she has. Yes, you should be satisfied with life and the ability in which you may have to work, and enjoy the opportunities of being promoted and hold a job. It's okay to want a home, clothes, a nice car and these are all possessions yet be satisfied with what you have whether it be a little or a lot. You are to practice being content, satisfied with your present condition even if it's good or bad you are to be secure in Christ and not in the things you possess. If you learn to do this you will see that God is making provision for the season in which you are in. Things come and they go. Remember:

> To every thing there is a season, and a time to every purpose under the heaven: A time to be born, and a time to die; a time to plant, and a time to pluck up that which is planted; A time to kill, and a time to heal; a time to break down, and a time to build up; A time to weep, and a time to laugh, a time to mourn, and a time to dance; A time to cast away stones, and a time to

gather stone together; a time to embrace, and a time to refrain from embracing; A time to get, and a time to lose; a time to keep, and a time to cast away,; A time to rend, and a time to sew; a time to keep silence, and a time to speak; A time to love, and a time to hate; a time of war, and a time of peace.

Ecc. 3:1–8 kjv

You must understand and know the counsel of the Lord and you will be able to understand the season and the time in which you are in for what you may be going through for it's just for a season. So worship him in spite of what you may feel, knowing that God has given you a time to do things and a time to let things go for the will and plan in which he has for your life. Be encouraged!

Receiving the End of Your Faith, Even the Salvation of Your Souls

Throughout the Bible, we are warned that we will face trials, tribulations, and persecution, but we can conquer these obstacles by keeping our minds and hearts fixed on the salvation of our souls. What things, people, or single persons are your mind fixed on that has separated you from the living waters you once had flowing? And now because you chose to detour off the journey where living water flows in Christ, you are suffering some great loss. We are to keep our eyes focused on moving toward the salvation of our souls and are not to give into words or voices that come to hinder our walk with the Lord. When we stay focused on our goal, we become stronger and better equipped daily to stand against all obstacles that come against our very souls. This is what we are to do with temptations: reject and turn away from it, and conquer the trials of this life through patterning ourselves after the characteristics of God. If you are not established in God through patterning your life after him through the doctrine of his Word, shame on you. Listen carefully to this, and study it for yourself.

Of which salvation the prophets have enquired and searched

diligently, who prophesied of the grace that should come unto you: Searching what, or what manner of time the Spirit of Christ which was in them did signify, when it testified beforehand the sufferings of Christ, and the glory that should follow. Unto whom it was revealed, that not unto themselves, but unto us they did minister the things, which are now reported unto you by them that have preached the gospel unto you with the Holy Ghost sent down from heaven; which things the angels desire to look into.

1 Peter 1:9–12 (kjv)

We Have an Entrance

Blessed are they that do his commandments, which they may have right to the tree of life, and may enter in through the gates into the city.

Revelation 22:14 (kjv)

Wherefore the rather, brethren, give diligence to make your calling and election sure: for if ye do these things, ye shall never fall: For so an entrance shall be ministered unto you abundantly into the everlasting kingdom of our Lord and Saviour Jesus Christ.

2 Peter 1:10, 11 (kjv)

Notice in the Scripture we are told that there is an entrance that God will give to us and we shall be ministered to when we give diligence to making our call and election sure. Notice that there is a right that the believer has to the tree of life and an entrance we have to go through the gates into the city. While you are on this earth you sometimes in your life, you may suffer through trails, tribulations and persecution but, one day you to will have an entrance into the gate of the everlasting kingdom and all these things will be over for you will be in glory with your Lord and Savior Christ Jesus.

Just remember that, when God saves a person, he saves them

that call upon him from death and exalts them into his glorious heaven. Salvation is so glorious that angels desire to look into it and to understand what it means. Salvation requires chosen men, chosen prophets, to proclaim its truth in holiness. Salvation was a mystery that was given to those who were filled with God's Spirit, which was sent down from heaven.

> And Moses said, Hereby ye shall know that the Lord hath sent me to do all these works; for I have not done them of mine own mind.
>
> Numbers 16:28 (kjv)

Just like Moses was sent by God, there are men and women who are sent by God to lead the people of God into true righteousness and holiness. There are sanctified, holy, and righteous vessels in which God has set aside to live in his tabernacle. Yet, Satan himself has set aside false prophets who have been ordained by Satan in demonic things that don't pertain to God, and these are those who are sent to those who are sanctified and have a strategic plan ordered against the Word that has been given to them by the enemy to draw them away from the truth. False ministers have been teaching from one generation to the next, and they are able to camouflage their true identities by the Word of God, and the people of God are paying into these sorts of ministries to their detriment. They don't even realize that they are blinded and are assisting these camouflaged ministries. There are all sorts of Bible colleges that are erroneous and teaching false doctrine. If you go to school for something that you have a passion to do, you can master it, but you must be careful what Bible College you go to because its founder may teach a false theology. You must line up with the Word of truth, the Bible, to be led by the Spirit before you go to any school of theology or seminary school; be led by his Spirit first. Many Bible colleges don't believe the whole book of the Bible from Genesis to Revelations. They teach it according to a system in which a group of people (board members) agreed on and have set. Again, before you think about going to any school to be taught the Word, you must do your own research and history on that particular school and its beliefs. Don't go on what someone told you, for in your heart you have the issues of life; therefore, you need to guard your heart with all diligence.

> Keep thy heart with all diligence; for out of it are the issues of life.
>
> Proverbs 4:23 (kjv)

In these last days, these sort of men who have crept in unaware teaching false doctrine, if it were possible (if God would allow it), they would deceive the very elect.

Yet these men still proclaim the Word of the Lord falsely in their own self-righteousness and have been indoctrinated by false teaching. The devil knows that if a true prophet (prophetess) is allowed to come forth in the presence of this foolishness, the false prophet will be exposed. These false prophets have set up denominations and religious organizations with fake and phony history of the gospel; they have watered down the gospel with their own doctrine from one generation to the next.

How clever they are, just like their father, the devil. Who shall be able to clean up such a great spill? Who is able to come forth and expose such a great plot and strategic plan like this? No one can see through a man's heart and snatch the evil, wicked, damnable heresy out of a person but the Holy Ghost. It's going to take some men and women who have been preordained, called, chosen, and persevered for such a time as this. God is calling these true prophets and prophetesses to come forth now. The body of Christ must come together as one, just like these those who agree as one who are false prophets, who were sent by Satan himself and have established organized religion and have incorporated themselves, under the name of God, as nonprofit organizations for filthy lucre (greed and gain through taking money from the church and not ministering to the sheep of God according to the word of God and using the pulpit for things other than the work of God) (see: I Per. 5:2) Listen, we must diligently guard our hearts and make our elections sure so that the entrance to hearing the truth will continue to flow in us and through us from the living water from heaven. Yes, we do have an entrance into the secrets and mysteries of God, which is the revelatory knowledge of the true gospel of Jesus Christ, but we must be willing to be diligent about seeking the truth, searching for the truth, and to continually find the truth and hold it in our heart. The issues of life cannot flow out of a tainted well. Our streams of life are only clean when we dip our heart in the crimson blood of Jesus Christ through staying unspotted from false teaching in false churches and stay away from following and loving the world and embracing daily the real genuine truth in the Word of God.

The True Sound of the Holy Ghost

Now is the time to pull the strongholds off of the unstable souls who think they got it but learned to look, act, and dress like they have something but not the true sound of the Holy Ghost. There is a true sound of the Holy Ghost that weeps down on the inside of one's belly with groaning that cannot be uttered. There is a true sound of the Holy Ghost that will come down and dwell in the children of God. When the right sound is heard in the ears of God, the heavens will open up and the angels will come to behold the glory of the Lord. I declare and decree that in the name of Jesus Christ, the Son of the living God that every true apostle, prophet, and prophetesses will come out from amongst these false denominations and religious leaders to cry loud and spare not and weep for the cry of Hosanna. We must cry the cry of true worship to come forth and declare and command his presence to be ushered into the tabernacle of the throne room which sits in the hearts of the righteous. We have this power in us through Christ Jesus to loose the shackles off of those who are bound by sin and set men, women, and children free from the bondage of sin that comes from the spirit of witchcraft, which is a form of rebellion against the mission, purpose, and plan of almighty God.

When you exercise the gifts of the Holy Ghost, according to Genesis through Revelations, this is information that is revelatory to your future, and all of the Bible must be applied in order to stay in harmony and relationship to the journey in which the Holy Spirit desires to lead you into. You have been given truth through the doctrine of God to exercise daily, sound doctrine. You will have to exercise your faith to stay in harmony with your relationship you have in God, and there is the spirit of wisdom which will come upon you and in you to help you improve in having keen discernment and insight into the evil, wicked works of the enemy. It's vital to your journey with Christ Jesus to hear wisdom and adhere to living this life in Christ to allow the Holy Spirit to speak and impart secrets to the hearer. The true sound of Zion is to be in continued position of vertical worship.

There is a call from heaven for Zion to continually cry out against the camp of the enemy. Zion must go into the territory of the enemy and reach the lost at any cost. In case you missed this the first time I said it, when the true apostles, prophets, and prophetesses come together in unity, the presence of the Holy Ghost will then embody the children of God who sit, eat, live, move, and breathe the very essence of Hosanna (save now), the Son of David, our Messiah. We, the true apostles, prophets, and prophetesses of the Most High, are called to usher in the presence of God by crying the right sound. No more will we be divided by denominations and religious leaders who have placed a barrier with their finite minds by bringing in damnable heresies with false teaching and are ruled by the devil. Men, who strategically strategize against the works of our Lord and Savior, Jesus Christ, will be damned to the pit of hell.

And the devil who had deceived them was thrown into the lake of fire and sulfur where the beast and the false prophet were, and they will be tormented day and night forever and ever.

Revelation 20:10 (esv)

In i Corinthians 2:6–16, there is a great call to the mature saint to receive the impartation of the Holy Spirit's wisdom and accept the Spirit of God through the depths of God's mind. Those who are mature in spiritual things will understand the sound of the Holy Spirit to quickly understand the instructions in which the mind of God gives his secrets and hidden wisdom only to those who recognize the true sound of the Spirit. There is impartation from the Holy Spirit to how we are to correctly interpret spiritual truth. The mysteries of God are given to those who hunger and thirst after righteousness. Those who are in true harmony with the clarion call in the She-kina Glory of God.

As we see in Exodus 40:34–38, there was a glory of the spirit which took Moses and the children of Israel on their journey, and this same power will come upon the true worshippers who worship the Lord in Spirit and in truth. It's so revelatory to hear the sound of the Holy Spirit and know how to journey with him as he leads, guides, and directs the children of God into all truth.

We must proclaim Christ Jesus with a humble spirit and cry loud and spare not the truth as our King in our hearts that lives to rule, reign, and abide in, over, and throughout our lives as he has called us to do.

We Are Called Out of Sin to Live Unto Him

You are not working on a job just because you signed a W-2 form and never showed up to do what you agreed to do. You are not born again until you confess him as your Lord and Savior and then commit to the covenant relationship that you came into the knowledge of and confessed before man through Christ Jesus. It is by faith you believe. Now walk with him with that same belief as when you first turned away from sin. You can say you are a believer, a follower of Christ, saved, born of the Spirit, filled with the Spirit, but you must allow the Word to come alive in you and allow Christ Jesus to live vicariously through you. I could tell you I have a PhD, master's degree, doctorate degree, and know the Bible from cover to cover, but if my disposition is not of the characteristics of Christ Jesus, then he cannot use me because I must know him intimately for him to commune with me to hear his voice. I can't prepare for the mission, plan, and purpose of God until I submit to him sincerely and not go back to my old sinful ways. He needs a yielded vessel that is willing to allow him to use them. Even though he has ordained many before the foundation of the world to do his will, many are called and few are chosen because many don't want to give up all to follow the leading of his Spirit.

It's not about what I have achieved on this earth; it's about Christ Jesus being formed in me by me allowing his Spirit to be made perfect in me through the truth of his Word. Don't believe for one moment I am putting down those who have all sorts of degrees, but it's not about what you have accomplished or established through material gain, awards, degrees, and man-made books of theology, etc. Only what you do for Christ will last. My reward is not in being born again, doing good, and looking for man's approval. My reward is in suffering for Christ's sake and not because I backslide, detour away from God, turn away from God, and commit to people, places, and things, choosing to do something other than God's will. Now you find many in God's permissive will that have chosen to forget the ways of the Lord and take on someone else's desires and call stepping out of the journey in which God has set before them (these are those who are sidetracked and detoured by hearing the wrong call). God's permitting me to do wrong and go in my own way is not his will, and it sure isn't a testimony. You can testify when you have suffered for righteousness's sake and not for the sake of your sinful, lustful flesh. Every thing you go through is not because of the cause of Christ Jesus; many things we go through are because we turned away into our own lustful desires and have forsaken the truth! That is not a testimony to come out of three, five, ten, twenty, one hundred plus relationships or jobs or from dealing with some entity that you could have avoided if you would have just listened to the voice of God through studying the world through humbling yourself under the mighty hand of God. You can get so use to seeing people do things wrong for so long you think it's the right way.

We often get ourselves into things or relationships we had no business in and then want to testify that God brought us through. That's not a testimony. I will say this again, we often on this journey, get off track, and suffer losses, havoc, hell, and chaos in our lives often because we choose to turn away from God and go in our own sinful, lustful, fleshly desires. We choose the wrong people over God's plan for our lives and allow them to take over our minds, our bodies, our homes, and then we get disillusioned by someone who is confused but clever enough to lure us into their own world. That's why we have people in Christendom with degrees, good jobs, have high positions in the church, and are doing crazy things by living a false lifestyle with someone they have no business with. If you really want to know if someone is sincere about their walk with the Lord, see if they will show some fruit for their labor in Christ. Who is it that will willingly minister with you as if you were doing this anyway when you're out having a good time, whether eating, at the movies, park, or just hanging at the mall. Do you and can you pray for someone while you are in a relationship with someone that you get together with every now and then, or do you have to put the ministry aside to cater to them and not be a testimony while you're with them and others? Okay, we all sin and have and will fall short of the glory of God. Who are you having sexual relationships with? Oftentimes, we get played on and played for a fool when we enter into these so-called friendly relationships because people prey on our weakness for what we tell them we're going through, and then you have a leach that preys on your sexual desire, and you find yourself over and over again in bed with someone who is not even your wife or husband. Most people who are not truly saved will lure you further away from your faith by using a little prayer and a few encouraging words, and then you all of a sudden are drawn away and enticed to think, *This may be my mate, my soul mate.* Well, they are with someone who claims to be born again, yet from the beginning of the relationship, they started off in the flesh, and it's ending in the flesh. It was not their fault but yours for taking your armor off and not being clothed in his righteousness. Instead, you where unclothed and disarmored, and now you have an STD and don't know how to be an effective witness because you got yourself in something that you should have known better not to do. Okay, let me give the women a Scripture, and the men can take some pointers from this.

> But understand this that in the last days there will come times of difficulty. For people will be lovers of self, lovers of money, proud, arrogant, abusive, disobedient to their parents, ungrateful, unholy, heartless, unappeasable, slanderous, without self-control, brutal, not loving good, treacherous, reckless, swollen with conceit, lovers of pleasure rather than lovers of God, having the appearance of godliness, but denying its power. Avoid such people. For among them are those who creep into households and capture weak women, burdened with sins and led astray by various passions, always learning and never able to arrive at a knowledge of the truth. Just as Janne and Jambres opposed Moses, (Ex 7:11) so these men also oppose the truth, men corrupted in mind and disqualified regarding the faith. But they will not get very far, for their folly will be plain to all, as was that of those two men.
>
> 2 Timothy 3:1–9 (esv)

Whatever excuses you make to live in the flesh, walk after the flesh, live after the lust of your flesh, and walk after the lust of your flesh, there is no excuse. You can continue in what you have learned and have firmly believed, knowing that since a child you knew the holy Scriptures, and turn away from sin, turn back to God, and do right; or you can be self-destructive and take out as many people as you choose to prey upon because you are so angry at others who did you wrong in the past, and keep on being impatient with what you believe you should have, and miss your journey with God by being ignorant of the truth. It's your choice, and you have a right to do with your life whatever you choose to do with it, but you will answer to God after you take your last breath. Maybe you don't care and you need to have the Spirit poured upon you. I will pray for you and ask God to redeem you if you will humble yourself for a moment of prayer.

Lord, we come to you to say thank you for another day. We thank you Lord for allowing us another chance to worship your holy name. We glorify your name for sending your Son to die on the cross for all of our sins. We thank you, Lord, for forever making intercession for us when we chose to go in our own selfish ways and not take the time to pray for our own lives. Lord, we ask for you to redeem us back to you through pouring your Holy Spirit down on the inside of us and give us the strength to endure the things we are facing. Show us and teach us how to be at peace and content with where we are, and no matter how it looks, we praise you; no matter how we feel, we worship you; no matter what infirmity we have, we repent for murmuring and complaining for the things that have happened to us. Oftentimes we chose the wrong people or person to be with and refused to take heed to the warning signs; therefore, our disobedient spirit has caused us to become like children that have to suffer for a season, and now we don't want to face ourselves. Therefore, we often hurt others because others have hurt us. Now Lord, heal our minds, as the thorns in your head were for all of our psychological, mental, and emotional problems. The thorns in your head were for all the evil and wicked thoughts that we think that cause us to sin. The thorns in your head are for all the games the many voices of the evil one continually throws at us like darts. The thorns in your head are for all the hate, regret, and unforgiveness we oftentimes try to not forgive others for doing wrong to us or those we love. The thorns in your head were for all the lies the enemy and those who were against us said to us that think they know our destiny and try to speak negativity into our minds, but you were wounded for our transgressions. You were bruised for our iniquities. The chastisement of our peace was upon you, and with your stripes we are healed (Isa 53:5, kjv) from all things that pertain to unrighteousness, ungodliness, and death. We are healed, and our hearts are set free from all those who hurt us and used us intentionally and unintentionally because of their own issues and frailties. As they pierced you in the side and water and blood came running out, you, Lord, you washed us through the living water that ran out of your body and cleansed us with your blood that was shed for all of our sins and for all of our hang-ups and for our shortcomings. You where hung high and stretched wide as a symbol that you were Lord of lord and King of kings and that you were high and lifted up, and your train filled the temple of the body in which you humbled yourself to the point of death that we would be healed, delivered, and set free by the renewing of our minds that is in Christ Jesus. We know that by faith when we separate from this old, wretched body—for those who have confessed you as Lord and Savior—we will go to heaven to be with you forever and ever. We repent for all the things that we have been ungrateful for and for falling away from the truth of your Word and not adhering to your Word that brings life and that more abundantly. We will not be moved, for we know that; Henceforth there is laid up for us the crown of righteousness, which the Lord, the righteous judge, will award us on that day, and not only to us but also to all who have loved your appearing (2 Tim 4:6, esv). We come against principalities, powers, the ruler of the darkness of this world, spiritual wickedness in high places (Eph. 6:10-18). And in the name of Jesus Christ, we put off our old ways, old nature, and thoughts that are not of you and receive the mind of the Spirit to walk in your nature, your Spirit, and choose to be free from our evil thoughts and ways to press into the kingdom of God and do your will for your glory. In the name of Jesus we pray. Amen.

I pray you receive this prayer, and you should pray it as often as you see yourself being made daily into the image of God. Don't ever forget you are called to walk in the mind of God through the mind of the Spirit, which you can only find when you search the Scriptures for truth and live in them.

It's not a degree that helps you or I achieve the things that God has called us into through salvation in Jesus' name. These accomplishments can help only when applied with the Word according to God's will for our lives. We must know the truth, and the truth will then set us free. Our degrees and our achievements that are tangible and material gain are nothing compared to the words in which God wants to speak into our lives to prepare us daily for his purpose. Be careful! No longer will men who have been called by their father—Satan himself, the devil, and the prince of the air—be able to decoy the true saints who have been reserved to pull the truth out of the lying mouths of all evil, wicked, and ungodly rulers who sit upon their thrones to lure the children of God away from the truth. Many are called to live to cry loud and spare not, speaking the words of truth in the Holy Ghost. If you are still reading this book, you must know and be able to recognize those who are working against the truth. These are those who chose the wrong way and have turned back away from the truth. They will continually answer to the call of Satan, and he also has called and chosen, appointed and anointed through demonic power and the craftiness of his subtle ways a cunning and crafty plan to take God's glory from those who are the righteous. It won't work! Watch those who are into being the founder of a cult unto themselves. These will bring quick damnation and sudden destructions upon themselves. It is time for the remnant, chosen, and called elect of the most high God to take a stand for righteousness and holiness, declaring the true works of our Master and Savior, our Lord Jesus Christ.

> And the disciples went, and did as Jesus Commanded them, and brought the ass, and the colt, and put on them their clothes, and they set him thereon. And a very great multitude spread their garments in the way; others cut down branches from the trees, and strewed them in the way. And the multitudes that went before, and that followed, cried, saying, Hosanna (save now) to the son of David (Messiah): blessed is he that cometh in the name of the Lord; Hosanna in the highest. And when he was come into Jerusalem, all the city was moved, saying, Who is this? And the multitude said, This is Jesus the prophet of Nazareth of Galilee. And Jesus went into the temple of God, and cast out all them that sold and bought in the temple, and overthrew the tables of the moneychangers, and the seats of them that sold doves, And said unto them, It is written, My house shall be called the house of prayer; but ye have made it a den of thieves. And the blind and the lame came to him in the temple and he healed them.
>
> Matthew 21:6–14 (kjv)

Until the ministers come together in the body of Christ Jesus, there will be a hindrance of the presence of true worship.

We won't have time to play church and be so busy doing things that don't pertain to heaven's call, when we learn to humble ourselves to the true call of God which is found in following after his word through The Mind of the Spirit.

The Desperate Mind

Have you ever been desperate for anything? Desperate: having a very great desire; need; driven to do something, be some great person, or achieve some accomplishment. What in life has caused you at one point or another to become desperate? Could it be you want to move out from home, knowing that you're nearing eighteen? Are you desperate to go to college because you believe you will be successful in the career that you desire to pursue? Have you gotten married and your relationship with your spouse is mentally, sexually, emotionally, physically, or financially abusive and you are desperate to get out? The house that you live in, you were not ready for the responsibility but you thought you were; now you have no where to go and you are desperate to get out? Have you been lied to about a job that is not taking you anywhere and you're desperate to change jobs, but you can't afford to quit at this time? Do you have some sort of drug addiction, alcoholic addiction, or are gambling with money or your body, changing sex partners, and you have no one to talk to, but you are desperate to get out of this kind of lifestyle?

Maybe you play or sing and are desperate to be on television. You might have just gotten pregnant and are desperate to know what you're having and can't wait to find out! Or you could be in love and are desperate to know if the one you love is the right one for you. What are you facing right now today in your life that has caused you to take some desperate measures?

I may not have covered every problem or circumstance, but you may be a kid or a teenager that has parents or a parent who won't allow you to be all that you could be because they have been abusing you and you are desperate to get help and don't know where to go or who to tell. Maybe you have a stepparent that enjoys causing confusion between you and your biological parent, and you are desperate to tell your biological parent how you are being treated when they're alone with you, and you're afraid to say anything because they won't believe you. Whatever you are desperate for—you may be born again or just searching for answers—I hope for you to get some answers concerning your desperate situation in this chapter. You have an urgent crisis that has caused you to want to give up, take your life, or even take the life of someone who seems as though they could care less about the way you feel. Don't think like that. Those sorts of thoughts are not going to get you anywhere, but you are losing time that you could be spending seeking the Lord and doing his will.

Desperate to Pursue Your Dreams

As children, in spite of what we are going through, it's important to remember when you become desperate to fulfill something you have dreamed of becoming, accomplishing, or you wish could happen, you should never ever stop dreaming. Good dreams of becoming someone or something turns into reality. When you're desperate enough to pursue what you believe in, it can become reality. When you became an adult, somewhere in your mind you still have some of those same wishes, dreams, and ambitions at times. They just seem like they're so farfetched to accomplish now that you are an adult when they really aren't. You have to think back to what's down on the inside of you that you wanted to do. Somewhere you have lost hope. Don't ever lose hope just because of your past hurts and loses. Be desperate enough to let go and let God use you in whatever gifts, talents, and abilities you have. It's not about what you did not do or become, nor is it about what you could have, should have, and did not have because of some situation you did not ask to come upon you as a young child. You will always have dreams, and don't ever, ever stop dreaming. You must become desperate enough to envision what you want and make it become a reality. You may want to leave a legacy for your name to be remembered for doing something good that no one else has ever done in this life. Well, whatever the case may be, you must be desperate and apply yourself to make it happen. You have to not watch others make things happen. You can't just lie down and dream and watch someone else make it happen. You must get up and pursue what it is that you want and be desperate about it, and one day it will happen. God has called you to do his will, but you have dreams, ambitions, ability, gifts, and talents that only you can bring to reality. It's God's gifts inside of you waiting to be revealed to the world so that God can get the glory out of your life.

The word *dream* is written in the Scriptures more than fifty times. There are true stories of how dreams can be good and dreams can be evil. There are dreams that warn us of tragedy, sickness, death, or about someone or something that we may question. Also, there are dreams that lead us into our purpose or mission in life. We often find our talents and gifts through dreams. God speaks to us and gives us directions through dreams. There are evil dreams that come to blind us from the truth, and there are dreams that are given to us to protect us from something or someone, showing details to how to deal with certain circumstances that befall us. Dreams are a part

The Mind of the Sprit

of our desires sometimes that we have because we are thinking or worrying about someone or something we need to do and are trying to figure out what to do but find ourselves drifting into a daydream or falling asleep, and we find ourselves dreaming and suddenly wake up. Sometimes we can fall asleep from reading, writing, watching television, talking to someone, and we go into a dream. Sometimes we dream that someone is chasing us or some loved one is talking to us and in the room present. There are dreams where we feel we are walking somewhere or are surrounded by something that is not usual or familiar to us. There are even dreams of angels showing or telling us something or taking us somewhere. Even as children and into our adulthood we have to go to the bathroom and dream that we have gotten up and find ourselves waking up out of a wet dream. We can dream about having sex or sleeping with someone we have no business with. There are so many types of dreams, and because our self-conscious is always thinking, sin is always lurking. But, God is always watching and showing us how to live free from anything—even a bad, horrible dream that may wake us up. We have been given the Word to interpret many dreams.

Therefore, the believer must not be lazy, complacent, or ignorant of the many dreams that come in ways for a certain reason, purpose, or just to deceive us into doing something our flesh desires; or the enemy may come and try to enter our minds through an open door we allowed through what we may watch, see, taste, touch, or have felt before we fell asleep. Dreams are somewhat like this. You may be the type of person that needs to talk to someone just to be a sounding board. You may not mention this to them, but you know what you're trying to do. You're with someone and you just begin to think of what you need to do, and as you're trying to figure it out, you begin to talk it through. Then the person(s) you're around suggests to do it this way or go ask that one and say, "I'm just trying to help." Most of the time, that does not help if that person is just trying in their own way to figure out what it is and just throwing out opinions in hopes that you will do it their way. Sometimes a suggestion can turn into a dream. A plot to do something you have no business doing can turn into a dream. Oftentimes you desire to be some great person and that turns into a dream. Dreams are something that are quite normal but sometimes awkward because we can't seem to interpret the meaning, and, therefore, many dreams, good dreams, often are dreamed over and over throughout our lifetimes, and we often miss carrying out the instructions given in our dreams for lack of knowledge.

Therefore, it's important for you to know that there are many good things that come into reality through dreams. We do a lot of dreaming when our teachers—whether at school, Sunday school, or even on a date or with a friend or relative—may ask us, "What do you want to be in life?" or, "What do you want to do with your life?" The famous questions we all have to face one day is, "Where do you see yourself five, ten, or fifteen years from now?" "Do you know what you want to major in?" "Are you going to further your education?" "Do you want children?" and, "Do you plan to get married?" These and many other questions people have, or even the ones we have of our selves, cause us to daydream or dream the night away. Oftentimes, we pick movies that we can relate to because we have idols we have made of people who we consider successful, and we watch their lives day to day, often dreaming of being like them.

I have to speak on this for a moment. It's an unfortunate tragedy when someone thinks evil and is jealous of someone through envy (hatred) and wants what someone else has and it's on their mind all day, throughout the night. And oftentimes this is how you can cause yourself to dream of how to cause harm to someone, thinking that's the way to get over in life. You can dream an evil dream by wanting through the lust of the flesh what someone else has or desiring to be someone that you can never be. That's an evil dream that comes to a person that may have been abused or was raised in a home with some sort of abuse, and they find themselves locked up for life or in and out of jail or a psychiatric ward for having a thought that turned into a bad dream. You have to be careful who you allow into your thoughts and into your mind because the mind is powerful and we produce often what we have thought of, dreamed of, or what someone may have suggested if we were not thinking right but were thinking bad thoughts. We can find ourselves in trouble, thinking of how to get someone out of something when we did not get them into the trouble they are in, in the first place. All dreams are not from our desires, especially if we find ourselves with someone who is conniving, slick, deceptive, controlling, or manipulative.

Our dreams are often based on our environment. A dream can come out of a successful event and can also come through an evil situation. If it was bad in your past, don't worry about something so much to the point that when you fall asleep your dreams are geared toward what you have been feeling about someone or something for too long. Your future to dream must reflect the goals of your future. You cannot change your past, but you can change your future. Okay? Saved, born again, on the right road to recovery, don't let your thoughts to do evil to someone get the best of you and you dream a dream that you will soon regret later. For instance, you can desire someone else's mate, and you go to sleep dreaming or fantasizing of ways to get them all to yourself. That's evil, wicked, and divisive, and that sort of dream you need to not try to pursue. Interpret it as just what it is: an evil dream that turned into a bad scenario. You can start out in your self-conscious mind dreaming, and it, the dream, can take a turn for the worst by what's heavy on your mind before you fall asleep. You will then find yourself waking up in a sweat by the scenario, and those who don't exist are false illusions that you need to pray against and not let evil overtake your thoughts by going to sleep with foolishness on your mind. Remember, an idle mind is the devil's workshop.

Before we go into the Scriptures, let's define a few words and let me express what is imperative at this very moment.

Dream: a succession of images, thoughts, or emotions passing through the mind during sleep; an aspiration; goal; aim a series of images, ideas, emotions, and sensations occurring involuntarily in the mind during certain stages of sleep. A cherished desire; to have ideas or images in the mind while in the state of sleep; to experience sleeping visions; often with or; as; to dream of a battle, or of an absent friend.

Vision: to envision; the act or power of sensing with the eyes; sight; the act or power of anticipating that which will or may come to be: prophetic vision; the vision of an entrepreneur; an experience in which a personage, thing, or event appears vividly or credibly to the mind, although not actually present, often under the influence of a divine or other agency: ex: a heavenly messenger appearing in a vision: ex: The vision revealed its message.

When we allow our emotions to begin to have a negative effect upon us because of certain circumstances in our life that we face each and every day, we will dream often things that can be contrary to the will of God which is upon our lives. When we view our lives in our finite minds in how we think and it's against God's will for our life, we will then begin to allow our flesh to control our spirit instead of our spirit controlling our flesh. The mind can often dream of things that are of no significance to our purpose in life.

> (For the weapons of our warfare are not carnal, but might through God to the pulling down of strong holds;) Casting down imaginations, and every high thing that exalteth itself against the knowledge of God, and bringing into captivity every thought to the obedience of Christ; And having in a readiness to revenge all disobedience, when your obedience is fulfilled.
>
> II Co. 10:4–6 kjv

As believers we must allow ourselves the opportunity to experience the expression of dreaming dreams and envisioning the things that God has set before us by being humbled to his call with a willing heart and mind to serve him. Until we learn to recognize the leading, guiding, and directions of the Holy Spirit as being ordinary people led by a supernatural power, we will continue to grope in dark places which we have been called out of. We have been called out of darkness and into his marvelous light, but until we taste and see that the Lord is good, we often are betwixt in our minds as to what power we have to control our own destiny. To dream a dream and to envision the things in which God has already placed in our being, we must yield ourselves to the anointing as though our flesh does not exist. As believers, we are called to serve him in Spirit and in truth. The truth comes when we allow the Holy Spirit to lead, guide, and direct us into the truth which is found in the mind of God. Through dreams and visions, we can behold the mysteries in which God has ordained for us to know. We have a greater power that has been given to us to take a deeper glimpse into the supernatural through the mind of his Spirit. The mysteries of God are illogical to the natural, carnal mind, but to the new creature, dreams and visions keep us from perishing. When our emotions are mild and when we can recognize the difference between our emotions and what we know and believe in God, we can address each emotion rightfully by not acting on our feelings but reacting according to the Word of God. It is a must to facilitate our lives for the betterment of our journey. We are more apt to act out of our feelings in any given situation than to think of controlling our emotions according to the Scriptures if we often choose to walk in the flesh. It's in walking in the Spirit and not the flesh that we can constructively recognize the wrong voices and know how to cancel out or lay aside the feelings that cause our emotions to dream and envision things that have no significance to the mission in which God has designed us to walk in. Walking out the dreams and visions of God can only be accomplished when we step into our position as gatekeepers and watchmen to guard our hearts with all diligence. Then we must continually walk in the mind of Christ to take authority over the things that come to distract us from our duties that belong to him. The Scripture clearly states: "For who has understood the mind of the Lord so as to instruct him?" But we have the mind of Christ (1 Cor 2:16, esv).

Therefore, we are given the impartation as natural people to walk in the supernatural power, which comes through the mind of God being activated in our minds to dream the dreams and envision the things which have been declared and decreed into the atmosphere by God before the foundation of the world.

Paul said it this way:

> Howbeit we speak wisdom among them that are perfect: yet not the wisdom of this world, nor of the princes of this world, that come to nought: But we speak the wisdom of God in a mystery, even the hidden wisdom, which God ordained before the world unto our glory: Which none of the princes of this world knew: for had they known it, they would not have crucified the Lord of glory. But as it is written, Eye hath not seen, nor ear heard, neither have entered into the heart of man, the things which God hath prepared for them that love him. But God hath revealed them unto us by his Spirit: for the Spirit searcheth all things, yea, the deep things of God. For what man knoweth the things of a man, save the spirit of man which is in him? Even so the things of God knoweth no man, but the Spirit of God. Now we have received, not the spirit of the world, but the spirit which is of God; that we might know the things that are freely given to us of God. Which things also we speak, not in the words which man's wisdom teacheth, but which the Holy Ghost teacheth; comparing spiritual things with spiritual: But the natural man receiveth not the things of the Spirit of God for they are foolishness unto him: neither can he know them, because they are spiritually discerned. But he that is spiritual judgeth all things, yet he himself is judged of no man. For who hath known the mind of the Lord, that he may instruct him? But we have the mind of Christ.
>
> 1 Corinthians 2:6–16 (kjv)

Before we can understand the dreams and visions of God, we must first have a strong desire to seek the perfect wisdom of God. The wisdom of God is not for the world but for those who seek God's revealed wisdom. God's revealed wisdom can only be by God's Spirit. As in verses 10 through 13, we see that the Holy Ghost reveals the wisdom of God to man. The wisdom of God is not found in the world or those who rule the world. The wisdom of God must be first imparted to those who search for perfect wisdom in God by a preacher or a teacher of the word of God, who speaks the perfect wisdom of God. He who speaks of these precepts must be a true seeker of truth and wisdom to humility of God's Word. When we look at the word *perfect*, it means finished and complete; fully developed, grown; mature; to reach one's end. We have to come to the end of ourselves to walk into the wisdom of God through his revealed truth.

A person who desires to one day be in heaven is a person who daily seeks after God and presses into the wisdom of God by making a choice everyday to die to himself and stop, arrest, and annihilate his end (his flesh, putting it to death) by seeking the wisdom of God. The wisdom of the world says that there is no God; he just can't exist. The wisdom of the world believes that long ago, back as far as the finite mind can think, that an element, molecule, atom, or a gas appeared and all of a sudden man came into existence with everything else we see and don't see. It's thought by the world that there was nothing, no such place as earth, no force no conditions ever existed. Well, that's not the case. We must understand clearly that our destiny is in our own hands. The wisdom of the world is to be wishy-washy and double-minded. Yes, God exists, and then something happens—some catastrophe—and then no, he does not exist because if he did, this or that would not have happened to me or to the one I needed to make it through life. Those who choose to go along with this world belief are left on their own to depend on science, technology, education, and man's effort to defend their religion. The wisdom of the world is vain, foolish, and passes away like a rose in a garden. As the Bible states, the wisdom of the world will one day come to naught (nothing); it will be nonexistent; it will cease to exist.

For the wisdom of this world is foolishness with God. For it is written, He taketh the wise in their own craftiness. 'And again, The Lord knoweth the thoughts of the wise, that they are vain.

1 Corinthians 3:19–20 (kjv)

Professing themselves to be wise, they became fools.

Romans 1:22 (kjv)

Beware lest any man spoil you through philosophy and vain deceit, after the tradition of men, after the rudiments of the world, and not after Christ.

Colossians 2:8 (kjv)

God's wisdom is proclaimed in a mystery. This means that the wisdom of God cannot be ascertained by natural men but only by God's wisdom. No man has gone into the heavens to enter and obtain God's wisdom that comes in truth. The material world can only know the spiritual world through God, and it's by his Spirit that he reveals himself and his spiritual world. The gospel is in the reconciliation that was according to the death, burial, and resurrection of Jesus Christ. The mysteries of God are not hard to understand for the spiritually mature man.

Therefore, as we understand the wisdom of God through his revealed truth, it's only then that we can dream the dreams of God and envision his plan as it unfolds to him from glory, to glory.

"But we all, with open face beholding as in a glass the glory of the Lord, are changed into the same image from glory to glory, even as by the Spirit of the Lord" 2 Cor 3:18, (kjv).

When the believer is transformed into the image of Christ, it's from glory to glory that he daily beholds, understands, studies, and lays hold on the glory of the Lord, which is the truth of God's Word in his wisdom. When the believer beholds the glory of the Lord, the progress is to grow more and more by stages of the glory becoming higher and higher by us understanding who he is in his truth. We are to grow in Christ from day to day, moving and pressing into his glory. We are not to entangle ourselves by going backwards, staying carnal and worldly, but we are to press into the wisdom of God through his truth. "For now we see through a glass, darkly; but then faced to face: now I know in part; but then shall I know even as also I am known" (1 Cor 13:12 kjv).

Even though this scripture is talking about love, man can only experience perfect love when he comes face-to-face with God. We experience this when we come closer and closer through the wisdom of God that is found in the mysteries of God, and then we go from glory to glory, giving us the truth to experience the spiritual love that is perfect because his Word is perfect and true. Having a perfect consciousness and knowledge of him is what our present relationship is comparable with when we look at our reflections in a dark mirror. We can, through the love of God in ourselves, only see at a glimpse it's just a figure. We won't see the fullness and the clear distinction of who we are (as also I am known) until we come to know him through death and the love of perfection becomes a reality. The death of us coming into the perfect knowledge of truth is through the wisdom of God; then and only then will the reality of perfection to man concerning God become truth.

We see God by faith, and faith is something we cannot see, but we believe that God is love, and no greater love than a man laying down his life for his friends. Therefore, no matter what gifts we have, the greatest gift was that God so loved the world that he gave his son to die that we, by faith, could come into the love of God through receiving the love (his son) that continues through his Word (the love we have of him and only have in him) to be made perfect through him.

It's in all of this that we can dream the dreams and envision the truth of his will for our lives. We cannot dream the dreams of his will and be visionaries by our own strength and our own desires. When we die to our own desires and experience the perfect love of his Word through understanding the mysteries of his Word, we will then be able to yield fruit to the mysteries that are only found in the perfect knowledge and truth of who he is in his wisdom. Dreams are not just for fun; they are a part of God's perfect plan of liberty. We are free in Christ to dream the dreams of righteousness and to envision our purpose in life as we pattern our minds after the wisdom of God. In the book of Job, Zophar speaks on this wise:

This is Zophar's answer to Job as he was pleading to God in Job 10: 8–22 (kjv).

> "Why did you bring me out from the womb? Would that I had died before any eye had seen me and were as though I had not been, carried from the womb to the grave. Are not my days few? Then cease, and leave me alone, that I may find a little cheer before I go and I shall not return to the land of darkness and deep shadow, the land of gloom like thick darkness, like deep shadow without any order, where light is as thick darkness."

> Then Zophar the Naamathite answered and said: "Should a multitude of works go unanswered, and a man full of talk be judged right? Should your babble silence men, and when you mock, shall no one shame you? For you say, 'My doctrine is pure, and I am clean in God's eyes' But oh, that God would speak and open his lips to you, and that he would tell you the secrets of wisdom! For he is manifold in understanding. Know then that God exacts of you less than your guilt deserves. "Can you find out the deep things of God? Can you find out the limit of the Almighty? It is higher than heaven what can you do? Deeper than Sheol what can you know? Its measure is longer than the earth and broader than the sea.

> Job 11:1–9 (esv)

As Job was pleading to God and complaining that he would have rather died before he came forth out of his mother's womb. We often times face the plea of help yet, speak as to babble on in our distress and anguish at times of loneliness, disappointment, despair, feelings of abandonment, not being understood by those we know and when facing a crisis it's often we complain and so soon forget the scriptures that we should walk in them and not just forget them in these times of need. As Job felt he did not deserve to go through the pain and suffering he did at that time, we often in a time of need question God saying, I don't deserve to go through the storms of life, trials, tribulations and persecution yet, these are all a part of life and its follies. We as believers cannot fathom the truth that lies in the bosom of an almighty God. If we would look around the world and see more than ourselves and what we suffer from time to time, there would be no wander to why we go through things as though we are in the darkness of death. If we would learn to think like God and not like our old nature staying away from our own selfish desires (the flesh), we then could gather much wisdom and truth to discern the grope in the dark that has no relevance to understanding the truth of his word. A mightier and more powerful than our flesh wants to have preeminence in our heart mind and soul yet; for a little foolishness we choose to walk in vain (in the flesh). Problem free will never exist in the flesh for the flesh is never satisfied, but when the spirit is awaken to heavens call there's life through the call of wisdom and we should forever learn to draw from it's well. "In his hand is the life of every living thing and the breath of all mankind. With God are wisdom and might; he has counsel and understanding" (Job 12:10, 13, esv).

> Does not wisdom call? Does not understanding raise her voice? On the heights beside the way, at the crossroads she takes her stand; beside the gates in front of the town, at the entrance of the portals she cries aloud: "To you, O men, I call, and my cry is to the children of man. O simple ones, learn prudence; O fools, learn sense. Hear, for I will speak noble things, and from my lips will come what is right, for my mouth will utter truth; wickedness is an abomination to my lips. All the words of my mouth are righteous; there is

nothing twisted or crooked in them. They are all straight to him who understands, and right to those who find knowledge. Take my instruction instead of silver, and knowledge rather than choice gold, for wisdom is better than jewels, and all that you may desire cannot compare with her. "I, wisdom, dwell with prudence, and I find knowledge and discretion. The fear of the Lord is hatred of evil. Pride and arrogance and the way of evil and perverted speech I hate. I have counsel and sound wisdom; I have insight; I have strength.

Pro. 8:1–14 esv

For the Lord giveth wisdom: out of his mouth cometh knowledge and understanding. He layeth up sound wisdom for the righteous: he is a buckler to them that walk uprightly.

Prov. 2:6, 7 kjv

Happy is the man that findeth wisdom, and the man that getteth understanding. For the merchandise of it is better than the merchandise of silver, and the gain thereof than fine gold. She is more precious than rubies: and all the things thou canst desire are not to be compared unto her. Length of days is in her right hand; and in her left hand riches and honour. Her ways are ways of pleasantness, and all her paths are peace. She is a tree of life to them that lay hold upon her: and happy is every one that retaineth her. The Lord by wisdom hath founded the earth; by understanding hath he established the heavens. By his knowledge the depths are broken up, and the clouds drop down the dew. My son, let not them depart from thine eyes; keep sound wisdom and discretion: So shall they be life unto thy soul, and grace to thy neck. Then shalt thou walk in thy way safely, and thy foot shall not stumble.

Pro. 3:13–23 kjv

If any of you lack wisdom, let him ask of God, that giveth to all men liberally, and upbraideth not; and it shall be given him. But let him ask in faith, nothing wavering. For he that wavereth is like a wave of the sea that is driven with the wind and tossed. For let not that man think he shall receive any thing of the Lord. A double minded man is unstable in all his ways.

Ja. 1:5–8 (kjv)

God Speaks to Us through Dreams

And it shall come to pass afterward, that I will pour out my spirit upon all flesh; and your sons and your daughters shall prophesy, your old men shall dream dreams, your young men shall see visions: And also upon the servants and upon the handmaids in those days will I pour out my spirit.

Joel 2:28, 29 (kjv)
See also Acts 2:17.

The believer should not believe that every voice is from God. We are not to believe that every dream and vision is from God; of course they're not. Until one truly comes into the maturity of wisdom in Christ, there is no question the enemy knows how to strategize through a schemed plan to get into our minds if we allow him the entertainment of doing so. We do have a choice not to and the power to put the enemy to flight. We have to resist him, and he will flee. We are to be careful what and who we entertain in our minds. We can't watch any and every thing, we can't listen to certain music, and we have to be careful who and what we touch because you can sin in your thinking, and your thoughts can easily be altered by what you touch, taste, feel, and see. If you want to be mediocre, living a watered-down salvation, you will have to answer for that. But to those who choose to submit to the call of Christ, there are definitely some things that must be put away and cast off, and, through annihilating sin, it can be done.

For though we walk in the flesh, we are not waging war according to the flesh. For the weapons of our warfare are not of the flesh but have divine power to destroy strongholds. We destroy arguments and every lofty opinion raised against the knowledge of God, and take every thought captive to obey Christ, being ready to punish every disobedience, when your obedience is complete.

II Corinthians 10: 3–6 (esv)

As we look at this scripture, Paul is reminding the believer that we walk in the flesh but we take control of the spirit of the enemy through spiritual warfare. The enemy knows that in our carnal mind and in our flesh dwells nothing good. Therefore, we must recognize that we need to stay in the Spirit as much as we can think to because spiritual forces attack and prey upon the imaginations and thoughts of men. Through mere words and things around us, they daily force their selfish and devilish ideas as darts against you and God in you to lure you away from thinking in the authority of the Spirit in truth. Every selfish, evil, and lustful thought are mental and immaterial ideas that are not physical and material substances. They are invisible and mental substances that we cannot see. By nature, this is not God's nature, but the devils nature. Any thought that is of such sort is opposed to God and anti-God. Yes, we as believers live in a body like other ordinary people, but we do not war in the flesh like the world. We don't fight our struggles we have in life in our own strength but, in the strength in which the Lord gives in the power of his might. Evil forces are immune to sin, evil, disorder, corruption, deterioration, havoc, hell, chaos, and death therefore we don't fight in the natural or fleshly mind but in the spiritual mind and spiritual things of God.

Paul put it this way:

Finally, my brethren, be strong in the Lord, and in the power of his might. Put on the whole armour of God, that ye may be able to stand against the wiles of the devil. For we wrestle not against flesh and blood, but against principalities, against powers, against the rulers of the darkness of this world, against spiritual wickedness in high places. Wherefore take unto you the whole armour of God, that ye may be able to withstand in the evil day, and having done all, to stand. Stand therefore, having your loins girt about with truth, and having on the breastplate of righteousness; And your feet shod with the preparation of the gospel of peace; Above all, taking the shield of faith, wherewith ye shall be able to quench all the fiery darts of the wicked. And take the helmet of salvation, and the sword of the Spirit, which is the word of God: Praying always with all prayer and supplication in the Spirit, and watching thereunto with all perseverance and supplication for all saints; And for me, that utterance may be given unto me, that I may open my mouth boldly, to make known the mystery of the gospel.

Eph. 6:10–19 kjv

Instant text messaging is like instant gratification: easy to receive, hard not to respond to. Many things we so quickly respond to cause us to miss the directions of the Lord because we are living in a world of gadgets. We respond too quickly to decisions and things of other matters in which we ought not even be bothered with or have on our minds. We need to be aware that as technology has so swiftly given us easy access to the whole world, we are caught up in the world of spiritual blockage by being enslaved to the world of technology.

We cannot dream the dreams of God and envision the will of God because there's always a phone call to receive, a text to answer, or something being downloaded into our minds other than the signs of the time. We need to watch and pray and be careful what we allow our minds to experience on a daily basis.

We cannot equip our minds for spiritual warfare if we are soon taken away by our thoughts with something or somewhere to go other than the Word of God. It's time to read the Word, study the Word to know the Word to know the things that God has revealed to us through his message. Without being equipped in our minds, we miss the plan of God and abort the mission of God. If you do, the consequences can take you off of your journey, and you often find yourself waging war against the thoughts of your mind for what you face in the flesh mind and not the Spirit mind.

> For they that are after the flesh do mind (work to keep their minds upon) the things of the flesh; but they that are after the Spirit the things of the Spirit.
>
> Romans 8:5 (kjv)

> And be not conformed to this world: but be ye transformed by the renewing of your mind, that ye may prove what is that good, and acceptable, and perfect, will of God.
>
> Romans 12:2 (kjv)

Until we learn how to honor God for who he is, we will forever miss the call daily of Christ, who is come to give us life and that more abundantly. We are to present our bodies as living sacrifices to God and not to sin. Every day of our journey with God we are to present ourselves to him as to equip ourselves to live holy in him. When we do these things, we can then dream the dreams and be the visionaries in which he has equipped us to be.

Paul said it this way:

> I appeal to you therefore, brothers, by the mercies of God, to present your bodies as a living sacrifice, holy and acceptable to God, which is your spiritual worship. Do not be conformed to this world, but be transformed by the renewal of your mind, that by testing you may discern what is the will of God, what is good and acceptable and perfect.
>
> Romans 12:1, 2 (esv)

When God declared into the earth that our sons and daughters would prophesy and that our old men would dream dreams, he was not talking about worldly dreams and false, pretentious prophecy. He was talking about the revealed truth being revealed to us like never before through the mysteries of his wisdom and knowledge. Only when we let go, give up, and turn away from the world and the things of the world will we be able to fulfill the will of God. Yes, we are called to dream; yes, God speaks to us through dreams; yes, we are called to have visions, but without it, we will be apt to do the things of the world if we don't stop doing things as usual. We are ordinary people with a supernatural being who lives on the inside of us and will lead, guide, and direct us into the truth only when we submit to the call of his voice and respond in his Spirit to the truth.

God speaks to us through dreams, and dreams are one way that God shapes our lives into the person he has called us to be. Some have dreamed of being great writers; poets; singers; dancers; movie stars; artists; opera singers; models; reporters; sports commentators; pro-football players or pro-basketball players; hockey, tennis, or volleyball players; actresses or actors; preachers or teachers, missionaries of some sort; race car drivers, disk jockeys; counselors; psychiatrists; doctors; lawyers; court reporters; politicians; etc., a mate to fulfill the rest of our lives with, going far away on a trip, traveling the world dreaming of doing something that is against all odds, like being the first to break a score or record in the genesis book of records. Whether or not you choose to dream, God does speak to us in dreams.

God, through his Spirit, speaks to all humans in dreams throughout their lives. It's just that many don't know how to recognize it oftentimes. Every human being has had some sort of dream at one point or another. I can't cover it all, but dreams can become a reality. But, not all dreams. Sometimes we think we're dreaming and we're just fantasizing about something, and most of the time it's something so ridiculous we ought not repeat its folly. All dreams are not meant to be pursued. All things we think about in our subconscious are not dreams. Sometimes they're just mere thoughts or suggestions from the enemy; therefore, as believers, we must be very careful what we attempt to pursue, making sure we understand what the will of the Lord is first, and then we can decipher through what is right and what is wrong and what is evil and what is good. Let's take a journey through Genesis.

Even when we sin and choose to go in our own ways, God makes a way of escape.

God came to Abimelech in a dream to warn him that Sarah was Abraham's wife. This was after Abraham had lied and told Abimelech that Sarah was his sister because he was afraid that Abimelech would kill him and his wife, Sarah (Genesis 20:3–6).

God often brings us encouragement through a dream when all seems to be at stake, just like Jacob was called back to the Promised Land and faced many obstacles. God already had a way of escape from the dilemma in which Jacob faced. Read Genesis 31:11–55.

When you find time to read this chapter, you will notice there were many obstacles Jacob faced, yet God spoke to Jacob in a dream and gave him directions on how to keep himself in his will and be saved from the threat of Laban, who was his wives' father.

Just like Jacob, who faced some barriers and roadblocks and God intervened, we too can experience the intervention of God's providence through a dream.

Jacob faced the obstacles of threatening situations of family and their carnality, greed, covetousness, and anger of others. He faced the obstacle of his own selfish desire and the fear of losing what he had gained, the deception of taking a man's daughters without him knowing; yet, through all of this, God just spoke to Jacob in a dream, and he followed the directions given to him by God. You will see in verses 43–53 that Jacob made peace with Laban. We as believers must learn how to make peace when there are obstacles that we have to face. We must not think in our selfish desires that we can connive, trick, con, or deal wrongly with others and have the blessing of God upon our lives. We cannot go through our situation of losing a house, car, job, having an illness upon ourselves or a loved one, and be too stiff-necked and hardheaded to think of our own ways to fix things without waiting on the Lord.

Many times the temptation of resorting to evil and wicked acts is knocking and waiting right at the beginning of our obstacle, dilemma, or even if we are trying to help someone else. We are so quick to resort back to our flesh and those who are not born again; we may even think to call on them before we wait on God. God can and will speak to us through dreams, but we have to be willing and committed to waiting on him and accept the way in which he tells us to do something. Don't ever say, "I don't think God would have me to give this up or that up as hard as I worked for it!" That's pride, and if you lift up things before the Lord and don't think you won't take a fall, then wait and see if you will dream the dreams of God and envision the ways of truth without first giving up some things that don't matter for the journey he has set before you anyway. Yes, before the foundation of the world, the dreams you would dream had already been declared to the ends of the universe. You must learn to humble yourself under the mighty hand of the Lord and not be so quick to think that you won't lose some things to gain the things through dreams in which God would have you to see.

Dreams can be interpreted by those who walk in this office, just like Daniel who was able to interpret dreams, explain riddles and solve problems. Daniel interprets the writing which was upon the plaster of the wall of the king's palace. No astrologer or soothersayer (enchanter) of any sort was able to do what Daniel had done because he came in the spirit of excellence!

> The queen because of the words of the king and his lords, came into the banqueting hall, and the queen declared, "O king, live forever! Let not your thoughts alarm you or your color change. There is a man in your kingdom in whom is the spirit of the holy gods. In the days of your father, light and understanding and wisdom like the wisdom of the gods where found in him, and King Nebuchadnezzar, your father your father the king

made him chief of the magicians, enchanters, Chaldeans, and astrologers, because an excellent spirit of knowledge, and understanding to interpret dreams, explain riddles, and solve problems were found in this Daniel, whom the king named Belteshazzar. Now let Daniel be called, and he will show the interpretation. Then Daniel was brought in before the king, The king answered and said to Daniel, "You are that Daniel, one of the exiles of Judah, whom the king my father brought from Judah, I have heard of you that the spirit of the gods is in you, and that light and understanding and excellent wisdom are found in you. Now the wise men, the enchanters, have been brought in before me to read this writing and make known to me its interpretation, but they could not show the interpretation of the matter. But I have heard that you can give interpretation and solve problems, Now if you can read the writing and make known to me its interpretation, you shall be clothed with purple and have a chain of gold around your neck and shall be the third ruler in the kingdom."

Then Daniel answered and said before the king. "Let your gifts be for yourself, and give your rewards to another. Nevertheless, I will read the writing to the king and make known to him the interpretation. O king, the Most High God gave Nebuchadnezzar your father kingship and greatness and glory and majesty. And because of the greatness that he gave him, all peoples, nations, and languages trembled and feared before him. Whom he would, he killed, and whom he would, he kept alive; whom he would, he raised up, and whom he would, he humbled. But when his heart was lifted up and his spirit was hardened so that he dealt proudly, he was brought down from his kingly throne, and his glory was taken from him. He was driven from among the children of mankind, and his mind was made like that of a beast, and his dwelling was with the wild donkeys. He was fed grass like an ox, and his body was wet with the dew of heaven, until he knew that the Most High God rules the kingdom of mankind and sets over it whom he will. And you his son, Belshazzar, have not humbled your heart, though you knew all of this, but you have lifted up yourself against the Lord of heaven. And the vessels of his house have been brought in before you, and you and your lords, your wives, and your concubines have drunk wine from them, And you have praised the gods of silver and gold, of bronze, iron, wood, and stone, which do not see or hear or know, but the God in whose hand is your breath, and whose are all your ways, you have not honored.

"Then from his presence the hand was sent, and this writing was inscribed, And this is the writing that was inscribed: MENE, MENE, TEKEL, and PARSIN. This is the interpretation of the matter: MENE God has numbered the days of your kingdom and brought it to an end. TEKEL, you have been weighed in the balance and found wanting; PERES, your kingdom is divided and given to the Medes and Persians. That very night Belshazzar the Chaldean king was killed. And Darius the Mede received the kingdom, being about sixty-two years old.

Daniel 5:10–30 (esv)

It pleased Darius to set over the kingdom an hundred and twenty princes, which should be over the whole kingdom; And over the three presidents; of whom Daniel was first: that the princes might give accounts unto them, and the king should have no damage. Then this Daniel was preferred above the presidents and princes, because an excellent spirit was in him; and the king thought to set him over the whole realm. Then the presidents and princes sought to find occasion against Daniel concerning the kingdom; but they could find none occasion nor fault; forasmuch as he was faithful, neither was there any error or fault found in him. Then said these men, We shall not find any occasion against this Daniel, except we find it against him concerning the law of his God.

Daniel 6:1–5

When God wants to bring judgment, he will often use someone that is exiled (someone that has been forced out of their country or home through detrimental circumstances) to bring the truth to the light. As we see in this text, even the astrologers and soothsayers (enchanters) weren't able to read the writing on the wall. It took a man of God, an ordinary person without a title, just a man who was taken from his own land to walk in the excellent Spirit of the most high God. If you want to do exploits and know that God can, will, and does speak to you in dreams and gives you the power to walk in excellence even against all odds of being unknown, if you humble yourself to his Word and seek the truth of his Word through the mysteries which are given to those who seek his face and turn from their wicked ways, you will be one that can hear from heaven, and God will heal that which concerns you. He will cause you to dream dreams and be the visionary that you so long to be if you but be still and see the salvation of the Lord! Remember, dreams and visions in God are given to the righteous to interpret the times, days, and seasons we are in and to lead, guide, and direct us into all truth in his Spirit.

Now let's take a look at this passage of scripture.

> But God hath chosen the foolish things of the world to confound (confuse) the wise; and God hath chosen the weak things of the world to confound the things which are mighty; And base (low) things of the world, and things which are despised, hath God chosen, yea, and things which are not, to bring to nought (nothing) things that are: That no flesh should glory in his presence. But of him are you in Christ Jesus, who of God is made unto us wisdom, and righteousness, and sanctification, and redemption: That, according as it is written, He that glorieth, let him glory in the Lord.
>
> 1Corinthians 1:27–30 (kjv)

Listen, my sisters and brothers. God is a God of purpose. He chose you in spite of what you have done and who you have done it with. Whatever it was is no more because you are now saved and your life is hidden in Christ Jesus. Remember, the word *saved* means that you have been redeemed from all of your sins. Therefore, where you used to go and what you use to do while you were yet on your way to hell, Christ died for you, and you are now saved and have eternal life in Christ Jesus. Amen. You have been chosen and predestinated to do God's will so that he will get the glory out of your life. Where you have been, how you think, and when you were in your mess, Christ had already paid the redemption price for you to be saved. Hallelujah!

If you were being abused. Christ died for you; if or when your family abandoned you, Christ had already died for you. If ever someone told you you would never amount to anything, Christ died for you too. If you were strung out on drugs, Christ died for you. If you were gangbanging, dope slinging, pimping, and always tripping, Christ died for you too. If you were acting the fool, always trying to be a thug, or thought it was cool not to go to school, Christ died for you. If you were sneaking around, living a double life and hating everybody and did not want to exist in life, Christ died for you. If you were despised and disowned by family and your so-called friends turned their backs on you, Christ died for you. If there were many, many times you thought you were going to lose your mind, Christ died for you. If you were violated, raped, molested or mentally, physically, financially, and emotionally out of control with no one to call, you ought to know by now that Christ died for you.

Your Lord and Savior, Jesus Christ died for you. All that you have been, said, and done while you were out in the streets doing what you did best (living in sin) in the flesh, Christ died for you. Through your ups and downs, ins and outs, bad days and heavy pains, he knows and he still chose you to do his will so that he will get the glory out of your life. Just remember, Christ died for you. You have a purpose. You don't have to die and stop living, even if you are on your sick bed. Know this one thing to be a fact: Christ died for you. If you are in prison, physically locked up or mentally in prison because of a satanic or demonic attack has come up against you, it's important to know and believe Christ died for you. He has given you a reason to live and not die because he died for you. The reason Christ died for you is 1) that he would get the glory out of your life, 2) you were lost in sin and shame and on your way to hell and, 3) to redeem mankind back to himself.

I pray this is helping someone, or maybe it's not you I'm helping, but you may know someone who has been desperate to change and has not found a way out of their desperation. Maybe someone's mother left them or father walked out on their family; maybe a mother chose drugs over you or your father was a womanizer or chose to gangbang because he did not have a mother or father and had you at a young age. Remember, Christ still loves, cares, and he died for you too. You may have had a mother, father, stepmother, or stepfather that treated you wrong, talked really badly to you, using all sorts of foul language and may have violated your body, and you as a little boy, or girl, look back and can't find it in your heart to forgive. Remember, Christ died for you and loves you enough that he wants to give you your assignment to help someone who may be still in an abusive situation. Just as myself, I was brought up in church yet, my father was abusive—mentally, physically—and my mother turned her head and ignored the abuse; yet, I got saved and was set free from all my miseries because I found out that I had a purpose and I am fulfilling my purpose right now. I know that some things are hard to let go of, but even though I was molested, used, abused, and it did not look like it, I let go of all my hurts, sorrows, and pains and gave it to the Lord, and he set me free because I found out, even with the messed up family that I was born into, that Christ died for me. If you want to read about what happened to me, I have been able to write my autobiography; it will be coming very soon.

Listen, I did not get delivered over night. It took many days of going to church, praying, crying, and forgiving myself for thinking it was something wrong with me. Then, there came a time where I took time off from church and got alone with the Lord for myself to find my purpose through being voracious about the Word. But as I got older and went through a lot more things that were thrown at me that I was not ready to handle, I got over it too, and through having a relationship with God, my life hasn't been the same. I have had my struggles, and it hasn't been easy; but through it all, I know I am delivered from the things that were done to me and against me. Forgiveness is the first step. I read the Word for myself and received revelation knowledge on this great problem with so-called family members. I did not have to be like my biological parents or my step-sisters and brothers, nor my one and only biological brother, for I have a new lineage in Christ. I have been blood-washed and blood-bought. My bloodline comes from the redemptive blood of Christ Jesus. It's so important to know that if you come from a family that is all messed up, dysfunctional, filled with demons of hatred, jealousy, strife, malice, backbiting, and revenge that no matter what you do, if you are talked about, you must leave your natural family and receive the spiritual family that you have in God.

Wherever God sends you, he will have a person or a few people that will love you unconditionally and not find fault with you. If not, God has given you the Holy Ghost, his Spirit, and his Son's redemptive blood to keep you from the snare of the enemy. Yet, when you learn that you were created for a purpose and you have been preordained, called, and chosen before the foundation of the world and you have been handpicked by God, it don't matter what they say about you and what weapons they try continually to use against you. God said, "No weapon formed against you shall prosper." It's up to you to let go of past hurts and love them at a distance and not feel lonely. Even though you may be physically alone, you are never spiritually alone. Remember, the Spirit can live without the body, but the body cannot live without the Spirit. You are a new creature in Christ Jesus, and you ought to say, "I will let nothing separate me from the love of Christ."

You can read my autobiography that I will be releasing soon because many times people see the glory and never know the story. I know I'm the only one that can tell my story, and there isn't a human being that can write this story like I can write my story. Nor can anybody tell the story of your life like you can, but you must know that; even after all that I've been through, I took care of my mom and my dad in spite of all the destructive things that had been done to me—not only me but all my other siblings. My father and mother were so messed up they allowed incest to live in our house, (when I began to write my Autobiography, I found out they both had incest in their own families and never dealt with it). I am the youngest of 9 but 7 are step-siblings, I had other brothers who did not try to stop the abuse. They even occasionally tried to force me to do sick things with them and use what was happening to me as a joke. Some of them made fun of me and other's had their own problems, instead of helping me some often laughed at me being sexually abused by one of my stepbrothers from 9 to 18, on and off until I got into the word and demanded to be left alone. It took the Holy Spirit to give me the strength to say what I needed to him and forgive him to be set free and delivered but, my deliverance did not come over night. Yet, the day I knew I was set free I was set free and had forgiven all my family members who did not care.

Did you know that if you have read this far, it's no accident that you are reading this book? Christ died for you, and he came to set you free so that you can live for him and let it be known to the world that you are alive, born again, and filled with the joy of the Lord. The joy is that you now have eternal life and if you were to die today you would be with Christ in glory. Amen.

There might be someone who might say, "I was living in sin, was down and out and could not see any way out, trying to commit suicide, trying to find love in all the wrong places, looking here and running over there, yet there was nothing that seemed to satisfy me." Christ died for you to give you the opportunity to live for him and serve him with all your heart, mind, and soul. You were not a mistake. You may have been rejected and left for dead, and at a very young age you were told many lies and tricked, tampered with, and your self-esteem might have been tampered with through the lies that have been told to you about you, yet tell yourself, "Christ died for me that I might have life and have it more abundantly. He died that I could tell of his miraculous healing power." Amen.

You are now saved, and God is right now ready for you to have your mind made up that for God you'll live and if you have to die doing his will, you'll go where he wants you to go. You'll do what he wants you to do. You'll be what he wants you to be because Christ died for you and all that you are and have is because of Jesus. He is the reason why you live and can now walk in his love knowing that you have a purpose and he has work for you today right now. Amen.

Listen, nothing that you have done or nothing that has been done to you will change the fact that Christ has a purpose for you. You have been given the power in Christ Jesus to determine the destiny you have in the newness of Christ. Someone you know may not have made it, but you're still here because you have a purpose and God has an assignment for you that no one else can do but you. He called you, and you came and gave your life to him. It's not about where you have been, it's about where God is taking you. He wants you to know that he loves you and has drawn you out of darkness into his marvelous light. He is your redeemer; he is your provider; he is your mother, your father, your friend. He is your door that has opened, and no man can shut the door or take away the God that lives inside of you. Many people use to envy me because I was always dressing up in brand new clothes and shoes and had my biological parents living in the same house. They would have never understood that I was a little girl that always felt like the only child because I was the youngest of nine children and was forced to go to church when none of the other children had to go. My mom would dress me up and fix me up to look pretty, yet I was broken, scorned, torn up on the inside because my father used to beat all of us badly, and it got worse when it was just me and my other two stepsisters moved out. Listen, I did not commit suicide or kill my parents because the Holy

Twila Williams

Ghost would not allow me to. God already, before the foundation of the world, had my life planned out. I did not get on drugs, alcohol, or become a prostitute, but I did look for love in all the wrong places.

You may have lost a lot of things, but tell yourself, "I will never lose Christ, for he died for me, and I am alive in him to do his will. He has put inside of me purpose to do what he has called me into existence to do. Amen. And whatever it is that God wants me to do, I will know it and understand it to pursue my purpose to do his will for the rest of my life and for the glory of the Lord. Hallelujah!"

You Are God's Choice

God did not choose the wealthy, great men and women in power, philosophers, or eloquent speakers, but the Scripture said he chose the base (low) things, things that were naught (nothing), things which were despised. God has chosen you to bring his Word, his promises, and his healing to those men, women, boys, and girls who folks have treated like they were nothing. Those things that are empty, lost, hollow, he is calling you to prepare the way of salvation and speak his Word in truth. When you do the Lord's will, nobody, not even you, can glory in saying it was them (the flesh), for he said no flesh will glory in his presence. You will give him the glory for what he has done, will do, and will continue to do. For he has called you, chosen you, predestinated you for his will to be done in your life, as he has purposed his will for you to do that he will get the glory. Hallelujah!

> Moreover whom he did predestinate, them he also called: and whom he called, them he also justified: and whom he justified, them he also glorified. What shall we than say to these things? If God be for us, who can be against us. He that spared not his own Son, but delivered him up for us all, how shall he not with him also freely give us all things?
>
> Romans 8:30, 31 (kjv)

God chose the weak, low, scorned, uneducated men and women to confound the learned. He chose weak things to confound the mighty; he chose you to usher in the grace and peace of his salvation, which only comes through or Lord and Savior Jesus Christ.

Before we go on, I would like for you to pray another prayer.

Lord Jesus, I come to you first to say thank you. Thank you for choosing me and not allowing anything or anyone to stand in the way of what you have for me. I thank you, Lord, for saving me. I thank you, Lord, for keeping me when I could not keep myself. I thank you, for I know it is you that brought me out of darkness and placed me in your marvelous light to show forth praise and glory to your most precious, holy name. Oh, Lord, I ask for your forgiveness for not wanting to live for you in the past. I know that it's you, Lord, who has given me eternal life. Oh, Lord, just like I have been desperate for the wrong things, right now I understand your plan of salvation causes me to be desperate to do your will. I know that in you I live and move and have my being. I have everything in you to live for, and in the name of Jesus I accept your peace and assurance. According to your Word, I know that I have been saved for a purpose. Forgive me, Lord, for every sin and for the things I chose to do and people I committed sin with that was not your will for me to do and for every negative and evil thought that I acted on or believed that someone may have spoken over my life. Now Lord, I ask that you continue to lead, guide, and direct me into your truth that is found in your Word. I ask that as I continue to read and study your Word that I will continue to know the truth and the truth shall set me free. I ask in the name of Jesus that I will grow in the fullness of your strength to know you the way you want me to know you. Help me to be who you have created me to be. For I know that I have been chosen for a purpose, and as long as I stay connected to you and obey your Word in love, you have already made the way for me to stay focused on my purpose. I believe you have ordained me before the foundation of the world. I know that you have my life planned, and

I will do your will so that you will get the glory out of my life. Thank you, Lord, for hearing me when I pray, and according to your will as it is in heaven let it be on earth. I pray in Jesus' name. Amen.

There may be someone that does not know how to pray and communicate to the Lord many things that are on his or her heart. Therefore, as I am leading throughout this book, I have been instructed to lead the sinner and born-again believer in prayer each chapter. Amen.

The Purpose of the Holy Spirit

The Holy Spirit is God's Spirit that draws us to God, and without his Spirit we would be lost. Did you know that you could not even come to the knowledge of Jesus Christ if God's Spirit did not draw you to him?

> No man can come to me, except the Father which hath sent me draw him: and I will raise him up at the last day. It is written in the prophets, And they shall be all taught of God. Every man therefore that hath heard, and hath learned of the Father, cometh unto me.
>
> John 6:44, 45 (kjv)

Once we hear the Word and receive the Word, it is God's Spirit (Holy Spirit) that brings us to salvation. Therefore, you must accept and understand that you came to the knowledge of Christ only through the Holy Spirit, who drew you to God. There was a pulling and a pressing upon your spirit, God's Spirit that is already in you, which pleaded or pushed you to come to him. Don't ever forget how you came to God, for without him you would be lost.

The Holy Spirit is God's Spirit that was promised to us when Jesus was leaving the earth to go back to the Father. Jn. 14:26-28

> But we are bound to give thanks always to God for you, brethren beloved of the Lord, because God hath from the

beginning chosen you to salvation through sanctification of the Spirit and belief of the truth:

2 Thessalonians 2:13 (kjv)

As you felt the tug and pull of God's Spirit, the Holy Spirit, you believed the Word by faith and received the free gift of salvation that you have in Jesus, who gave his life for you, and you now are saved and have eternal life. Amen. When the enemy comes to tell you you're not saved, know that the hindrance is that he comes against you in your mind. You have to know that you don't have to answer the thoughts that come against your old man. You have been born again of the Spirit (new man, new nature.) God reconciled you back to him through his Son Jesus, and he sealed you with his Spirit, the Holy Spirit so that when the enemy comes against you in the old mind and fleshly thoughts, you have to know how to shift into the heavenly mind, which is the Holy Spirit that has power to cast down every imagination and thought that would exalt itself against the knowledge of God.

Remember, no matter where you are or what you are doing, you need to always be ready to shift in the Spirit, to walk in the heavenly mind that gives you power to come against any thought that is against who God says that you are. The cross is what you need to be in remembrance of because it was at the cross where Christ had a crown of thrones placed on his head, and it was for all the mental dysfunctions; evil thoughts; negative thoughts; and ugly, dirty, nasty memories that cannot destroy you anymore because they have been covered in Jesus' blood. Did you know that when he died on the cross, your deliverance of any mental dysfunctions; evil thoughts; negative thoughts; ugly, dirty, and nasty memories were nailed to that old rugged cross and you are free in Jesus' name? Well, if you did not know, you need to tell yourself and every devil in hell that you are free from your past memories and healed by the blood of Jesus who died and rose again for your justification. You don't have to be hindered in your mind anymore now that you have been born again. Amen.

Your Thoughts

No matter how painful the circumstances may be for you, the victory is yours in Jesus' name. If the enemy can just get you to hear what ugly, negative things people are saying about you, he knows all he needs is your thoughts. The enemy is after your destiny, and he knows that if he can come in and eat off of God's time through your mind, he has hindered you by taking your mind out of the heavenly mind that was given to you before the foundation of the world. The enemy's purpose for you is to bring you down in your mind and try and bring you back to the old man that you have put to death when you received Christ. If he can just use your mother, father, sister, brother, coworker, boss, ex-boyfriend or ex-girlfriend, ex- spouse, grandchildren, or children, and whoever else he can use that he has access to, you cannot allow one word into your mind that is negative, unholy, and unrighteous to stand between you and your God. Circumstances, problems, situations, and interferences are going to come, but it's how you allow God to handle them for you, by walking into his mind through his Spirit (Holy Spirit), that will bring you through to bring you out of whatever seems to be that really is not to be. Amen.

> Casting all your care upon him; for he careth for you.
>
> 1 Peter 5:7

The word *care* means to suggest a weighing down of the mind; as by dread; apprehension, or great responsibility; a troubled or burdened state of mind; worry; concern; a cause of such a mental state.

Whatever it is or whoever it is that's causing you to feel sad, upset, disturbed, confused, or any kind of negative way in your life, you need to rid your mind and heart of all the unnecessary baggage and let it go. Move on with your life and don't allow what you feel about what someone has said, did, or is trying to do to bring you down. You must realize that people can only effect your moods when you walk by what you feel for them and not in what you know in God. God is going to be there for you and is right now with you if you call on his name and pray for strength to get through the storms, pains, heartaches, and shame that has come through many circumstances that cannot stop you from going on if you let it go. Let God heal you through worshiping him and not dwell on the person or situation that has come upon you. Don't hold on to some-one or something that is causing you pain; let it or them go. You will one day look back and see that it made you a stronger person, better person, and a wiser person, but don't be a bitter person.

Relationship with God

The Holy Spirit

Have you ever wondered who the Holy Spirit is?

> In the beginning God created the heaven and the earth. And the earth was without form, and void; and darkness was upon the face of the deep. And the Spirit of God moved upon the face of the waters.
>
> Ge. 1:1, 2 kjv

1. The Holy Spirit is a real person. He is God in action that is from the beginning. God is the person who began time and placed His Spirit upon the waters, moving over the waters.

What was the day of Pentecost?

> All of them were filled with the Holy Spirit and began to
> speak in other tongues as the Spirit enabled them.
>
> Acts 2:4 niv

2. The day of Pentecost was a very special day, an event that made
   history.

That day was when the Holy Spirit came and it was the birthing of
the new church. It was the promised word corporately filling a body
of believers with God's spirit. It was the day in which the presence
of the Holy Spirit would corporately fill a body of believers with the
presence of Christ. This day was when the presence and power of
God came and filled, gifted and equipped the believers to be able to
go out and proclaim the message of salvation to the world.
  Jesus spoke of men receiving the Holy Spirit by prayer:

> If ye then, being evil, know how to give good gifts unto your
> children: how much more shall your heavenly Father give the
> Holy Spirit to them that ask him?
>
> Lk. 11:13 kjv

Even Joel prophesied of the coming and the baptism of the Holy
Spirit.

> And it shall come to pass afterward, that I will pour out my
> spirit upon all flesh; and your sons and your daughters shall
> prophesy, your old men shall dream dreams, your young men
> shall see visions. And also upon the servants and upon the
> handmaids in those days will I pour out my spirit.
>
> Joel. 2:28, 29 kjv

We see in the book of Matthews where John the Baptist spoke on this wise:

I indeed baptize you with water unto repentance: but he that cometh after me is mightier than I, whose shoes I am not worthy to bear: he shall baptize you with the Holy Ghost, and with fire:

The Ephesian believers received the gift of the Holy Ghost.

> And when Paul had laid his hands upon them, the Holy Ghost came on them; and they spake with tongues, and prophesied.
>
> Ac. 19:6 kjv

Cornelius was accompanied with those who spoke in the Holy Ghost.

> While Peter yet spake these words, the Holy Ghost fell on all them which heard the word.
>
> Acts 10:44 kjv

Also, the Samaritan Christians receive the gift of the Holy Ghost.

> Then laid they their hands on them, and they received the Holy Ghost.
>
> Act. 8:17 kjv

> Before Jesus ascended into heaven he said, "John truly baptized with water, but ye shall be baptized with the Holy Spirit."
>
> Acts 1:5 kjv

The most important event that took place was on the day of Pentecost because both Jewish and Gentile believers were present and the bible clearly explains this. God's historical plan was for both Jew and Gentile to be baptized by the Holy Spirit and this took place, placing both into the body of Christ, His Church. On that day the disciples where also filled with the Holy Spirit. In the book of Acts 2:16–18; we read of the spirit being poured out on the believers.

> As we read about the Holy Spirit and the experience the believer had, it is evident that, God gave the gift of the Holy Spirit to them. He promised to give the Holy Spirit to the believer today, if we just asked Him.
>
> Lk. 11:13

> For by one Spirit are we all baptized into one body, whether we be Jews or Gentiles, whether we be bond or free; and have been all made to drink into one Spirit.
>
> I Co. 12:13 kjv

The Holy Spirit baptizes or immerses the believer into the body of Christ and places them in the universal church of God. God's church is universal and that he is not a denomination but, his church is for all nations, tongues and creed. This is why, when a man, woman, boy or girl believes in their heart that the gospel is true and confess Jesus as Lord and Savior. The Holy Spirit enters into the life of the believer. This is a heavenly act that God does and it takes place in heaven. God opens the door of eternal life and his spirit comes into the believer. The position is that of eternal son-ship.

> But when the fullness of the time was come, God sent forth his Son, made of a woman, made under the law, To redeem them that were under the law, that we might receive the adoption of sons. And because ye are sons, God hath sent forth the Spirit of his Son into your hearts, crying Abba Father. Wherefore, thou art no more a servant, but a son; and if a son, then an heir of God through Christ.
>
> Ga. 4:4–7 kjv

Why is the Holy Spirit called the spirit of truth?

The Holy Spirit is God's spirit and his spirit is holy, just, righteous and pure. And can go into the deep parts of a man and clean him up from sin, purifying his heart and mind through the power of Himself. Therefore, it's the power of Christ Jesus who is the word of God's spirit which came to save mankind in the flesh. Let's look at some of the scriptures that confirm that God's Spirit is the Spirit of truth.

> Even the Spirit of truth; whom the world cannot receive, because it seeth him not; neither knoweth him: but ye know him; for he dwelleth with you, and shall be in you
>
> Jn. 14:17 kjv

> Howbeit when he, the Spirit of truth, is come, he will guide you into all truth: for he shall not speak of himself; but whatsoever he shall hear, that shall he speak: and he will shew you things to come.
>
> Jn. 16:13 kjv

> We are of God: he that knoweth God heareth us; he that is not of God heareth not us. Hereby know we that spirit of truth, and the spirit of error.
>
> I Jn. 4:6 kjv

The Holy Spirit Dwells in the Believer

> But ye are not in the flesh, but in the Spirit, if so be that the Spirit of God dwell in you. Now if any man have not the Spirit of Christ, he is none of his.
>
> Ro. 8:9 kjv

> Know ye not that ye are the temple of God, and that the Spirit of God dwelleth in you?
>
> I Co. 3:16

But the anointing which ye have received of him abideth in you, and ye need not that any man teach you: but as the same anointing teacheth you of all things, and is truth, and is no lie, and even as it hath taught you, ye shall abode in him.

I Jn 2:27 kjv

The Holy Spirit is a Teacher

But the Comforter, which is the Holy Ghost, whom the Father will send in my name, he shall teach you all things, and bring all things to your remembrance, whatsoever I have said unto you.

Jn 14:15 kjv

Which things also we speak, not in the words which man's wisdom teacheth, but which the Holy Ghost teacheth, comparing spiritual things with spiritual.

But the anointing which ye have received of him abideth in you, and ye need not that any man teacheth you: but as the same anointing teacheth you of all things, and is truth, and is no lie, and even as it hath taught you, ye shall abide in him.

1 Jn. 2:27

After a person is saved they are to continually be filled with the Spirit (Holy Spirit). God's desire is for all who are believers in him to continue in him bearing fruit and doing good works until he returns. He wants us to increase in his knowledge, strength and live in the glorious power with much patience and walk in longsuffering having joyfulness and to always be thankful to the Father. For he has made us partakers of his inheritance this includes all the saints who are in the light leading the way to deliver those out of darkness because he has delivered us out of darkness therefore, because we have been translated into the kingdom of God we have redemption

Twila Williams

through his blood to receive the forgiveness of sin in Christ Jesus for he is the invisible God and the firstborn of the dead among all creatures (people). So, we understand that God is preeminent above all for in him all fullness dwells and this is what God is well pleased with. Therefore we aught to allow the Holy Spirit to fill us daily with his truths to continue to grow in the spirit and in the knowledge and wisdom of God through the Holy Spirit.

> For this cause we also, since the day we heard it, do not cease to pray for you, and to desire that ye might be filled with the knowledge of his will in all wisdom and spiritual understanding; That ye might walk worthy of the Lord unto all pleasing, being fruitful in every good work, and increasing in the knowledge of God; Strengthened with all might, according to his glorious power, unto all patience and longsuffering with joyfulness; Giving thanks unto the Father, which hath made us meet to be partakers of the inheritance of the saints in light: Who hath delivered us from the power of darkness, and hath translated us into the kingdom of his dear Son: In whom we have redemption through his blood, even the forgiveness of sins: Who is the image of the invisible God, the firstborn of every creature: For by him were all things created, that are in heaven, and that are in earth, visible and invisible, whether they be thrones, or dominions, or principalities, or powers: all things were created by him, and for him: And he is before all things, and by him all things consist. And he is the head of the body the church: who is the beginning, the firstborn from the dead; that in all things he might have the preeminence.
>
> Co. 1:9–18 kjv

> To be filled with the spirit is what God desire of all believers. Be filled with the Spirit
>
> Eph. 5:18

The characteristics of God's spirit (Holy Spirit). Yes, God has a nature and this is that of a inward character which is to be exemplified in the believer to all.

> But the fruit of the Spirit is love, joy, peace, longsuffering, gentleness, goodness, faith, meekness, temperance: against such there is no law."
>
> Gal. 5:22, 23 kjv

Anyone who says they are born again and does not exemplify or pattern themselves after the characteristics of God have denied the true nature of God and are walking after the flesh and not after the spirit. We as believers are to be as God and to be like him is to walk in his nature by staying filled with his spirit.

> If ye love me, keep my commandments. And I will pray the Father, and he shall give you another Comforter, that he may abide with you for ever; even the Spirit of truth; whom the world cannot receive, because it seeth him not, neither knoweth him: but ye know him; for he dwelleth with you, and shall be in you.
>
> Jn 14:15–17 kjv

The New Nature

The new man is found in living in the mind of God through the Word of God. In God, you have to fellowship with him by living in the fruits of the Spirit. You walk in the fruits of the Spirit by not walking in the old man, old ways, and old nature that only brings sin and death. The fruits of the Spirit in Galatians 5:22 is the nature of God. The only way to know if a person is truly genuine in Christ is to know through the Word that they are living in the characteristics of God through walking in the fruits of the Spirit (God's nature). The only way to walk in the nature of God is to not walk in the old nature of the flesh. You must bear the fruit of God. The fruit of God is the Spirit of God, and God's fruit only has one nature. The first nature of God is love. When you have God's Spirit in you, you will love like he loves. You will walk in love bearing God's nature. You will walk in God's nature, exemplifying to the world that your flesh has been crucified. You will love by God's Spirit and not by your feelings. You love your enemies; you love those that don't even deserve to be loved, including yourself. Yet, you love all people because you once were a sinner in need of a Savior and you did not deserve to be loved. Yet, God loved you in spite of all he knew you would do before you ever came into the revelation knowledge of who he is.

Yes, there or many family members who will come against some of you, but you have to love them anyway. You cannot hold grudges against family members, neighbors, or any ex-relationship that you are no longer in. You have to let it go like you throw away an old pair of shoes. That's old news; last weeks special is not today's special. God wants you to live in forgiveness through the love he has given to all the world. I don't think it's going to be hard for God to forgive you unless you carry old baggage of hate, revenge, and wish for things to happen to those who have done you wrong. Many people may have done you wrong and in your future will do you wrong, but you can't live this new life with unforgiveness in you. Why you? Why not you? You are chosen; that's why. Many are called and few are chosen because all want to go to heaven, but no one wants to pay the price to sacrifice the things of this world to live holy and righteous before the Lord. Forgiveness is not a choice in Christ; it's a command (see: Mk 11:24-26, St. Lk. 6:32-38).

You have to have the love in which Jesus had on the cross—the agape love for all God's people. It's not the person you should not love; it's the sin in the person that you should not love. God loves you but hates the sin that you allow to control your life through the lust of the flesh. You will sin, but any sins you will commit, you must repent and turn away from them. Don't be a habitual sinner (read: Ro. chapter 6). Sin is everywhere; you cannot get away from it. You were a sinner and look where God has brought you from. Don't let the sinner bring you to their level and lose your reward in heaven. It's not worth it. Or don't allow the sin in you to control you for you ought to have self-control and not be out of control.

> This is my commandment that, you love one another, as I have loved you.
>
> John 15:12 (kjv)

> For if, when we were enemies, we were reconciled to God by the death of his Son, much more, being reconciled, we shall be saved by his life.
>
> Romans 5:10 (kjv)

We were reconciled to God, even when we were enemies because of sin. When we accept God, we accept his love. To know God, you have to love like God by experiencing his love through salvation. God's love pours out on us every day and every moment. Even when we are not thinking about loving, God's love comes through his grace and mercy that he has shown toward us because while we were yet sinners, Christ died for all. His love overflows in us and spreads so far that no one can ever take away the love that God has placed in our hearts. If you are a new creature in Christ Jesus, you have experienced the love of God. This is the same love you are to pour into others. Overflow that same love into others and spread this love that is in your heart to others, which no one can ever take away. Yet, there are so many born-again believers that refuse to forgive others or refuse to let go of what someone has done to them in their childhood or adult life. Now the same old nature has been kept alive, and the love of God has not flowed out to others, poured on to others, or flooded others because many stop the pouring of God's love, the flow of God's love, and the flooding of God's love by holding unforgiveness, hatred, and animosity in their hearts and have not given God their hearts to take God's heart that has love that over flows, love that floods, and love that pours out into the heart of the world for the forgiveness of sin.

If this is you, repent and change your ways to walk in the new man, which is found in the love of Christ Jesus, who died for your justification and forgave you of all your sins, loving you more than you could ever know. The next fruit that comes in having a personal relationship with God by experiencing his love that came through salvation is joy. The joy of God's nature is an inner gladness that is so deep that when you have it, you give it to all that come around you or anyone that is in your presence knows that they are in God's presence because you will show a cheerful heart and you will exemplify the characteristic of having joy in your behavior. The fruit of peace is next to love and joy. This peace is a peace that God has joined you to his body, and you are bound and woven together in peace to give to others when they seem to not have peace. It's by your presence they feel God's presence because the peace of God is in you that comes in the behavior of all who have accepted the Lord as their Savior. You will give peace, show peace, and express peace in spite of those who don't have hope because they have not received the hope of glory as you have. Now we have peace of assurance, and we are confident that the peace we have the world cannot take out of our hearts, but we can give it to the world because God left us peace and we are to give it willingly in spite of our conditions or other's conditions. Even in sorrow, sickness, and pain, we still, as those with the nature of God, have the peace of God. Amen.

> And, having made peace through the blood of his cross, by him to reconcile all things unto himself; by him, I say, whether they be things in earth, or things in heaven. And you, that were sometime alienated and enemies in your mind by wicked works, yet now hath he reconciled.
>
> Colossians 1:20, 21 (kjv)

God made peace with us through the blood of the cross, and we are to give peace to our fellow man and not show our enemies hatred, contention, and or division, but show our fellow man the peace of God.

> And let the peace of God rule in your hearts, to the which also ye are called in one body; and be ye thankful.
>
> Colossians 3:15 (kjv)

> Peace should rule your heart, especially in the body of Christ. How can we say we know God and we have no peace? We should have peace, walk in the peace of God, and leave the spirit of peace when no one else can express peace. For the rest of the fruits of the spirit see.
>
> Ga 5:22,23 (kjv)

Do You Need to Be Baptized Again?

Our nature should exemplify God's nature through our characters walking in God's character. It would not hurt you to be baptized again. If you don't agree, get someone that you confide in that is familiar with baptism, and you can decide if it's necessary or not. I don't want to discourage you; I want to help you. Amen.

If you have been baptized, you may have this question in mind. "I have been baptized; how do I live in the new man?" These are questions that need to be addressed because baptism is a choice just like anything else in life. It's important to do even though some have repented on their deathbeds and their spirit went to heaven without being baptized.

> When Jesus was on the cross one of the thieves asked Jesus to remember him when he comes into his kingdom. Jesus said unto him, Verily I say unto thee, today shalt thou be with me in paradise.
>
> Luke 23:42,43 (kjv)

His Spirit went to heaven right then, and he was not baptized. To be baptized with the understanding of why you are doing it is to know that you are identifying yourself with the death, burial, and the resurrection of Jesus Christ. You can go to heaven without being baptized, yet it's better to be baptized. How many people have you seen or heard of repent on their deathbeds? These are those who folks say waited to the last minute to repent, and many will say, "I don't know if he or she was saved. They repented on their deathbed." We just have to wait until we get to heaven and see for ourselves. Then they want to criticize their pasts even more by saying, "I know they lived a bad life and this or that." Why is it that people try to make decisions on where someone is going to spend eternity when they are closer to going to hell than the one they are trying to bring judgment upon? Why can't we let God continue to do his will as he sees fit and leave his judgment to his determination? These are the folks that want to change the Word of God.

There are all sorts of beliefs, and you have folks in the church that believe that if someone dresses a certain way, drives a certain class of car, and can quote every Scripture in the Bible that they are definitely on their way to a glorious heaven. Yet, there are some hidden things that only God knows about and some things we will have to let God's Word be done in and let go of other folks and their business, leaving unanswered questions to God to judge. We have our own issues and problems that we need God to bring us through. Don't be a gossiper, but be desperate to know and understand the things of God for you to make it into the kingdom.

I know that there are things that many will disagree with, but whatever you are called to do, just do it in the name of the Lord and let him be the judge of what you did on this earth. I am grateful to say I did write as God has given me the ability and pray that you have received something out of this thus far.

Now I will finish this up by saying these words. When you are baptized, you are making a covenant to God. Baptism is a reminder to you that you are a new creature in Christ. It's an act of confession that you are dead (your old nature) with Christ and now alive in the new man. When you are baptized, you should walk in your confession as a believer in Christ and be an example to the unsaved that you are a new creature in Christ. It's in the new birth of being born of the Spirit and water that you are buried with him and raised with him, being alive in the new man. Baptism does not bring salvation. Baptism is an obedient act of faith after you have been converted (saved) and are dead to sin through salvation, and the baptism symbolizes what you have confessed. When you repented and gave your life to Christ, you were giving up sin to live free from sin. When you are baptized, the act portrays the symbolic washing away of your sins. When you are baptized, you are in obedience to God's Word, and by baptism you identify yourself with Christ's death, burial, and resurrection, and then you continually walk in the new man through obedience to God's Word. Amen.

If you were baptized and did not understand why you were baptized, you will have no significance in knowing what you did because you did not understand what you were doing, and you will not walk in covenant with God. If you were baptized and never acted on the obedience of God's Word, it was in vain (of no effect). You may have been baptized, but have you grown by showing the symbolic act that you have been changed? Or, did you continue in sin and you went down in the water dry and came up wet, dried off, and talked, walked, and acted like you had never been baptized? Did you know that when you are still operating in the flesh and still doing things as the world, you have not fully accepted your covenant with God? Baptism must be understood for what it is, and if you have accepted the Lord Jesus Christ as your Lord and Savior and have not been baptized, you should be baptized as soon as possible. Baptism is your covenant with God in that you are buried with him in baptism and are dead with him (the old man, flesh). When you come up out of the water, you have risen with him (your Spirit is alive in him, the new man), and through the faith in the operation of God, who has raised Jesus from the dead, you are alive in him. Hallelujah!

Buried with him in baptism, wherein also ye are risen with him through the faith of the operation of God, who hath raised him from the dead.

Colossians 2:12 (kjv)

Know ye not, that so many of us as were baptized into Jesus Christ were baptized into his death?

Romans 6:3 (kjv)

For by one Spirit are we all baptized into one body, whether we be Jews, or Gentiles, whether we be bond or free; and have been all made to drink into one Spirit.

1 Corinthians 12:13 (kjv)

But now we are delivered from the law, that being dead wherein we were held; that we should serve in newness of spirit, and not in the oldness of the letter.

Romans 7:6 (kjv)

Just in case you missed it or got distracted, I will go over this with you again. I know that the devil does not want a new convert to understand the significance in this lesson and the devil is a liar, and in the name of Jesus, I will repeat this again. I apply the blood of Jesus to your mind and command you to hear and recognize the revelation knowledge that God has given to you this day in Jesus' name. Amen. Many get baptized and don't understand why they needed to be baptized. Then, the enemy comes in and misleads them in their thoughts. Therefore, they never learned or knew the significance of baptism.

Baptism is essential for it represents the new man that we are in Christ. Baptism is a symbolic act that by faith your old nature is buried with Christ. By faith, when you come up out of the water, you are a new creature in the Spirit. You are baptized into Christ's death as signifying that your old life of the past is dead and you are free from sin that once had you bound. I want to assure you that baptism is necessary, and it's important to understand the reason for baptism. You need to know what baptism symbolizes, stands for, or represents, just as anything else in this world. We have people who are not saved in the world today and will be saved one day, and they understand what certain things represent from the world's standpoint. For example, the American flag, different cultures, colors of different baseball caps, football symbols, even gang symbols that are represented by different signs, rags, and colors. If the world can represent each other and stand for something, don't you think you need to know what we have in Christ that symbolizes to the world that you are saved? Therefore, you have come out of the world, and you need to know what baptism in Christ Jesus represents. Amen.

Now that I know you should have a clear understanding of the significance of baptism, you need to walk in the new man and represent God. Jesus fulfilled being baptized to identify with His Father's perfect will for salvation. He was our example. He was not baptized, because He was a sinner (see: St. Matt 13-17).

> What shall we say then? Shall we continue in sin, that grace may abound? God forbid. How shall we, that are dead to sin, live any longer therin? Know ye not, that so many of us as were baptized into Jesus Christ were baptized into his death? Therefore we are buried with him by baptism into his death: that like as Christ was raised up from the dead by the glory of the Father, even so we also should walk in newness of life. For if we have been planted together in the likeness of his death, we shall be also in the likeness of his resurrection: Knowing this, that our old man is crucified with him, that the body of sin might be destroyed, that henceforth we should not serve sin. For he that is dead is freed from sin. Now if we be dead with Christ, we believe that we shall also live with him: Knowing that Christ being raised from the dead dieth no more; death hath no more dominion over him. For in that he died, he died unto sin once: but in that he liveth, he liveth unto God. Likewise reckon ye also yourselves to be dead indeed unto sin, but alive unto God through Jesus Christ

our Lord. Let not sin therefore reign in your mortal body, that ye should obey it in the lusts thereof.

Romans 6:1–12 (kjv)

In Romans 6:1–12, Paul goes on to explain how we are to live in Christ. Paul asked the question, "Should we continue to live in sin that we might say we are free by grace?" No, we are not free to sin because of God's grace. Just because we have the grace of God does not give any believer the right to just sin. As Christians, we are not free from the duty or obedience to God's law. The word *Christian* means to be Christ-like. Your characteristics will reflect God's Spirit because it is his Spirit that dwells in you. Therefore, by following Jesus through obeying his Word, what you say and do should reflect a Christ-like spirit. When you find that you do not resemble Christ or imitate his ways, the Holy Spirit will convict you through the Word. The Holy Spirit reveals to you the truth and shows the believer how to live a life that is pleasing to God. Amen. The Holy Spirit is the new man in you working inside of you to lead and guide you toward the will of God.

When you are baptized, you are dead to sin and the new man comes alive in you because you are serving God from a new prospect. You now walk after the Spirit (Holy Spirit) in the new man and not after the flesh as the old man. Now that you are saved and baptized into Jesus' death, you acknowledge walking in the newness of the Spirit because you are awakened to the truth that you have in Christ Jesus. We must obey the laws of the land also and not think that it's okay to disobey them because of the grace of God. We are free spiritually from the bondage of sin and Satan and from ceremonial law, yet we are servants of God. As believers in Christ, we are free from Satan having any power or dominion over us and free from the laws of condemnation, free from the wrath of God, and from the duty that was under the law that we could not keep because of our sinful natures.

Grace

> For by grace are you saved through faith; and that not of yourself: it is the gift of God: Not of works, lest any man should boast. For we are his workmanship, created in Christ Jesus unto good works, which God hath before ordained that we should walk in them.
>
> Ephesians 2:8–10

There is no way that we could make it to heaven and live as born-again believers if it was not for the grace of God. Amen.

Never Forget, You're Saved!

Therefore, we are not threatened by the terrors of death. Now that you are saved, you are no longer under the power of Satan anymore. This is why you are to live unto God and not unto the deceitful desires of sinful flesh. Now that you are saved, it is important that you die to sin and live to righteousness, put off the old man, and put on the new man. Stop doing evil and learn to do good according to the Word of God. Mortify the deeds of your flesh means to put off the old man by not living in sin. Don't be as you use to be or do the things that your flesh desires to do. No one is without sin, yet you don't have to live in sin. You have to stop old patterns of the past and live life in Christ. You have to use the Word by applying the Word to your life. In feeding your mind spiritual food, you can overcome the deeds and desires of the flesh by not walking in the flesh. You can mortify, give up, let go, and not look back at the old man and his desires. The old man is dead because you were buried with Christ in baptism and now you are alive in the new man with Christ. Amen.

We do not have to live a life of corruption because we dwell in these bodies of sin. We have many parts and members, yet we have to put our bodies under control by what we see, hear, touch, and taste. We have to stop sinning by submitting to the Holy Spirit, and he will lead, guide, and direct us into all truth. We have to change our habits and our appetites by not satisfying the works of the flesh. You must put restraint on your flesh and take heed to do God's will God's way. Amen. Though, there is sin all over the world, we must not give into sin and allow sin to control our lives. You must allow the Word of God to penetrate your mind, heart, and body to come under subjection (obedience) to God. You have to practice everyday submitting to God's Word and preventing every measure of sin by crucifying and killing the flesh through meditating day and night in the Word of God. Have you ever heard the saying that practice makes perfect? What you practice every day, you will become perfect in doing. In other words, you will have to break, get rid of, and stop doing things that your flesh enjoys and turn away from sin. Give up all to follow Christ by applying the Word and feeding your Spirit the new man, life in Christ. Don't think for one moment that you can live saved without reading, studying, and living in the new man. Just when you might think that you can skip a day or a week or a month out of the Word, you will find yourself in an unholy, unpure, unrighteous state without God.

It's not what we do for Christ; it's how we do what's holy and righteous through our love and gratitude for what Christ has done for us. We cannot keep traditions passed down from one generation to another and think for one moment that this is our ticket to heaven, nor should we ever be deceived to believe that it pleases God. God wants us to love him with all our hearts, souls, and minds. He requires us to accept that we are free from laws, rules, and regulations of men and that we serve him because of love and gratitude, which requires the believer to be alive in newness of spirit. Don't get confused think for one minute that I'm saying you don't have to obey things like running red lights, not stopping at stop signs, going into a store and stealing, or not obeying a court order. You have to obey the laws of the land in that respect.

I'm talking about traditions of how to serve God, and many have made their own religions and false doctrines and beliefs, taking away from the Word and adding to the Word of God. Let me inform you that to every sin there is a Word from God to explain the things we should do and should not do. I want to reassure you that nothing is new to God that a man can do.

> The thing that hath been, it is that which shall be; and that which is done is that which shall be done: and there is no new thing under the sun. Is there any thing whereof it may be said, See, this is new? It hath been already of old time, which was before us.
>
> Ecclesiastes 1:9, 10 (kjv)

God sent his Son to die for all the sins of the world; therefore, there is nothing that is done, has been done, or will be done that will surprise or shock God. The Scripture says that those who add or take away from God's Word will be plagued and taken out of the Book of Life.

> For I testify unto every man that heareth the words of the prophecy of his book, If any man shall add unto these things, God shall add unto him the plagues that are written in this book: And if any man shall take away from the words of the book of this prophecy, God shall take away his part out of the book of life, and out of the holy city, and from the things which are written in this book.
>
> Revelations 22:18,19 (kjv)

This means exactly what it says, just as anything else that is written in the Word of God. You have a right to listen to anything, and you will pay the consequences of your choices, good or bad. This is the freedom you have as a newborn believer. God does not take your right to choose which way you will go, but he leaves you the right choices to make the right decisions. You should not make an effort in keeping up with other people concerning their beliefs about the Bible. You need to hear and accept the truth that is only found in the Word of God. Amen. It's not man that died for you, but Christ who died for all and is forever making intercession for us to the Father.

> Wherefore he is able also to save them to the uttermost that come unto God by him, seeing he ever liveth to make intercession for them.
>
> Hebrews 7:25 (kjv)

> For to this end Christ both died, and rose, and revived, that he might be Lord both of the dead and living.
>
> Romans 14:9 (kjv)

It's so imperative to know and believe as a believer that Christ, being the only living and true God, is not just our Savior but also our Lord. If you are a newborn believer, it is one thing to pursue and stand firm in and to know who your God is and why he died for you and rose again. Understanding the new birth is your blueprint to having a solid foundation to continue daily walking in the new man. Isn't it wonderful to know that Christ's death and resurrection brought us free salvation through Jesus Christ?

When All Hell Breaks Loose

Keep the Devil Out

Shall I remind you once again the importance of staying connected to God by walking in the mind of the Spirit? You should already know how to keep the devil out of your thoughts. He just desires to take your thoughts away from what God's Word says, and he can only do it by stealing from your thoughts. Therefore, you have the power in the name of Jesus to resist the thoughts of the enemy by pleading the blood of Jesus over your thoughts, knowing that the Spirit (Holy Spirit) forever is interceding for the saints according to the will of God. You must keep your mind renewed in the Word to stay connected to the mind of the Spirit. Amen

> Likewise the Spirit also helpeth our infirmities: for we know not what we should pray for as we ought: but the Spirit itself maketh intercession for us with groanings which cannot be uttered. And he that searcheth the hearts knoweth what is the mind of the Spirit, because he maketh intercession for the saints according to the will of God.
>
> Romans 8:26, 27 (kjv)

When you plead the blood of Jesus against Satan, you keep the enemy, negative thoughts (that have been formed in you through your past), and evil speakers (people that speak against the God you serve) out of your thoughts. You have the victory in Jesus' name. Jesus already died and rose again over the battles that will come up against your mind through thoughts. You just have to walk in the mind of the Spirit (the Word of God). Your greatest battle is to overcome the way you think and what you think about yourself. Being defeated in your mind about who you are in Christ is no longer an issue with the devil, but when you walk in the flesh and allow him (Satan, your adversary) to plant thoughts of negativity through evil devises into your mind and his trifling demons to come in and speak negatively, you are not allowing God to fight your battles. You are entertaining thoughts that you have no business thinking. You have to learn how to plead the blood of Jesus with authority. God has given you that authority and power in him.

When you accept Christ, Satan no longer has control over you. If Satan can continue to get you to believe the lies of the past, he will continue to make you believe that he has defeated you. He knows that you are not defeated, but he will continue daily to assign demonic spirits to come against you and play games with your mind, even though he knows that he already has been defeated. Did you know that Satan is powerless? Satan has to eat off of your thoughts to produce the desires that only come when you walk in the old, sinful nature, the flesh.

And the Lord God said unto the serpent, Because thou hast done this, thou art cursed above all cattle, and above every beast of the field; upon thy belly shalt thou go, and dust shalt thou eat all the days of thy life.

Genesis 3:14 (kjv)

Without your cooperation, Satan cannot operate in you or through you. He has to first get permission from God, and then you have to give in to his tactics. Now you know what his job is, and that is to keep you distracted by causing confusion, havoc, hell, and chaos at whatever means. He will do this through your spouse (or someone that you desire to be with that you should not be with), children, coworkers, boss, when you go shopping, and many other areas of your life, but that's if you let him. But, you have power in the name of Jesus to resist the devil, and he will flee from you. "Submit yourselves therefore to God. Resist the devil, and he will flee from you" (James 4:7, kjv).

Don't allow the devil into your imagination. He will enter in any kind of way he can. Stay on your job because Satan and his cohort of demons are always on their job twenty-four hours a day, trying to trip you up and get you out of the connection you have in Christ. Satan will steal time away from the work that you have in the kingdom of God when you allow him into your thoughts. As long as you stay involved in all sorts of ungodly activity, you are defeating your purpose to being effective in walking in righteousness to win souls for the kingdom of God. Therefore, leave, avoid, and get rid of anything that distracts, hinders, or comes between you and your relationship with God.

For though we walk in the flesh, we do not war after the flesh: (For the weapons of our warfare are not carnal, but might through God to the pulling down of strong holds); Casting down imaginations, and every high thing that exalteth itself against the knowledge of God, and bringing into captivity every thought to the obedience of Christ; And having in a readiness to revenge all disobedience, when your obedience is fulfilled.

2 Corinthians 10:3–6 (kjv)

Satan operates off of your desires, and if you give in, you will be beguiled (deceived) just as Eve was in the book of Genesis. He tempts you by the sin that is in you, and if you give in to the temptation, you pay the consequences. Satan is plotting day and night and assigning all sorts of demons against you to tempt you over and over. Satan's desire is to destroy you by whatever means it takes. Don't make it easy for Satan to come in by not resisting his temptations. Remember this scripture? "Submit yourselves therefore to God. Resist the devil, and he will flee from you" (James 4:7, kjv). You have to walk in the mind of the Spirit to not fulfill the lust of the flesh. If you stay connected to the mind of the Spirit, you will not operate in sinful flesh. "But put ye on the Lord Jesus Christ, and make no provision for the flesh, to fulfill the lusts thereof" (Romans 13:14).

The Word tells you, the believer, to put on the Lord Jesus Christ. You put him on by waking up and putting on the whole armor of God found in Ephesians 6:13–18. And then put on the nature of God, which is the fruits of the spirit in Galatians 5:22–25. Satan will always attempt to distract and intimidate anyone he can and try to make them believe a lie. And until you learn how to operate in knowing who you are in Christ, you will continue to yield your mind to the entertainment of negativity and all manner of evil thoughts if you don't quickly learn how to operate in the mind of the Spirit. You are to control your own environment and not let anyone or the environment you are in control you. Whether at home, on the job, at school, or wherever you go, you are in control through the Spirit, but if you walk in the flesh, you will be controlled by flesh and how it thinks in your old nature. You are to pattern yourself after the things of God that he may be formed in you from day to day. You have to apply the Word of God to your situation daily.

Keep Running the Race

We know that there is only one way to God, and that is through his Son, Jesus Christ, and when you learn to follow him and not man, you will do exploits, moving daily toward the Lord Jesus Christ, who is the author and finisher of your faith. Whether sun, rain, storm, blizzard or hail, you will not be moved!

> Wherefore seeing we also are compassed about with so great a cloud of witnesses, let us lay aside every weight, and the sin which doth so easily beset us, and let us run with patience the race that is set before us, Looking unto Jesus the author and finisher of our faith; who for the joy that was set before him endured the cross, despising the shame, and is set down at the right hand of the throne of God.
>
> Hebrews 12:1, 2 (kjv)

We are surrounded by men and women in the Bible through faith that received not the promise but obtained a good report through faith. If you forget to walk in the nature of Jesus Christ and come into fellowship with the nature of the devil, the spirit of error can corrupt your very soul. One way that all hell breaks loose is when your very soul has been corrupted by false teaching. You may feel you're being taught right by your own emotions and thought. You may even think because you are serving in an auxiliary that you're doing the will of the Lord. Yet, hell is running rampant, and if you don't get a grip on the truth, you will be the last one to know it.

My family and I went to visit a church, and there was a cult spirit sitting in the building. I felt the strong hold of deception hovering over the pulpit. I told my children, "Let's go. This is not God's Spirit that is operating in this building; let's go." Then we went to another church where the anointing was ushered into the sanctuary of the people of God, yet the pastor was under a bishop that did not believe in women pastors and wouldn't ordain or install her as a pastor. The church called her pastor, but the organization that she was in had a statement of faith, a doctrine of belief; they were incorporated and had many followers. Since there is an affiliation with certain associations, many feel it's better to belong to a denomination or religious organization to be acceptable according to who knows who. Yet, God is not satisfied with men who have chosen to follow a doctrine of faith just to have the benefits of the organization, yet they teach, preach, and do whatever they want because the bishop is not going to sit in his services to agree or disagree with what the person is doing that is against the organization. In other words, there are women who are preaching the gospel, and they stay under certain denominations because these denominations are big and powerful and they have the funds, banks, and equipment to give to them to keep their ministry going. But, the organization will not accept these women as pastors even though their church congregation calls them pastor. To compromise with man is to deny the faith, and that's another way all hell is going to break loose because this sort of ministry is coming under subjection to man and not God. God is not pleased with those who use his anointing to go into places they are not welcome nor accepted as who God called them to be. God says this:

> For thou hast possessed my reins: thou hast covered me in my mother's womb. I will praise thee; for I am fearfully and wonderfully made: marvelous are thy works; and that my soul knoweth right well. My substance was not hid from thee, when I was made in secret, and curiously wrought in the lowest parts of the earth. Thine eyes did see my substance, yet being imperfect; and in thy book all my members where written, which in continuance were fashioned, when as yet there was none of them.
>
> Psalms 139:13–16 (kjv)

> But thou art he that took me out of the womb: thou didst make me hope when I was upon my mother's breast. I was

cast upon thee from the womb: thou art my God from my
mother's belly.

Psalms 22:9, 10 (kjv)

Thus saith the Lord, thy Redeemer, and he that formed thee
from the womb, I am the Lord that maketh all things; that
stretcheth forth the heavens alone; that spreadeth abroad the
earth by myself; That frustrateth the tokens of the liars, and
maketh diviners mad; that turneth wise men backward, and
maketh their knowledge foolish; that confirmeth the word of
his servant, and performeth the counsel of his messengers; that
saith to Jerusalem, Thou shalt be inhabited; and to the cities of
Judah, Ye shall be built, and I will raise up the decayed places
thereof: That saith of Cyrus, He is my shepherd, and shall
perform all my pleasure: even saying to Jerusalem, Thou shalt
be built; and to the temple, Thy foundation shall be laid.

Isaiah 44:24–28 (kjv)

God never intended for man to start having organized religion.
What I mean by this is for men to put God on a schedule and to
keep people from developing and growing to the extent of moving
in their gifts and talents. When men become too manipulative over
God's children, this is a form of rebellion against God, and we are not
to be controlled but taught the laws, covenants, and statutes of God.
Eventually this sort of church turns into false religion, man-made
denominations, and doctrines of the devil. This is another form of
hell breaking loose. God called us to himself to empower mankind
to go out into all the world and to preach the gospel. Not to preach,
teach, and start a ministry unto one specific denomination, but for
all to be saved, to have teachers who will teach God's people about
Jesus Christ and to exercise daily the gifts of prophetic revelation,
being filled with the fullness of the Godhead body and equipped
unto every good work by being filled with the Holy Ghost, being

baptized into Christ's death, burial, and resurrection, then many can go out into all the world to proclaim the gospel.

> For as much then as we are the offspring of God, we ought not to think that the Godhead is like unto gold, or silver, or stone, graven by art and man's device. And the times of this ignorance God winked at; but now commandeth all men every where to repent: Because he hath appointed a day, in the which he will judge the world in righteousness by man whom he hath ordained; whereof he hath given assurance unto all men, in that he hath raised him from the dead.
>
> Acts 17:29–31 (kjv)

> For the invisible things of him from the creation of the world are clearly seen, being understood by the things that are made, even his eternal power and Godhead; so that they are without excuse; Because that, when they knew God, they glorified him not as God, neither were thankful; but became vain in their imaginations, and their foolish heart was darkened. Professing themselves to be wise, they became fools.
>
> Romans 1:20,21 (kjv)

When true prophets are sent by God, they will be in the forefront to declare and decree the works of the Lord, yet the enemy will do everything in his might against them to tear down, destroy, and completely annul their calling. False prophets will be used by the enemy until the Lord returns. False prophets will go to the grave and die for the assignment they are chosen by Satan to fulfill. The devil will take out whom he pleases to carry out his mission, plan, and purpose that he planned against the children of God before we even realize there is an enemy. He has already assigned demons against everything that God created in us to do. The devil will even go as far as sending his co-host of demons assigned against God's children, using one of his elite bishops, pastors, and leaders to come after you. Even though it looks like they are walking with you and your God, make sure it's not someone camouflaged. Satan does not always come to you with evil; he covers up the evil with good first. It seems that an individual is nice, caring, and giving, and they appear this way and sound like they don't mean any harm, yet all along they are helping Satan plan a downfall of one of God's chosen leaders.

Satan often is sending his messengers, which are demons camouflaged and hidden in the spirit of men who allow this sort of entrance. They will live in the halfhearted so-called believer but carry a chameleon spirit that is filled with all sorts of demonic activity. Satan transforms himself into an angel of light, and if you are too soon to go with the majority and their opinion and forget to hear from God on your own, then the assignment that the enemy has planned against you will come to pass. All hell breaks loose, and lots of time we don't know why our homes are being torn apart by being under hellish ministries. False ministers are not being held accountable as the Bible teaches and are often chosen because they have finished school by man-made teaching and not the Holy Spirit's teaching. It's a difference. You can go to school to learn any subject and master it. That doesn't mean it's being taught right. If someone has the ability to be taught the behavior and the characteristics of how to behave, act, and talk a certain way, you can easily be deceived by this sort of character. Oftentimes demons can hide and go under like cancer that goes into remission. Often you don't even know or are not aware that they have attached themselves to someone's spirit without the spirit of discernment.

And you wonder how he or she missed that. They did not see it coming. Demons don't come out and say they are that. They go into a cleaned and garnished vessel that chose to not be alert and on the gate, or the gatekeeper forgot to arm himself, got caught sinning and without his armor on, and, therefore, he or she slipped into sin and the enemy just needed a moment to slip into action just like a virus. He enters unaware, and you don't even realize you're going out with someone that is camouflaged yet all dressed up with a chameleon-like nature. This is a person that will cause all hell to eventually break loose and bring with themselves havoc, hell, and chaos.

This happens to detour many who follow behind great leaders who are leading right, but, when hell gets a glimpse into the ministry, Satan says to his demons, "Go and do this and do that, and don't stop until your assignment is accomplished." He will deceive you into a great conspiracy, tricking you. Remember, he's very subtle and will use you for public display. You must know who you worship with and how to worship God according to the sound of how the Holy Ghost leads you and guides you and directs you into all truth. Many leaders who are truly sold out for the cause of Jesus Christ are clear on how to usher in the anointing, but if the people have been taught the wrong way for decades and decades, it's a battle on how to turn the heart of man back to the heart of God. Unless the people obey the Word, they will fall away to serve another god and lose the way to righteousness and holiness.

If a person who teaches or preaches the gospel is aware of what has been going on in the church and chooses to go forth with the wrong covering or overseer—a false overseer who is camouflaged by using the right words and taught the doctrine from cover to cover those who know and see it are responsible for exposing sin if the leader is corrupt. The false teacher is one that can not be easily detected, yet, those who walk close to this sort of Shepherd should not support his or her ministry. And expose that person; or their just as responsible as them for they know because, they eat, fellowship and spend time with the Shepherd being that they are clergy. For every true worship service and true worshipper, there is a strong demonic séance. Yet, we must stay on guard and not be naïve. We must not allow our mind to be reprobate by ignoring false teacher's and supporting their evil, wicked works (see 2 Jn. 10,11).

Moses said that the works that he did were not of his own mind but he knew it was the mind of God working through his mind. This is the great problem in men throughout history. They try to control the anointing and allow their own finite thoughts, their own agendas, man-made programs, religious beliefs, formalism, and self-righteous purposes to get in the way of God's plan. When God brings forth someone who has the vision of God's mind and heart inside of their spirit through the divine nature of God, God is able to move miraculously in the order of his nature through the death, burial, and resurrection of Jesus Christ's Spirit to live inside the mind, soul, and heart of all men who allow Jesus Christ to live in them vicariously to do his will through worship to usher in his glory. The humanity of Jesus Christ can only be moved into position to call into place the destiny of the church when he is released corporately to live inside of the minds, hearts, and souls of those who worship him in spirit and in truth.

The mission, purpose, and plan of God was never to have denominations, formalism, or man-made religion because when this type of atmosphere is inhabiting the people of God, the prophetic, glorious experience cannot inhabit the praises of those who worship God with another. Many of these leaders need to be put out the church, and the tabernacle of God needs to be rebuilt the way the Bible told the people of God to build it (1 Sa. 35, He. 5:10). God said that he would pour out his Spirit upon all flesh, and this is the activating of the divine nature of God's Holy Spirit showing up to do what he has given to us to do. God cannot give many of his people the full, complete anointing because your call from him needs to be lived through him vicariously as proof of your conversion. God said that he wants no other man, no other person, no other idol worshipped over the experience of the conversion you have through his Son, Jesus Christ.

God can't give you the mission, purpose, or plan for your life by false doctrine, denominations, or a church that quenches the divine order of God. It is God's Spirit that fills the spirit of man with the power of the Holy Spirit to proclaim the Word of salvation. It is mandatory to fill the tabernacle of God in Spirit and in truth through true worship. God's Spirit cannot move in the atmosphere if we continue to worship religions, doctrines made by man, formalisms, and man-made agendas. God's glory will not be given to another. It will take men and women on one accord in allowing the divine nature of God's Spirit to impact the tabernacle of the souls who will worship God in Spirit and in truth to bring in the deliverance, healing, and experience God's glory.

The Holy Spirit only comes into the temple of those who worship to the sound of heaven and obey the atmosphere of heaven's throne through worshiping God in Spirit and in truth. "This people honors me with their lips, but their heart is far from me, in vain do they worship me, teaching as doctrines the commandments of men" (Matt 15:8, 9, kjv).

Breaking the Covenant

When those who have corrupted the pulpit repent and start running the race right, get right, and truly consider their ways by making the right choice to examine their presumptuous ways and humble themselves under the mighty hand of God, then will God deliver the homosexual; heal the sick; deliver the liars, fornicators, thieves; raise the dead; and raise up his bride who he is preparing to meet him on that great day of his coming. There is a witchcraft spirit which fights against the church and sits in the church, which is called the Jezebel spirit. These are woman who are in the church, and their sole aim is to destroy good men who are not learned in the Word. As we know, men are visual, and these sorts of women seduce the innocence of man who has a desire to be married and faithful to one woman. I'm not talking about a bad man, but a good Christian man who decided he wanted to do the right thing but married the wrong woman.

> Have we not all one Father? Has not one God created us? Why then are we faithless to one another, profaning the covenant of our fathers? Judah has been faithless, and abomination has been committed in Israel and in Jerusalem. For Judah has profaned the sanctuary of the Lord, which he loves, and has

married the daughter of a foreign god. May the Lord cut off from the tents of Jacob any descendant of the man who does this, who brings an offering to the Lord of hosts!

Malachi 2:10–12 (kjv)

Just as the Lord had warned the men of Judah not to divorce their wives to marry these sort of woman, it's important for good men of God to beware of these sort of women also. I am not talking about the unfaithful and unworthy men who are preying on innocent, good women in the church, but the men who are worthy to be married to someone who appreciates them. I will talk more on this subject in my next book, *Let's Talk: Relationship God's Way*. But, in the interviews I've done for this up coming book, I've found that men choose wrong because they are not knowledgeable in the Word and they choose by outer appearance and don't look deep enough into the nature of that person. They make their own choices and don't want to recognize that some women they are just not compatible with. I will deal with the women later because there are many good woman who marry the wrong men too.

You shall not intermarry with them, giving your daughters to their sons or taking their daughters for your sons, for they would turn away your sons from following me, to serve other gods. Then the anger of the Lord would be kindled against you, and he would destroy you quickly.

Deuteronomy 7:1–4 (kjv)

These sorts are those who don't believe in Jesus Christ, and they serve idols, worshiping false religion. Be careful!

Those who have been mandated to usher in the coming of the Lord, Jesus Christ, must stay on alert daily because it is our duty to stay on alert. We are called to watch and pray. The rebellion against God's chosen remnant has been going on since the foundation of the world. We must pray often and fervently. Many have been chosen to bring in the Spirit of truth, but there is a Jezebel spirit of hindrance, and the strong hold of the devil is holding the anointing by men who are hiding the truth in a lie. If this is someone's struggle in the church, keep on running the race, and let God lead you through your relationship.

Remember these words that Job spoke in his distress:

> Man that is born of a woman is few of days full of trouble. He comes out like a flower and withers; he flees like a shadow and continues not, And do you open your eyes on such a one and bring me into judgment with you? Who can bring a clean thing out of an unclean? There is not one, since his days are determined, and the number of his months is with you, and you have appointed his limits that he cannot pass, look away from him and leave him alone, that he may enjoy, like a hired hand, his days.
>
> Job 14:1–6 (esv)

Therefore, as long as a child is born and the woman brings life into the world, there is always going to be a man that is willing to be used to mess up what God came to heal, hurting men and woman who married someone they had no business marrying.

We Must Be Skilled, Wise Master Builders

> According to the grace of God given to me, like a skilled master builder I laid a foundation, and someone else is building upon it. Let each one take care how he builds upon it. For no one can lay a foundation other than that which is laid, which is Jesus Christ. Now if anyone builds on the foundation with gold, silver, precious stones, wood, hay, straw-each one's work will become manifest, for the Day will disclose it, because it will be revealed by fire, and the fire will test what sort of work each one has done. If the work that anyone has built on the foundation survives, he will receive a reward. If anyone's work is burned up, he will suffer loss, though he himself will be

saved, but only as through fire. Do you not know that you are God's temple and that God's Spirit dwells in you? If anyone destroys God's temple, God will destroy him, For God's temple is holy and you are that temple.

1 Corinthians 3:10–17 (esv)

The Bible confirms that God is the origin of all churches. He is the source of all who are in the church, and his name is to be given the honor due as our source and origin who has founded the church. We are God's, and he lives in all of us for we are his people. Minister's are coworkers with God and are to assist him in his purpose, plan, and will. As ministers, their sole duty is to carry out the mission of God and to serve him as he leads them for he is God. As Paul wrote to the Ephesian elders in the book of Acts, so ought the ministers to walk and think in this like manner.

But I do not account my life of any value nor as precious to myself, if only I may finish my course and the ministry that I received from the Lord Jesus, to testify to the gospel of the grace of God.

Acts 20:24 (esv)

Someone who claims to be in the ministry, if they don't work with the Lord, is contradicting the true nature of God. As someone plants fruits and vegetable yet does not go out to work, they will not receive any income because they planted and never went to pick the crop they planted. The church is the body and the building of God. If the church does not do its duty toward working with God—and that is to bear fruit and to add to the church, which is the structure of God's body—then the church is useless and is not useful for God. If the minister of the Lord cannot work inside the church, then there is some danger, lack of security, and hazard which is causing the church to be attacked, and the Lord cannot use the building of the church through his minister due to those who choose to contradict the true nature of God.

The purpose of God building the church is for the believers to work together with the ministers of God. Everyone has a part to be of use in God's church, and the cry of heaven is for the body of Christ to cooperate and not deviate from the purpose, plan, and mission in which God has already established according to the Scriptures.

> So then you are no longer strangers and aliens, but you are fellow citizens with the saints and members of the household of God, built on the foundation of the apostles and prophets, Christ Jesus himself being the cornerstone, in whom the whole structure, being joined together, grows into a holy temple in the Lord. In him you also are being built together into a dwelling place for God by the Spirit.
>
> Ephesians 2:19–22 (esv)

> Behold, I am laying in Zion a stone, a cornerstone chosen and precious, and whoever believes in him will not be put to shame.
>
> 1 Peter 2:6 (esv)
> See also Matthew 7:24.

Just as in the church of that day, Paul declared to those believers that they were God's building, and his foundation is the only one that we can build our lives upon. The Corinth church was distressed. There were those who caused problems by being too self-righteous in their beliefs and their misinterpretation of the truth. They were cliquish and on a mission, though it seemed to destroy the church. We see the same formality and rebellious spirit interfering with the foundation of God today. Those who put the church in danger through vain words, actions, and think it's okay with God because someone gave them a little authority are tampering with the lives of God's children and their eternal destiny and, without a warning, will suddenly be destroyed because of themselves. God is calling for wise builders and not foolish ones.

We have the carpenter, architect, our Lord and Savior, Jesus Christ. He is the master builder, and he has a project that has already been put in place for us to work together and build upon, yet many believers refuse to take heed to "Behold." His glory has already been laid, and the foundation is structured toward us, identifying our lifestyles with the characteristics of his true nature through following the pattern in which he has already laid for us.

Paul was affirmed in that he was a wise master builder, which is one who is skillful. Do you consider what kind of builder your leaders are in the church? Are you working together with leadership that is assisting the Lord to be wise master builders? Or, do those who you fellowship with walk in the characteristics of pride and arrogance, being boastful in their own personal abilities and merits? Remember, there is only two ways to go in building on the foundation in which God has already laid: to be a wise builder or to be a destroyer of what has already been built upon. Yes, there are some foundations that have been re-laid that are not patterning themselves after the master builder who is the architect of all churches; yet, if they refuse to adhere to the ways of God, then they must answer to him through being tried with fire as the Scripture has said. Therefore, be careful where you settle for worship, making sure that God is being represented and the church is being strengthened upon the right foundation.

Remember, Satan did not just start being divisive, but he started scheming and being subtle in heaven. Then he was cast out of heaven into the earth and continued his divisiveness and scheming by deceiving Adam and Eve. The devil will always have a device, scheme, and a strategy-plotting day in and day out to how he is going to keep confusion, havoc, hell, and chaos in the church, which is God's body and building. He sends his cohort of trifling demons, in which he gives his assignments to night and day to conjure many evil and wicked devices against those who are saved. He not only attacks the saved, but he attacks those who even have a desire to be saved but are still under his control out of rebellion and being blinded in their minds by the tricks that he plays on peoples' mind through deception. Some are just under the strong hold of Satan's power. Satan does not fight fair. He starts on you as you are being conceived into the world by hereditary ties. He has no compassion or sympathy and definitely no remorse for the selfish crimes he commits when you are in diapers. That's when he's at his best to destroy you before you even realize that he really does exist. Satan is waiting to mess with you by the environment that you live in. Did you forget how he started on you as a child? Therefore, you must stay prayerful now that you are aware of his conjuring, evil, and divisive schemes.

Satan devises to manipulate your thoughts by a pattern of illogical thoughts and vain desires; he brings you no plan other than what his motives are, and that is to cause you to sin and stay bound by his commands. Sin is produced by the lust of our flesh, and when we live in this environment, we give the devil and his cohort of trifling demons access into our minds to run rapidly through us causing havoc, hell, and chaos. Even if you were tampered with as a child, he used those who where not obedient and yielding to God's Word, but sin reigned one way or the other out of order in the minds of many adults who have children; and many adults are not capable of dealing with their own demons less on trying to rear their children in the right path. Of course, it's unfair, but because of the fall of mankind, we must suffer in areas that we sometimes as children never had a chance because many are born into homes where they are unprotected because the predator often is someone that takes care of them or is close to the family.

Yet, once we come into the knowledge of Christ Jesus, we must forgive and pray for those who have wronged us. It's hard due to many that fight the fact that it was the parent or relative and that's just unforgivable. But, God commands us to forgive or we are accountable for not forgiving because we cannot change our pasts, but we can change our futures and have a greater life of peace and love through letting go of past hurts and pain. If you look at some of those who are actors, actresses, and have books out that were abused, they are successful not because they waddled in their past abuse but they went on to help other's in-spite of their past.

Those who choose to walk after the lust of the flesh give the enemy access to live his mission, plan, and purpose of evil and wicked devices out in their lives. You must know that the lust of the flesh is where the enemy cohabitates through getting into your thought pattern by the fleshly desires many times one chooses not to control. It just takes one thought of sin to create the action that goes along with its thought. The devil sends his assignments to great and power-ful men who have a strong desire to be something great. His wicked devices operate and prevail in great and mighty numbers through great and mighty men who are evil and wicked and will do anything behind closed doors to gain power, authority, and lordship over the people of God. The devil uses some of the most influential leaders to devise his schemes to steal the glory, honor, and praise away from God. This is why one has to be careful as to what kind of thoughts he or she is entertaining in his or her mind. The devil knows that he can-not be omnipresent at all times; therefore, his assignment is to molest the minds of men and to turn their wicked hearts through defiling their minds through persuasion. If this is not all hell breaking loose in the decrepit minds of men and woman, then what is it? When Satan gets into your mind at a young age, he knows that he can make you decrepit and wear you down in your thoughts where you don't want to think of what is rightfully yours, why you were born, and for what purpose. He wants to dismantle your thoughts before you start think-ing about what is right from wrong, good from evil, righteous from unrighteous. He wants your mind to be bound to hell and its evils. Yes, as young as you were when he was already doing things to your family, he began to work on you, and now you know better. Therefore, get into the will of God and don't let hell's desires take you away from who God has called and chosen you to be.

Satan deceived Adam and Eve through a thought that came from a conversation the serpent started with Eve. She should have never responded to his thoughts that began to engage her. He asked Eve a question, but she had a choice to not respond. But she chose to entertain hell, just as many do without even realizing the damage that is about to happen to them from one thought of evil. This is the way hell begins to break loose. All it takes is the wrong thought to persuade you into doing the wrong thing. Adam, in his foolish heart, seemed not to even take control but seemed to conform to Satan in spite of God's command and warning. It was Adam that God commanded to not eat of the tree of knowledge of good and evil. "Then God warned Adam to not eat from the tree of knowledge of good and evil or upon eating of this particular tree he would surely die." (Genesis 2:15–17, kjv).

Adam was commanded not to eat of that tree before God had made Eve. Then God did not want Adam to be alone, so he created him a helpmeet. God caused Adam to go into a deep sleep. God has power to do anything but fail, and before there was a physician, there was God. God took one of Adam's ribs and then closed Adam's flesh. Then with Adam's rib, God made the woman and then brought her to Adam (Genesis 2:21, 22, kjv). Adam named the woman Eve, and as you read the Word of God, Adam knew it was his position to give Eve a name and was knowledgeable in knowing what God had done because he said, "She shall be called woman because she is bone of my bones and flesh of my flesh."

Be aware that Satan forms his devices in the thoughts of man to turn him away from serving God through worship. If you allow Satan and his cohort of demons to get into your thoughts, you will find yourself worshipping him through worship also and not even realize it until you have been pulled in too far to get out. This has been exposed through revelation knowledge of many years of studying the true Word of God for the revealed truth. Listen, you worship Satan when you allow him to use any part of yourself to entertain evil, sin.

The Spirit of Subtlety

The devil and his cohort of trifling demons have pressed into God's mission, plan, and purpose through using a strategic tactic of demonic attacks of evil and wicked devices. Since the beginning of time, Lucifer had a mission, plan, and purpose to prey against God who created him. Notice in Genesis 3:1 that the scripture lets us know this one thing about the serpent: he was more subtle than any beast of the field which the Lord God had made. Through subtle devices and a plan to deny and betray God using mankind, he causes many to refuse to stay in his position. When Lucifer was in heaven, his position was to worship God through music. God created Lucifer with every color in harmony of stones and with pipes and tambourines that were prepared in him by God when he was created. God created Lucifer as an anointed cherub that was full of wisdom and perfect in beauty. Lucifer was the anointed cherub (angel) that covered heaven with the ray of colored brightness, and the sounds of music filled the heavens with harmony. God created this once-anointed angel perfect in accordance with the mission, plan, and purpose for which he was created. Yes, Lucifer was created by God and made to worship him until iniquity was found in him.

> Son of man, take up a lamentation upon the king of Tyrus, and say unto him, Thus saith the Lord God; Thou sealest up the sum, full of wisdom, and perfect in beauty. Thou hast been in Eden the garden of God; every precious stone was thy covering, the sardius, topaz, and the diamond, the beryl, the onyx, and the jasper, the sapphire, the emerald, and the carbuncle, and gold: the workmanship of thy tabrets (tambourines) and of thy pipes was prepared in thee in the day that thou wast created. Thou art the anointed cherub (angel) that covereth; and I have

set thee so: thou wast upon the holy mountain of God; thou hast walked up and down in the midst of the stones of fire. Thou wast perfect in thy ways from the day that thou wast created, till iniquity was found in thee.

Ezekiel 28:13–19 (kjv)

Lucifer was created with nine precious stones, and like a guardian angel he covered the heavens with his splendor! When iniquity was found in him, he ruined himself and tainted himself to the point that God had to throw him out of heaven. God created Lucifer with the glory of accession, and, because of his iniquity, he was dethroned down to hell and holds a very low position so low that he was cursed above all cattle and above every beast of the field; upon his belly he crawls and dust he eats all the days of his life. (Ge. 3:14) Remember, the devil is a spirit and needs a human body to cooperate with his evil and wicked devices in order to hide himself through familiar spirits inside the mind and hearts of man. This is why the Scripture tells those who are saved to be careful for nothing. This is why you must know the Spirit of God to be able to detect the spirit of Satan, divisive and subtle is he. Now the serpent was more subtil than any beast of the field which the Lord God had made. Ge. 3:1 kjv Therefore, beware of his divisive ways.

> Be careful for nothing; but in every thing by prayer and supplication with thanksgiving let your requests be made known unto God. And the peace of God, which passeth all understanding, shall keep your hearts and minds through Christ Jesus.

Philippians 4:6, 7 (kjv)

Those who reject coming to God with their whole heart can be seduced in the lust of their heart by Satan, who assigned demons to all and any human he had no selection that he picks out. He is greedy and wants to invade all who will allow him into their heart, mind, and soul. Those who are not careful cause themselves to turn further away in their heart to evil and wicked devices by refusing to recognize that Satan is real and is out to kill, steal, and destroy through bringing hell, havoc, and chaos at any means. Once they begin to fall away, they turn back because they never were a part of us from the beginning. Those who are not of God choose to rather get educated in the word, but their knowledge and wisdom is not of God but taught to them by man. They learn how to preach, teach, and speak in an educated way concerning the Bible to persuade as many as possible for their father, the devil. In hell there are demons that get their assignments daily from their father, the devil, and they wait for the time when they can manipulate the mind of a man who pretends to be saved and have the true mission, plan, and purpose of God almighty, yet he carries a hidden agenda and takes his knowledge to the unlearned and even those who are educated. Haven't you heard of an educated fool? These are people who believe that because they have some sort of degree that they are wiser and more knowledgeable than other's and can do greater things than those who do not have a degree. The devil knows the Word and how to manipulate the educated folks who have degrees in theology yet; teach the word from the mind of man's agenda and will. He does this by adding and subtracting and twisting and turning the Word of God into a lie using men who seek the pleasures of evil and wicked devices to gain power and notoriety. As Satan is quite persuasive in placing his personality in the minds of those who choose to come to God halfheartedly and learn the Bible and its patterns through serving themselves for lustful pleasures, it's no wonder that there are so many homosexuals in the pulpit, liars, adulterers, fornicators, thieves, etc.

God created a woman for every man. He told them to be fruitful and multiply and to replenish the earth. The devil knows that if he can pervert mankind into believing that they don't need to be with a woman, he can kill the human race and cause dissension in the church. The Scriptures has much to say about this sort of behavior.

If you can turn with me to; Acts 20:28–36, kjv.

Take heed therefore unto yourselves, and to all the flock over that which the Holy Ghost hath made you overseers, to feed the church of God, which he hath purchased with his own blood. For I know this, that after my departing shall grievous wolves enter in among you, not sparing the flock. Also of your own selves shall men arise, speaking perverse things, to draw away disciple after them. Therefore watch, and remember, that by the space of three years I ceased not to warn every one night and day with tears. And now, brethren, I commend you to God, and to the word of his grace, which is able to build you up, and to give you an inheritance among all them which are sanctified. I have coveted no man's silver, or gold, or apparel. Yea, ye yourselves know, that these hands have ministered unto my necessities, and to them that were with me. I have shewed you all things, how that so labouring ye ought to support the weak, and to remember the words of the Lord Jesus How he said, It is more blessed to give than to receive. And when he had thus spoken, he kneeled down, and prayed with them all.

In this text, Paul speaks his last words that were given to him as a mission to the Gentiles. To the church leaders, Paul wrote the first duty was for the leaders to guard themselves and the flock in which the Holy Ghost has made them overseers of. He told the leaders to feed the church of God that was purchased with his own blood. This critical message was not to be forgotten but studied over and over again, not giving into the grievous wolves who will enter in among them by deception and persuasion. A minister, servant of the almighty God, must watch, pray, and be diligent to confirm who he is through being honest, sincere, humble, and pure in his heart before God. He is not to let his character be tainted with the perversion of all sorts of man-made religions, doctrines, or formalism, which man has brought into the church through heresy. The word *heresy* means a religious belief, the rejection of a belief that is a part of church dogma, or any opinion opposed to official or established views or doctrines. If a man takes the Word of God and forms another religion based on his beliefs that women are not to be pastors—but they can be deaconesses, evangelists, missionaries—and that men can only do this and that, or, women are not to wear this, do that, and are to obey the authority and leadership in that organization that is only given to a bishop or a pastor, which can only be a male, this is something that one needs to research for themselves and find out clearly if this information is misinformation (see: 1 TIM. 3). Paul knew that Polygamy was common back then and the men needed to be corrected. Many churches take the Bible that was purchased with the blood of God, according to Acts 20:28, and they change it around to fit their agenda, plan, and get enough people to agree and form a cult (organization, corporation), and then before you can realize that the Bible did not mean it for what man has said, many are deceived and have allowed wolves to enter in among them and have grieved the very presence of God's glory out of the midst of his people. According to Acts 20:29, people are going to depart from the church while they are yet in the church through wolves entering in and not saving the flock but killing the very worship that belongs to God.

If someone was saved and found out later that God had called them to pastor, but they were committed to a man-made religion that was founded by a man that is dead, couldn't come back from the grave, or never resurrect himself without God who purchased the church of God with his own blood, then I would turn away from that false teaching of formalism and repent. Then I would ask the Holy Ghost to lead, guide, and direct me to doing his will without the validation of a man who has no power other than what God allows him to have.

A cult is a system of religious worship or ritual, a quasi-religious group, often living in a colony, with a charismatic leader who indoctrinates members with unorthodox or extremist views, practices, or beliefs, devoted attachment to, or extravagant admiration for, a person, principle, or lifestyle.

I have seen people die for the cause of a man that has no power to raise them from the grave. I have watched people in my lifetime worship the offices of men who are nothing but mortal beings and are filled with the breath of God and refuse to turn to God but have pleasure in keeping God's people in bondage.

> For God so loved the world that he gave his only begotten Son that who so ever believeth in him should not perish but have everlasting life. For God sent not his Son into the world to condemn the world; but that the world through him might be saved.
>
> John 3:16, 17 (kjv)

> There is therefore now no condemnation to them which are in Christ Jesus, who walk not after the flesh, but after the Spirit.
>
> Romans 8:1 (kjv)

> For he that is dead is freed from sin. Now if we be dead with Christ, we believe that we shall also live with him: Knowing that Christ being raised from the dead dieth no more; death hath no more dominion over him. For in that he died, he died unto sin once: but in that he liveth, he liveth unto God. Likewise reckon ye also yourselves to be dead indeed unto sin, but alive unto God through Jesus Christ our Lord. Let not sin therefore reign in your mortal body, that ye should obey it in the lusts thereof. Neither yield ye your members as instruments of righteousness unto sin: but yield yourselves unto God, as those that are alive from the dead, and your members as instruments of righteousness unto God. For sin shall not have dominion over you: for ye are not under the law, but under grace. What then? Shall we sin, because we are not under the law, but under grace? God forbid. Know ye not, that to whom ye yield yourselves servants to obey, his servants ye are to whom ye obey, whether of sin unto death, or of obedience unto righteousness? But God be thanked, that ye were the servants of sin, but ye have obeyed from the heart that form of doctrine which was delivered you. Being then made free from sin, ye became the servants of righteousness.
>
> Romans 6:7–17 (kjv)

Man-Made Doctrine

There are many in Christendom who preach, teach, and proclaim the gospel of Jesus Christ. These are those who have been called out of darkness into his marvelous light. Paul says we are not to live in sin, we are dead to sin, and that we are not to allow sin to reign over us. It is a sin to say you believe the whole Bible, yet belong to a church system that teaches contrary to what you believe. You cannot sit or associate with the enemy and believe you are going to justify why you do what you do by saying you are going to convince them to change. They may pretend to go along with you, but you are still under their denomination and cannot differ with them too much or you will be insulted for what you say you believe. (see: 2 Jn. 10, 11) Man-made religion and those leaders who run their churches by formalism and you are aware of it, you are just as wrong as they are for belonging or participating with them. You are casting your pearls before swine's. "Do not give dogs what is holy, and do not throw your pearls before pigs, lest they trample them under foot and turn to attack you" Matt 7:6, esv.

Those who criticize the gospel, God say's that, they are unworthy of it. Christ is telling us to not be fools and think that we can jeopardize our beliefs for those who are against what we stand for. If a person will not receive you or allow the Word to be preached or taught correctly without adding or subtracting or misinterpreting it wrongly due to false teaching, then you need to leave that church or person alone. We are taking what is plainly stated from Christ to justify to ourselves and God why we are socializing with those who are not true believers, even though they claim to be like us. If we are like Christ and walk in his characteristics, then those who say they believe as we do ought to exemplify those same characteristics. We often choose to go against what we believe to reach out to someone that we think we have the power to convince and convert; yet, they normally try to hurt us by criticizing our character and defaming the very characteristics of God in us, just as Christ was adamant about these words, telling us to not give what is holy to dogs. There are some unbelievers who are so evil and cruel that they will say anything just to manipulate you into believing they are born again and a worshipper of Christ when they are really worshipping their father, none other than Satan himself.

Those who are unworthy of the gospel are people who defy, rage, scorn, revile, and openly despise God by their lifestyles, not honoring God by exemplifying his ways but utterly living, talking, and doing whatever sinful pleasures they please, and then come to church or fellowship among those who are true believers, daring anyone by their arrogant ways to rebuke or correct them. These are those who are unworthy of the gospel.

They may not have their hands in all of these sins and others I did not list, but they have the characteristics of living as stiff-necked, hardened, and judgmental criticizers of the gospel so that they can do what they please.

> But understand this, that in the last days there will come times of difficulty. For people will be lovers of self, lovers of money, proud, arrogant, abusive, disobedient to their parents, ungrateful, unholy, heartless, unappeasable, slanderous, without self control, brutal, not loving good, treacherous, reckless, swollen with conceit, lovers of pleasure rather than lovers of God, having the appearance of godliness, but denying its power. Avoid such people.
>
> 2 Timothy 3:1–4 (esv)

> But these people blaspheme all that they do not understand, and they are destroyed by all that they, like unreasoning animals, understand instinctively.
>
> Jude 10 (esv) (read 11–13)

> For this people's heart has grown dull, and with their ears they can barely hear, and their eyes they have closed, lest they should see with their eyes and hear with their ears and understand with their heart and turn, and I will heal them.
>
> Matthew 13:15 (esv)

If these churches were believing the whole Bible, then why are some women denied access to minister? If you go back into the history of who founded many of these sort of churches, you will find that they have based their beliefs on a man's doctrine and the founder most likely is dead and has been for several decades, yet they are still living under that curse.

The church has been purchased with Christ's own blood, and he has called you, chosen you, foreknew you, and predestinated you for such a time as this; therefore, there isn't any kind of formalism, doctrine of faith, or man-made cult of men who hide behind the truth that can cause you to change your title and take a title that is not even in the five-fold ministry. (see: Eph. 4:11) If you are a leader, you ought not to be a sellout to a man that has not shed his blood for you. If you think the Scripture is right and you have been called to be a woman pastor, then you ought to step away and turn from following after the traditions and rudiments of false teachers. God is bigger than an organization. God is greater than man-made doctrine. God is more powerful than the duties that are made by a man. God's Word says this:

> And it shall come to pass afterward, that I will pour out my spirit upon all flesh; and your sons and your daughters shall prophesy, your old men shall dreams, dreams, your young men shall se visions.
>
> Joel 2:28 (kjv)

> Wherefore the law was our school master to bring us unto Christ, that we might be justified by faith. But after that faith is come, we are no longer under a schoolmaster. For ye are all the children of God by faith in Christ Jesus. For as many of you as have been baptized into Christ have put on Christ. There is neither Jew nor Greek, there is neither bond nor free, there is neither male nor female: for ye are all one in Christ Jesus.
>
> Galatians 3:24–28 (kjv)

Maybe some of those who are under the bondage of a man-made doctrine need to be reminded that we are in a covenant with God, who purchased the church of God with his own blood and not man who has no power to bring anyone back under the bondage of sin. But by faith we are all in one in Christ Jesus.

> If you have spiritual Son-ship, why are you bound by the traditions of men?
>
> Ga. 4:26–31 kjv

But Jerusalem which is above is free, which is the mother of us all. For it is written, Rejoice, thou barren that bearest not; break forth and cry, thou that travailest not: for the desolate hath many more children than she which hath an husband.

Why are you travailing to birth out of your spirit things that God has freely given to you? If you would give the devil back his false, fake, perverted, man-made doctrine and walk in the doctrine that was given to you by Paul, then you could bring forth the people that are enslaved to sin and all unrighteousness, when you realize that God is your covering. Don't worry about those who leave the ministry because you know if you leave they will leave. God places those who are true worshippers in spiritually perverted doctrines to be bold in these last days to usher those who are blinded by man-made doctrine out of these false religions. If it's you, then it's time to bring yourself to a place that you will walk by faith and do like the Bible tells you to do. Come out from among those who are not of the fold but are playing church at the expense of souls being deceived, lied to, and confused about their calling. Peter says this:

> Therefore, brothers, be all the more diligent to make your calling and election sure, for if you practice these qualities you will never fall. For in this way there will be richly provided for you an entrance into the eternal kingdom of our Lord and Savior Jesus Christ. Therefore I intend always to remind you of these qualities, though you know them and are established

in the truth that you have. I think it right, as long as I am in this body to stir you up by way of reminder.

2 Peter 1:10–13 (kjv)

And he said unto them, Go ye into all the world, and preach the gospel to every creature. He that believeth and is baptized shall be saved; but he that believeth not shall be damned. And these signs shall follow them that believe; In my name shall they cast out devils; they shall speak with new tongues; They shall take up serpents; and if they drink any deadly thing, it shall not hurt them; they shall lay hand son the sick, and they shall recover.

Mark 16:15–18 (kjv)

I would not even waste God's time preaching in or down below someone's pulpit that did not honor the Holy Ghost that sent me. If God told you to do something, then you need to do it. There are signs and wonders that follow those who are called, chosen, and are willing to go, and if you choose to be damned by going where those who don't believe that God can send you forth to do what he told you, you are delivering his Word in vain. If the anointing is upon you, then you will heed to the Word instead of being filled with zeal to preach where men are reluctant to receive you but are willing to use you as a tool to convince people that they do believe enough to let someone who is anointed to; but they have a hidden agenda, believe it. Instead of equipping newcomers in the kingdom of the Lord, they are enslaving people from this bondage into another kind of bondage, control, and manipulation. You are putting your stamp of approval on the doctrine of man's will when he has formed his own religion and built it off of using women to serve where he places them but not where God sent them. Your will is to do God's will first. Do this in the name of Jesus Christ. Right now, I command every woman who has accepted that it was okay to follow after man when you know what God has told you to be free to be delivered right now in the name of Jesus Christ of Nazareth.

He gave gifts to all those who are his children, but not for people to form their own doctrine of faith. I believe the whole Bible, and to add or subtract anything within the beginning of it or the end is not righteous or holy, but evil and wicked in the sight of God. God already laid the foundation, and we need to be cautious of how we follow those who have rebuilt the foundation over in their own man-made doctrine of faith. Many leaders ought to be ashamed of themselves for selling out to a paid position, and it seems that if the bishop does not see it and I can have a place in leadership, then I'll take it! I don't think God is going to reward those who hold the truth in ungodliness; this is living a double life! I would never change my position that God called me into for any man or woman. I would not use the gifts of God to the glory of man but only to God.

There are many who are anointed and taking a bribe to deny the very identity of God's Spirit and aborting their mission.

You might say, "How is that?" If someone has given you wrong advise and you know you have been destined to carry a certain task out until you complete it, yet you are still searching for all the right answers, but everyone you socialize with has told you this is how you do it because bishop heard a word from the Lord and this is what the Bible says about you, then you can be deceived into compromising your anointing. Remember, bishop is just a mere man! He is not always anointed and walking in discernment. Neither are we. It's God that we all must answer to. Be sure you know what you are called and chosen to do with an anointing, and you will not be misled. Use your intuition; be wise as a serpent, and always harmless as a dove.

To Worship Him

As we look at the word *worship*—to honor, reverence, adore, glorify, to submit and express great respect to God—there are many things other than God that people worship, like cars, houses, jobs, jewelry, clothes, shoes, etc. Then there are people who worship their children; men worship their wives; women worship their husbands; children worship their parents or their parent for the things that they do for them; people worship other people like people in the entertainment business, professional sports icons; gadgets such as cell phones, iPods, DVD players, movies, porno; elicit sex; and all sorts of music. Some people worship boating, fishing, camping, traveling, animals, food, and themselves, and there are all sorts of things, people, and places that are very ceremonial to people that are like a ritual to them. It's not a sin to worship some things, but the sin is when you go against the purpose and plan of God by being unbalanced and unmindful of the way you give honor to people, places, and things with no balance of putting God first before you get too far away from him and began to be vain in your worship by not giving him the praise, honor, and glory due to his name. There also has to be strong morals in your life, then you won't become corrupt in what you worship that is not okay.

How often do you take time out in a day to worship the Lord? When do you set aside time to tell the Lord thank you, I praise you, I love you, I worship you, I honor, adore, and lift up your holy name? Or, is it only when some tragedy strikes and after you come out of it that you may say, "Lord, thank you," or, "Lord, help me get through the pain, and I will give you praise for when you bring me through"? Or, do you bless the Lord as often as you can think on his name through the good times and the not-so-good times?

Let's talk worship in a church setting. Praise, worship, and prayer are three necessary requirements that we are to give unto the Lord. We are not asked to do this, but God, who is our King, commands us to worship him in Spirit and in truth. Notice that it is only through the Holy Spirit that we can accomplish such a beautiful task. Our praise, worship, and prayer can often become just lip service and not from our hearts. This is why it is essential to allow the Holy Spirit into our hearts with all due reverence because he is called to teach us all things that pertain to God.

At the beginning of a church service, notice that the first thing done is prayer, praise, and worship; then there are other parts of the service which happen, but most services start off in this order. As the worship and praise leader begins to serenade in worship unto the Lord, the beautiful harmony in the atmosphere begins to fill our hearts to call on his name to worship with them. We are welcome to sing, clap our hands, lift up our hands high above our heads, and worship our God. As I reminisce on the times I sang and led song service or was in the choir, I remember worship songs like "I will enter his gates with thanksgiving in my heart. I will enter his courts with praise. I will say this is the day that the Lord has made. I will rejoice for he has made me glad. He has made me glad; he has made me glad. I will rejoice for he has made me glad," "We come to glorify his name; we come to glorify his name; we come to glorify the name of the Lord. We come to glorify his name," "I'm so glad that Jesus lifted me; I'm so glad that Jesus lifted me; I'm so glad that Jesus lifted me, we're singing glory hallelujah. Jesus lifted me," and, "This is the day, this is the day that the Lord has made, that the Lord has made. I will rejoice, I will rejoice and be glad in it and be glad in it. This is the day that the Lord has made. I will rejoice and be glad in it. This is the day, this is the day that the Lord has made."

After the clapping, jumping, and shouting unto the Lord in high praise, we go into worship and sing songs like this: The songs are slowed down into a softer tone and calmer setting to prepare the hearts and minds of the people to worship the Lord and thank him for all the things he has done with a feeling that involves emotional expression and the heart being sincere through humility and a willingness to recognize that he is a God who deserves to be worshipped. This is to bring the congregation into an atmosphere of worship and honor. Songs like this:

> He touched me.
> Yes
> He touched me.
> And "Oh"
> The Joy
> That floods my soul.
> Something happened
> And now, I know
> Jesus touched me
> And he made me whole.

As I envision the church vocalist singing worship, his or her voice goes into a higher range and tears often begin to fall from his or her eyes as she looks up toward heaven, and those in the audience began to stand with their arms stretched wide—some with their eyes open as tears fall from their eyes, some with their eyes closed crying, and some trying to hold back the tears; yet, the heavens have opened, and the Holy Spirit has been welcomed into the worship service. Then the vocalist goes on to sing, "Amazing grace, how sweet the sound that saved a wretch like me," "Hallelujah, Hallelujah, Hallelujah, Hallelujah, Hallelujah, Hallelujah," "Lord, I love you. Lord, I love you. Lord, I love you. Lord, I love. Lord, I thank you. Lord, I thank you. Lord, I thank you. Lord, I thank you. Lord, I worship you. Lord, I worship you. Lord, I worship you," "Thank you, Jesus. Thank you, Jesus. Thank you, Jesus. Thank you, Jesus," "Lord, I praise you. Lord, I praise you. Lord, I praise you. Lord, I praise you," "Hallelujah, Hallelujah, Hallelujah, Hallelujah, Hallelujah, Hallelujah."

As the atmosphere is filled with worship, adoration, and praise, oftentimes the vocalist goes into a song that brings one to fall on their knees. singing:

Everybody say, "Yes!" "Yes!" "Yes!" "Yes!" "Yes!" Yes, Lord!" "Yes, Lord" "Yes, Lord!" "Yes, Lord! Have your way, have your way, have your way, have your way, have your way have your way." All of a sudden, the anointing is so strong in the building all there is left to do is worship him with words that are in the Spirit, and only the Holy Spirit can translate these mere words to our father who is in heaven.

As the weeping, wailing, and humility unto God goes forth for God just being God, for him waking one up in the morning, being able to see, hear, walk, and talk, being alive one more day, being able to feel his presence, being able to think on his name and know that it is he that has made us and not we ourselves, acknowledging him for breathing breath into our vile bodies, the worship is high in the building, and all of a sudden from the pulpit to the church doors the Lord's presence is indescribable and many are in bowed-down position. Even the children are worshiping and praising God in their own way, with their hands lifted high. Some are on their knees, some are laid out on the floor crying, and some are bowing down before the presence of the Lord. The atmosphere is so beautiful and wonderful, and everyone in their own way is magnifying, worshiping, and lifting up the name of the Lord. This is when healing begins to take place. Deliverance is all in the atmosphere, and the supernatural power of the Holy Spirit is present in this place. This place is where God can work his miracle power, this place is where God can set the captive free, and this place is where those who desire to be saved can cry out and ask the Lord to save them. This place is a place where no altar call needs to be made because the Holy Spirit has come into the presence of genuine, true worshippers who are calling upon the Lord with a contrite and humble spirit. In this place, there is an outward expression by adoration, praise, worship, and words that cannot be uttered because the anointing is flowing in the building where the vessels are open unto receiving from the Lord, and the spirit is sweet, and the power of the Lord is so strong in the building that the musicians are no longer playing but are on their knees, worshiping the Lord and giving him glory for who he is—Lord of lords, King of kings, Alpha and Omega, the beginning and the end. He is the first and the last, the soon coming King. He is the great I AM, the Bright and Morning Star, the Prince of Peace, the Rock of all ages, a Balm in Gilead, the great Physician, our Redeemer, our Healer, the Lord our God is he.

The call to worshiping God is very simple, and it involves those who love the Lord to participate by showing an outward expression of their appreciation of who he is through worship, praise, prayer, and adoration. There are many verses in Psalms which speak about worshiping and praising the Lord. Let's look at a few.

> Ascribe (give) to the Lord the glory due his name; worship the Lord in the splendor of holiness.
>
> Psalms 29:2 (esv)

> Bless thee our God, O peoples; let the sound of his praise be heard.
>
> Psalms 66:8 (esv)

> Oh come, let us sing to the Lord; let us make a joyful noise to the rock of our salvation! Let us come into his presence with thanksgiving; let us make a joyful noise to him with songs of

praise! For the Lord is a great God, and a great King above all gods.

Psalms 95:1- 3 (esv)

Oh come, let us worship and bow down; let us kneel before the Lord, our Maker! For he is our God, and we are the people of his pasture and the sheep of his hand.

Psalms 95:6, 7 (esv)

Exalt the Lord our God; worship at his footstool! Holy is he!

Psalms 99:5 (esv)

Enter his gates with thanksgiving, and his courts with praise! Give thanks to him; bless his name!

Psalms 100:4 (esv)

We are to praise the Lord because he commands us to (Psalms 150:1); He inhabits our praises (Psalms 22:3). Like Paul and Silas in Acts 16:25–31 prayed and sang praises unto the Lord and there came an earthquake that loosed their bands and opened the prison doors, when you learn to pray and worship the Lord as he has commanded you to do for your benefit, he will loose your bands of bondage and open the prison doors of whatever it is that has held you captive and set your free. The people of Israel obeyed the words of the Lord and did what Joshua told them. They marched around the walls of Jericho and on the seventh day; when the priest blew the trumpets the people shouted and the wall fell down.

So the people shouted when the priests blew with the trumpets: and it came to pass, when the people heard the sound of the trumpet, and the people shouted with a great shout, that the wall fell down flat, so that the people went up into the city, every man straight before him, and they took the city.

Jo. 6:20 kjv

Twila Williams

We see clearly that, the Bible says that as soon as the people shouted a great shout, the wall fell down flat so that the people went up into the city, every man straight before him, and they captured the city. If we could learn how to be obedient to the commandments of the Lord, no matter how awkward or strange what he wants us to do may sound or seem, if we would learn to shout unto the Lord through our praise, worship, pray, and give adoration unto his holy name, he would do just what he says, and we could then do exploits in his name. For there is great power, and it's not just natural but supernatural power through the Holy Spirit that our bands of bondage can be loosed and the prison doors of our minds can be unlocked for we can praise our way out of the prison of deceit, distress, trials, tribulations, and persecution and into a glorious worship, prayer, and adoration to the joy of every Jericho wall coming down flat so that we can take our city back from the enemy by praise, worship, prayer, and adoration unto the Lord our God. Jehovah is his name. Hallelujah!

The Enemy False Worship

Are you aware of why Lucifer was created? He was created to usher in worship unto God; by harmonizing music in heaven that would forever bring adoration, glory, honor, and praise to God in heaven. Just as he has a spirit which characterizes him and his true nature, we as believers must be wise to understand his strategy of how he uses music to fulfill his corrupt nature to cause those who worship God to serve him and they don't even know it. Satan knows that he will never, ever be able to worship the Lord and he will never ever be equipped with the musical instruments that he had in himself. For when Lucifer was created, he had instruments that he was created with to praise him and to worship God. At one time before his great fall, he orchestrated the heavenly music unto the Lord our God in all heaven. Many do not know him, cannot identify how he causes things to happen, and there are too many who will not do any research on his character and his true nature that Lucifer once held in heaven. Yes, before his fall he had a place in heaven that could be adored, cherished, and a privilege to hold, but he chose to demoralize, debase, and defame literally to his detriment his gifts, and they are no longer his. Lucifer turned on God by choice, his free will, then as he chose to turn away from serving the Lord through the instruments that God had created him to worship him with, he was kicked out of heaven. It's imperative that we take a look at how the enemy uses music to distract many from worshipping God, and they don't understand how they are being deceived because they choose not to know the demonic, wicked, evil devices of his ancient character. Not until it's often too late do many find out after their life is over that it really was a Lucifer, Satan, the prince of the air, the devil himself, until it's too late.

Satan hates for there to be praise, worship, and adoration to God through music with singing, without singing, with instruments and singing, without instruments and singing. This is why the Bible says let everything that has breathe praise the Lord! For it's at the name of Jesus, every knee shall bow in heaven and on earth and under the earth, and every tongue confess that Jesus Christ is Lord to the glory of God the Father.

I will give several Scriptures to look up on your own time for when Lucifer fell and was put out of heaven, and I will not elaborate on him because he has no power other than what you give him. He is not omnipresent, yet he does dispatch demons, and if you're not careful of whom you allow into your life, these demonic imps can impose themselves on those who have not accepted Jesus as their Lord and Savior. The devil needs a body to use, just like God will use us when we yield ourselves unto him willingly.

Paul put it this way,

> But thanks be to God, that you who were once slaves of sin have become obedient from the heart to the standard of teaching to which you were committed, and, having been set free from

sin, have become slaves of righteousness. I am speaking in human terms because of your natural limitations. For just as you once presented your members as slaves to impurity and to lawlessness leading to more lawlessness, so now present your members as slaves to righteousness leading to sanctification.

Romans 6:17–19

Okay, the Scriptures you want to study are:

Genesis 3:1. It speaks of Satan's subtlety and how he is the craftiest, keen, slickest, and sliest creature that God ever created. He is skillful, and you must learn to strategize against him, not with him.

Isaiah 14:1–23 (his fall): The king of Babylon punishment that is described here is a far worse punishment spoken than the punishment that would befall mankind for his sins. The word used in these few chapters is *morning star*. Did you know that the name Lucifer is the Latin word for "morning star?" (See verse 12). Here, the sinful nature describes the king of Babylon having the very character of Satan himself, which derives from the depths of hell. This king wore pride as if he was Satan himself. He was driven to be looked upon and worshipped as the most high God. He was filled with pride and arrogance; a wicked, evil and corrupt nature is what possessed this king. Therefore, this depiction is the very distinction of Satan's characteristics and the judgment he will face when it is time.

Daniel 10:20 speaks of Satan assigning princes, or fallen angels, to nations that he has targeted to influence the leaders in these countries to go against the plan, purpose, and will of God. The spirit of rebellion is the demon that is in these countries to bring havoc, hell, chaos, and confusion to detour them from obeying God.

Revelation 22:16 reveals his character of pride to desire God's position and to take control of the world. Satan is a copycat and enjoys duplicating what he will never be. He can transform himself into an angel of light but will never ever be an angel of light again.

How we are to be mindful of what he use to be in his character before his fall? This is why we must be careful what sort of music we sing, listen to, and allow into our homes and lives because we just might be worshipping the lyrics of Satan. For every song is not heaven-sent but can be hell bound by the chains of its lyrics!

The word *lyric* means having the form and music quality of a song; the character of a song, like outpouring of the poets on thoughts and feelings, as distinguished from epic and dramatic poetry; having a pleasing succession of sound; melodious; or relating to the lyre or harp.

The definition of *lyrics* is a word of poetry that can be spoken or song.

When we hear the melody of a song in a band, the first thing that is taught about how to play is harmony. This is why the enemy has made a massive plan to corrupt the music and use it in sexual content, porno movies, phone sex, between intervals of plays, television shows, cell phone rings, and iPods with millions of songs easily downloaded. These are the enemy's weapons against the mind to keep mankind from hearing the truth. He uses music in such a subtle form that it's accepted in society as a way to be. Our children are targeted by parents not regulating what they hear. So many people are not going to hear the trumpet sound because they are listening to the wrong lyrics. *Lyrics*, as the Greek definitions states, is "singing to the lyre." Or singing to the harp. Lucifer was clothed in instruments and every precious stone.

> Your pomp (splendor) is brought down to Sheol, the sound of your harps; maggots are laid as a bed beneath you, and worms are your covers, "How you are fallen from heaven, O Day Star, son of Dawn! How you are cut down to the ground, you who laid the nations low!
>
> Isaiah 14:11, 12 (kjv)

Satan's name in the book of Ezekiel is king of Tyre for he transformed himself into this being. In Hebrews, the Scriptures warn us to be careful, for we might be entertaining angels unaware (see Heb 13:2).

Moreover the word of the Lord came unto me, saying, Son of man, take up a lamentation upon the king of Tyrus, and say unto him, Thus saith the Lord God; Thou sealest up the sum, full of wisdom, and perfect in beauty. Thou hast been in Eden the garden of God; every precious stone was thy covering, the sardius, topaz, and the diamond, the beryl, the onyx, and the jasper, the sapphire, the emerald, and the carbuncle, and gold: the workmanship of thy tabrets and of thy pipes was prepared in thee in the day that thou wast created. Thou art the anointed cherub that covereth; and I have set thee so: thou wast upon the holy mountain of God; thou hast walked up and down in the midst of the stones of fire. Thou wast perfect in thy ways from the day that thou wast created, till iniquity was found in thee.

Ezekiel 28:11–15 (kjv)

Look at the end of the thirteenth verse in Ezekiel that God created him a perfect angel and had placed in him the tabrets and the pipes in which God prepared and placed in him the day that he was created.

The word *tabrets* is a small tabor drum formally used to accompany oneself on a pipe of fife.

The definitions of *pipes* is "a set of flutes as in panpipes, the sound of a voice used in singing."

The Scripture speaks of the viol, a musical instrument coming from the family of string instruments. In the Bible, Lucifer had been given the sounds in his voice and instruments that God created and prepared in him to play as the harp, and he made his music within himself. He was a work of splendor. Satan was the first musician, and he was his own orchestra; therefore, he knows how to orchestrate all sorts of sounds to distort music and cause mankind to create false worship by not knowing the art of heavenly music. Satan comes against the kingdom of God by using people to play distorted music and songs that have no meaning or significance for what man was created to do, and that is to praise, worship, and magnify the Lord. He strives and is driven to disrupt the harmonious gift of music in which God has given to man to use for his glory. But instead, out of ignorance and lack of knowledge and wisdom, there are so many different kinds of music, and it all belongs to God and God alone, yet God is not pleased with all music for he knows the evil which Satan uses to deceive many to worship him in music that is dirty, filthy, and full of words that distain the truth in why music was created.

Lyrics (in singular form lyric) are a set of words that accompany music, either by speaking or singing. The word *lyric* derives from the Greek word *lyrikos*, meaning "singing to the lyre"

The word *lyric* came to be used for the "words of a song." This meaning was recorded in 1829. The common plural predominates contemporary usage and used the singular song word as a "lyric."

Combination of words when spoken or sung in a musical fashion would create in the ear of the recipient the combined effect of the sound of a musical instrument in the voice and the delivery of a message in the words which would have a succinct and direct intention to evoke thought or emotion.

This is why we must be careful what we listen to as believers because the sound of music evokes actions through thought or emotion.

Music is a beautiful way to express oneself to God, yet the music in the church has become distorted and worldly because of the leadership and how its leader have chosen to allow any kind of music to be played, and this is the downfall and a great detriment to true worship in the church. The Word must be taught by and through the Holy Spirit, speaking into the minds and heart of those who choose to bring the Word, but the Word must be brought forth out of a vessel that is sent by God and not sent by Satan. Therefore, those who are singing and playing music for many churches are so busy trying to make music without hearing from the Lord. They have not been taught how to usher in the true worship of the Lord through the right sound of harmony in the music they play. It's a certain kind of sound that ushers in the true worship of God's Spirit, and it cannot be tainted by those who have unclean vessels. An unclean vessel sings praise and worship unto God in vain. The Bible speaks of these sorts of people only have praise and worship on their lips and not in their hearts. Some people go to church to let their gifts go forth, and they are doing anything and everything contrary to the Word of God before and after they sing and play church. Then these same people believe they can come to serve the Lord by singing and playing instruments, yet there is a lack of harmony in the flow of the music in many churches due to sin and unconfessed sin. Many will repent and know they can't wait to run swiftly back home or out somewhere to go to do whatever they were doing before they repented. They go and do the same thing, even text messaging right in the middle of services and taking phone calls as if God is just another person. How many musicians play music and, if you needed them to speak a word into the atmosphere to give free course to the anointing coming into the building, they would be reluctant to do so because they haven't completely repented for things that they are into and are easily able to keep to themselves because they are so busy playing music and they hardly can hear the Word. How many young people are placed in front of an instrument and have learned how to master the music but not their thoughts, actions, or conversations that bring many sinful things that interfere with them serving the Lord in righteousness to give God the praise and honor that's truly due to him? It would be good if there was a required class for musicians in the church and all choir members and those who lead worship service to take weekly to remind them of how it's necessary to praise, worship, and pray to God in the spirit of humility. Many times those who have these talents are so busy trying to learn a new song and the musicians are trying to find a gig here and there to earn a living that there is little focus on how the expressed worship to God through music must be correctly communicated for the heavens to open up and send down the anointing of his presence.

Get an understanding, and later on I will speak on this subject. The word *Sheol* is Greek for Hades and also means grave or pit. In the Scriptures, it's not always used for the meaning of hell itself. Sometimes the word *Sheol* is referring to hell but also is a place of punishment, suffering, and agony. This is why it's so important to study the context in which a passage of Scripture is used so that the Word will not be taught out of context with its meaning and the events of that day for this era. If we misinterpret the Word or allow someone else to speak into our lives a false meaning of the truth, we are accountable to God for our own souls. And if we will not study the Word, if we want the truth, we must go deeper into the mind of God through his Word on our own time. We study what we think will bring us closer to someone or something we really think we want, yet years later that desire seems to fade away and the desire to know the truth is more important than anyone or anything you think you could ever have. Never forget, heaven and earth shall pass away, but the Word of God shall stand forever. God's Word shall never, ever pass away. Therefore, in all your getting, be wise enough to get an understanding.

You Will Know Them by the Fruit That They Bear

But you want to know what nature a person has, look at the fruits they bear. The root of a tree is in the soil in which it lives. What kind of root is in the nature of the person you are allowing into your life? Is it God's seed, the root, or is there another root with another kind of seed planted down in their spirit? What is the nature you discern as they exhibit the fruit of their tree? Life in the Spirit starts with one acknowledging and being aware that their soul has a new root and has been replanted by a new nature, which is Christ Jesus. One must recognize how someone moves, lives, and in what spirit they have their being planted in. You must listen to people when you engage with them. You cannot ignore even the slightest word or phrase. Even their body language can be discerned when you are seeking to know and do what's right. Don't ignore the small talk. What you miss might be the very thing that snares you and catches you off guard. If you are watering a plant wrong, it will die. If you don't learn how to nurture a plant, it won't grow and then it will die. If you don't know what kind of plant to plant in its season, it will not blossom. Therefore, souls are people with minds that have a season to be blossomed, and you must water them right, feed them the right food (soil), and then you will see the tree blossom. This is what a soul-winner and a mind-saver does.

Corrupt communication corrupts the heart; good communication nurtures, grows, and develops the mind. Therefore, if there is not a plant that is nurtured right according to the mind of God and how we are to think Christ-like and act Christ-like, then we will not be capable of winning those who have been corrupted by those who have bad natures and corrupt fruit.

Everyone that wants to be in your life, speak into your life, and have your undivided attention is not meant to be in your life. You must choose your associates and those who are around you with caution. It's your responsibility to choose your surrounding soil wisely. Guard your heart, and the heart of God will sustain you. Plant good soil with those who choose God first so that the trees you have planted with care can flourish with those with likeness. If the tree is not bearing the fruit in which you have to offer, then you must leave the corrupt tree and its fruit and embrace that which desires to be good soil to produce good fruit. In one way or the other, you must be aware of those who are not walking with the same Spirit of God and avoid damages at all costs. Stop, and if you haven't started making up excuses for those who are not fully developed and choose not to grow, let the dead fruit alone if it's dead.

If you are a soul-winner and desire to let your mind think of good ways to save others, yet there is someone that refuses to go in the same path, if you see that they are rejecting what you live for, you have to leave them alone. It is vital to know the nature of a person, and then you will know how to win the nature of that person or leave them alone if they have a wicked and nasty nature. Some bad fruits won't even acknowledge you even if you do abide in the soil of God's Word. This is why you must keep yourself from the wickedness of those who refuse and reject the good soil in which you offer them. You have to work, go to school, do something to make a living, and you will always have someone that is around you one way or the other. But be wise and know how to adjust to your environment without being too conflicting. Be humble, kind, and gentle yet firm when necessary with care. You will be a soul-winner and a mind-saver by first saving yourself.

We are to be true believers, sincere in our hearts, following God in all reverence to him, and if a person reveals anything concerning their identity in their conversation and lifestyle that is contrary to the Bible, just don't mingle with their conversations if they are too ungodly. Don't follow after those who walk contrary to what you believe. You are to be a soul-winner and a mind-saver, and you cannot save the world, but living the life is more important in some situations and environments. If they don't appear to exemplify by faith that they believe in the only true and living God, the Father of Jesus Christ, the Son of Mary, the divine Creator of the universe, don't force your beliefs on anyone. If they inquire, then that's different.

"Every tree that bringeth not forth good fruit is hewn down, and cast into the fire. Wherefore by their fruits ye shall know them" (Matt 7:19, 20, kjv). Also see Luke 3:9, 6:43–44; John 15:16; Acts 2:30; Romans 1:13, 6:21, 22; 15:28; and Ephesians 5:9.

Don't Forget Who You Are Required to Worship

Many people who say that they are born again, saved, called, and chosen of God seem to worship the creature more than the Creator who is blessed forevermore. It seems to me that from one decade to the next, people want to be in church, have a desire to be saved, because they don't want to go to hell.

Then it's been too many times from one decade into the next that men, women, and children continually wind up in a backslidden state of mind due to the lack of studying the Bible incorrectly to no avail, with the understanding of how to actively apply the Word of God into their own lives. Many people are given the invitation to go down to the altar to receive salvation, and only a few are chosen correctly according to the Word of God because most people do not want to pick up their cross and follow Jesus Christ, the Messiah. Instead of those who think they have a call on their lives choosing to follow the teachings of Jesus Christ, they choose to follow human flesh. Many people turn away from the truth and go with the majority, choosing this way out of ignorance. These are those who are deceived out of desperation to know the will of God yet, fall into the line of obeying a duty of service for a man who stole the mission of God, turning the plan and purpose of God's will into organized religion that has stipulations, standards, formalism, and customs in which God commanded the saints to steer clear away from, avoid, eschew evil and all manner of false doctrine and teaching of devils (study: Matt. 23).

To all the saints of the most high God, don't compromise the gospel just to hold a position in a false, fake, and phony church that has false doctrine being spoken in the pulpit. Many men who made up their own doctrine by using the Bible to form a religion and an organization will try to use you for a front to cover up their evil ways. These are false teachers who have flocks yet, have founded their own established position for greed; they have their on vision and leave it for others to carry on their work. We are to carry on the work that Jesus Christ left here on earth and sent back the Holy Ghost to lead, guide, and direct us into all truth. Anything else that people choose to do other than this have formed their own agenda, religion, organization, doctrine of faith, and is a cult and a form of rebellion, which is like witchcraft, and those who carry on this are doing an abominable work that is in vain unto the Lord. He did not ask for anyone to be worshiped after they are dead and gone; then folks choose to put a dead man on their agenda to have ceremonies, to keep his dream alive. He is not the Lord of lords, but many denominations have been formed against God, making their own doctrine by stealing the Scriptures to fit into a statement of faith and a board of trustees, secretary of state, chairman of the board, etc., and they worship a idol, which is the man who formed the denomination by using the name of the Lord in vain to deceive billions of people.

Be very careful whom you worship with because you may be worship a false god who placed himself on his own throne to be worshiped; even after he is dead and gone, people take a whole day to fly here and they're faithful every year, and in every sermon they honor the wrong lord and god that has the last say over their organization. But "What did God say?" is my question.

> The elders which are among you I exhort, who am also an elder, and a witness of the sufferings of Christ, and also a partaker of the glory that shall be revealed; Feed the flock of God which is among you, taking the oversight thereof, not by constraint, but willingly; not for filthy lucre but of a ready mind; Neither as being lords over God's heritage, but being ensamples to the flock. And when the chief Shepherd shall appear, ye shall receive a crown of glory that fadeth not away.
>
> 1 Peter 5:1–4 (esv)

There is no man or woman who deserves the glory that belongs only to God. If there is a mortal man who has died and has risen from the dead to take away the sins of the world other than God, let him arise at any time. He who is born by God's power and given God's breath to breathe, once death comes to take his breath, he is dead and gone, never to return in the work that was never finished. But if some group of people chooses to gain that power, prestige, and keep the flow of his vision going, that is on them. God can resurrect the dead, God is coming back for the saints, and God sent his Son,

Jesus Christ, to die on the cross for all mankind. If God calls, can a man stop him from his time of meeting his Maker? God resurrected his Son. If this man can resurrect himself, then he must be the Lord himself. Therefore, God is not going to share his glory with any mortal, finite, simple-minded man who thinks he can be covered from the things he did that were hidden agendas behind closed doors. This statement is dedicated to the only true and living God who has reserved a day of judgment for the day of the wickedness of men, who choose to use the name of God, his Word, and anointing to build his own memorial and leave a legacy unto himself to deceive many who can't seem to grasp or perceive the truth.

Never will God give his glory to anyone. You should see that from the fall of Lucifer, the power is God's, the spirit is God, and the might of all things belongs to God. By God the Father of all things were created, and without him nothing was made. Yet the majority of his followers choose to distort the truth of the Bible. Building an organization, corporation, or religion being used by man to serve in an organization that was set up by a mortal man was never God's plan from the beginning. We have a duty to serve the Lord, only to find that once we have found our calling of service unto him, we die and go back to him to be judged. There are many who are spiritually impregnated by the true revelation knowledge of the Holy Ghost; there are those who have been given an anointing to reach the lost at any cost, yet they are in organizations that are corrupt, and they know it. Get out! You still can resign, get out, and write a book about it so that others can be set free. Following after the will of a man, the mission of a man, and the vision of a man who has his own agenda, doctrine, religion, and purpose going against the very epitome (a short statement of the main points of a book) of the Bible will cause you to self-destruct, especially if God has revealed the truth that lies behind that particular religion, organization, or man who founded it.

The devil does not have a problem with anyone who opens up his mouth to confess Jesus Christ as Lord and Savior, for the Scripture enlightens us to this fact that many confess him with their mouth and their heart is far from him. Thou believest that there is one God; thou doest well: the devils also believe, and tremble. Ja. 2:19 kjv

What makes the devil angry and swift to unleash a legion of demons is when someone gets saved and chooses to follow the only true, righteous, and holy way of God's Word. The believer's road map to lead, guide, and direct the believer by faith into the revelation knowledge that is true is only found when the Bible is rightly divided by truth. There is a reason why many people cannot find God though he is not far from them, and it's because those who don't want to go to hell, the majority, get saved and search for the truth in people. Then they're often misled to believe that they need to quickly get to work in the church, thinking it's the right thing to do, when what they really need is to search the Scriptures diligently, pressing into the Mind of God. You're not chosen to look for God through a ministry.

Through many wicked devices, the devil and his cohort of trifling demons continues to send his vicious cycle into the environment of the church through the tactics of deception and subtleness. In past generations, people did whatever they're sinful flesh desired to do, and even today folks continue to do whatever they think in their finite minds is okay to do. When we leave these old mortal bodies of sin, people will still continue to do and say whatever they choose to. Mortal men and women only choose to repeat history in their hearts that are filled with much corruption and wickedness. When will men ever learn sinful living will not void the truth that to no avail of escaping the truth, the soul that sins eventually will die? Even though there is God's judgment, commandments, statues, ordinances, thus saith the Lord, woe unto man etc., people still refuse to adhere to the truth of who God really is. As knowledge increases, evil enters into the stony hearts of men and creeps into the mind of man's perception of what they think God is saying in his Word. Instead of many people having a hunger and thirst for righteousness, they allow their flesh to control them and have a hunger and thirst to become twisted in their finite minds.

There be many who live in sin and many who claim to be saved, yet they just mean it with their mouths and their hearts are far away from the Lord. So many people have made a choice to deny Jesus Christ and denounce that he is the Son of the living God. There are people changing the Bible by adding and taking away words from the Word of God. As if the Word is easy to escape, many people are self-destructing because they have made a choice to live an unrighteous and unholy life. Let me say it this way: many are approaching their own doom and damnation from following after this sort of rebellion against God Almighty. The Word commands those who are saved to be fruitful and multiply and to replenish the earth. Instead of men obeying these words from the Bible, they choose to be fruitless in their assignment that God has foreordained, yet the fact still remains that we must be born again of the spirit to enter into the kingdom of heaven. Therefore, it is vital for all men to consider their ways and actively live holy before the Lord in the position he or she holds to win the lost and dying at any cost. It would behoove all who live upon the face of the earth to continue in him (God). Yet we find in our times from one decade into the next and throughout history that men, women, and children choose to deny the Savior of the world, Jesus Christ, the Messiah. We don't have to go far to see people who live any kind of way; it's right in our homes.

What is pleasing to God? It is pleasing to God for the redeemed of the Lord to not just say so; but it's overdue glory and honor to the only living God for the redeemed of the Lord to live in the thoughts of God and to decree and declare the works of the Lord. Jesus Christ died for the believer to have eternal life and that on this earth the believer would live by faith in his Word. God's promises are for the believer, and they are for us to receive the inheritance of our Father. We are the called, chosen, and elected children of God. We are not to take God's Word lightly or the redemption that his Son Christ

Jesus has paid the price for all to have salvation. We as believers must live by what we believe and not just say it. Don't be deceived or let any man teach you how to be phony, fake, and untruthful or cause you to stray into being a false believer, which is being a hypocrite; that is someone who says they love God with their mouth yet, deny him in works. If you are a born-again believer for the sake of God's Word, don't be a hypocrite, just as the Sadducees and the Pharisees of Christ's time. You must adhere to God's Word and believe by faith that you shall do greater works in his name.

Don't ever forget that it is vital to be a genuine believer to receive the things the Lord has freely given to you. By living in his thoughts there will be nothing impossible to you if you believe. A believer is not to become reprobate in his mind by the influences of the negative entertainment, which comes against one's mind daily through his own thoughts or the thoughts that come through those who refuse and reject our God. This is why you must be careful of what you allow into your thought pattern and be careful about who you're around that you are listening to by feeding off of them through conversations that ought not be. When you least expect it, you can be caught off guard and by a phone call or knock on the door you can be at a store, on a bus, at work, at school, walking down the street (I'm sure you get the picture) then all of a sudden, someone out of nowhere starts a conversation with you; or you can be taking a class where a teacher is atheist and in that particular class you have to intermingle with other classmates concerning the assignment given, and the conversation is geared toward a subject that is not godly; then you have the obligation of participating in order to pass the class because you may be going to school to be a nurse, doctor, lawyer, social worker etc. In this sort of environment you can eventually, with no thought of it, allow your thoughts to go wherever the assignment is taking you, for the group discussion most likely will have nothing to do with God. Then you go farther into areas that disconnect you from the ways of God.

Be careful always with what you say with your mouth at all times. I'm not saying drop a class that is required for you to go into the field that you are pursuing, but when you are in any environment that you cannot express your beliefs in, be aware of your conversation at all times and don't allow your mind and behavior to adjust and adapt to the environment. You are to control your own tongue and control yourself outward behavior by your inward confession that you know who you believe in, which is the Lord. In this life we are in the world, but we do not mimic or pattern our lives after mankind; but we are to be Christ-like at all times. Through prayer and fasting you will strengthen your inner man, never to forget that you can meditate on God's word. The Holy Spirit will strengthen you to keep you focused on the Lord. "Who is a wise man and endued with knowledge among you? Let him shew out of a good conversation his works with meekness of wisdom" (James 3:13 kjv).

Did you know that your spirit has freedom to be controlled by what you choose to think about and if you are not very careful your thoughts will drift away from the Word of God? Or you can allow your feelings of wanting to do this or that to cause your emotions to be fixated (to direct and focus the eyes on a point or object) where you find yourself always thinking this or that which has nothing to do with the mind of God. You can find yourself in an atmosphere that you cannot control by yourself when you choose to allow your feelings, emotions, and thoughts or other people's feelings, thoughts, and emotions lead you away from the things of God. Let me give you an example of how we can allow something or someone to change our mind, causing us to respond in doing something we were not even thinking of doing. You can be at home, at work, at church, at school or just running some errands and then you get a phone call or you run into an old schoolmate, an old friend you have not seen in quite some time, or maybe you run into one of your relatives that you lost contact with; then they are not saved, or maybe back then when you knew them they were. Whatever the case may be, they invite you out or over to their place or maybe you tell them it's better for them to come over to your place because you have this or that to do; you may even have to be somewhere early in the morning.

How often we are sidetracked, our lives are interrupted, and we are detoured so unexpectedly when we don't seek God for directions? Well, next thing you know you have not prayed, sought the Lord, because the enemy knows when to catch you off your guard, causing you to make a decision in haste (quickly or precipitate movement or action, as from the pressure of circumstances or intense eagerness). Without any preservations we often make rash decisions only to our detriment of saying, "What was I thinking about at that time?" "How did they catch me off guard?" or "I cannot believe this has happened to me?" These sorts of thoughts and conversations we tend to have only come when we choose not to seek the Lord but make decisions only to confuse our lives the more. If it's of God that you are doing this and you truly believe it's an innocent invitation yet, you find yourself later on down the line in more mess, farther away from the Lord and your reputation in a more sinful, condemning state because you got involved with someone and their intentions, then you're detoured away from the Lord. This can be devastating when you get involved with someone and you're not thinking of what God has to say about the decision to interact with them or not, and all of a sudden, this just happened or that just happened because you began to change your ways, gearing them toward them and what they wanted to do.

At times when you weren't thinking of ever doing this or that you were too naïve and passive to say no or at least let me pray, and many times we need to fast about this or that decision first. If it's something that is going to change your life dramatically and you may not see it while you are pressured or it could be the subtlety of some decision you make too quickly, then the snake does not show up until you have bitten the unforbidden fruit. See Genesis 3:1 kjv: "Now the serpent was more subtle than any beast of the field which the Lord God had made." Stay with this for a moment as I define the word subtle (craftiness, delicately skillful or clever, not dense or heavy; a subtle gas, marked by or requiring metal keenness; subtle reasoning, not open or direct). Listen to me carefully; learn quickly through the Word of God to be keen in the spirit. The believer is called to walk in salvation through living his or her life, hid in Christ Jesus. This means that we live in Christ through the inward man (the spirit of Jesus Christ) through the words of God. We live in his thoughts through his spirit, the Holy Spirit, which teaches us all things and he will bring all things to our remembrance, whatever it is that he has said to us.

> Can two walk together, except they be agreed?
>
> Amos 3:3 (kjv)

If you are walking together with God, you have no business walking with someone who does not agree with your God. Unless you have been given an assignment to try to help them understand the truth, you cannot be running buddies with God and running buddies with those who mock and laugh at the God you say you serve. You are owned by God; you have been purchased with a price that no other man, woman, boy, or girl could pay. There is no other excuse for being misled, deceived, or hoodwinked away from walking with the Lord, other than you made a choice without walking together with God and you did not have permission with God to do whatever you choose to do. Stop letting fables fool you, like, "Lord, if it's not your will, show me." His Word tells you his characteristics, and if you choose to do anything with anyone that does not exemplify the characteristics of the Lord, then it's not his will. He does not have to show you anything. His Word is close to you and tells you what you are to do and how you are to live and what you need to continue in until he returns.

Agreement means the act or fact of agreeing, or of being in harmony or accord, an understanding or an arrangement between two or more people. Based on what the definition of this word is, then you must at all times make sure beyond a doubt that the Father, Son, and the Holy Spirit is agreeing with you as you walk together with them, and you can only be accepted by faith in your works when you are agreeing with the Word of the Lord. The Word is not given to you for it to agree with you; you must agree with the Word and line up with its truths. In other words, when you came into covenant with God, you were placed in harmony with him through you making the right decisions daily to stay in harmony, with understanding the fact that you cannot walk with anyone who is not walking in agreement with the Word of God. You are to be committed to the fact that you are saved and you have made a covenant with God by confessing Jesus Christ as your Lord and Savior. Now from this day forward or whenever you made your confession of faith, you are to walk with him and agree to do exactly what he tells you to do. I've seen it often in the church where church folks always have to find their way into someone else's business and tell you that you ought to marry this one, be with that one, do this or that. Yet if you watch their lives closely, you will find that they don't know how to handle their own household, nor have they truly committed themselves to walking in agreement with the Word of God. Therefore, it is mandatory for you to continue to walk with him and remember you must walk with God, not God walking with you. The difference in you walking with God is that you follow him through obeying his Word and you have to choose every day to allow the Holy Spirit to lead, guide, and direct you into all truth. You cannot lead God anywhere because you are the creature and God is the creator of all things. Whatever you need to know about this new relationship, you have made a commitment to God. Then you can know it in God, but don't be foolish and think you can do it without God's hand upon your life. Every day you can have a new, renewed, and refreshed relationship with the Lord because his mercies are new every day!

But the Comforter, which is the Holy Ghost, whom the Father will send in my name, he shall teach you all things, and bring all things to your remembrance, whatsoever I have said unto you

John. 14:26 (kjv)

Howbeit when he, the spirit of truth, is come, he will guide you into all truth: for he shall not speak of himself; but whatsoever he shall hear, that shall he speak: and he will shew you things to come. He shall glorify me: for he shall receive of mine, and shall shew it unto you.

John 16:13–14 (kjv)

The Holy Ghost teaches us all things and brings all things to our remembrance, only if we have studied God's Word. You cannot remember or be familiar with anything or anyone until you spend quality time with them. You have to spend quality time with someone, and after so long of getting acquainted with a person, you can do things for them based on your knowledge of them concerning their likes and dislikes. You have to be willing to know God's Word and study his ways; then the Holy Spirit can operate through your willingness to do God's will. If you have a personal relationship with God and keep yourself intimately inclined to his commandments, statutes, and truth that are found in God's Word, it's only then that God's Spirit can do his job through you. It's solely up to you to make up in your mind that right now you must declare these words and say, "I am saved and my life belongs to God and I must pursue after Christ Jesus and be diligent to seek him daily and pursue to do God's will." Now that you have come into the family of God, you also must declare and decree that, "God's way is the only way, and all other people, places and things will not have preeminence over his will for my life. Always remember, you must be a genuine believer in order for him to get all the glory out of my life." You must be a doer of the Word and not a hearer only because if you are just a hearer of the Word and not a doer, you only deceive yourself.

> But be ye doers of the word, and not hearers only, deceiving your own selves.For if any be a hearer of the word, and not a doer, he is like unto a man beholding his natural face in a glass. For he beholdeth himself, and goeth his way, and straightway forgetteth what manner of man he was. But whoso looketh into the perfect law of liberty, and continueth therein, he being not a forgetful hearer, but a doer of the work, this man shall be blessed in his deed.
>
> James 1:22–25 (kjv)

For when you get acquainted with the scriptures through understanding the text, the history, and why it was written, who it was written to, and how to apply the Scriptures in the text to your life today, this is how you get acquainted with God and are equipped to walk in his mind because the Word is God's Spirit; not with ink, but with the Spirit of the living God. The Word is written to us to be placed in our hearts because our sufficiency comes in the fellowship we have with God in his Word and not from ourselves. Therefore, like Christ, you too can become a living epistle to others by sharing this living Word, which comes through understanding the Word of God.

Paul said it this way in 2 Corinthians 3:1–6,

> Do we begin again to commend ourselves? Or need we, as some others, epistles of commendation to you, or letters of commendation from you? Ye are our epistle written in our hearts, known and read of all men: Forasmuch as ye are manifestly declared to be the epistle of Christ ministered by us, written not with ink, but with the Spirit of the living God; not in tables of stone, but in fleshy tables of the heart. And such trust have we through Christ to God-ward: Not that we are sufficient of ourselves to think any thing as of ourselves; but our sufficiency is of God: Who also hath made us able

ministers of the new testament; not of the letter, but of the spirit: for the letter killeth, but the spirit giveth life.

We see in these verses that Paul is addressing a problem in those days of the church being seriously divided. Just as they were saved, they were yet in a carnal state because they were new to the faith. Just like some children when they are not taught how to behave tend to be silly, gravitating toward everything that is against the right that you try so hard to enforce in their minds, as soon as you turn your back they start gossiping, murmuring, and complaining, stirring up mess. The Corinthians were immature and not walking in the Spirit but saved and still choosing to walk after the flesh, not in the deep where God can flow. The carnal man is known by his conversation and actions and when you correct someone in making it clear that they ought not do this or that or say this or that, if they are mature they will humble themselves and grow gracefully in the Lord. If they are immature like the Corinthian church, they will murmur, complain, and talk about you for trying to correct their old nasty, evil, gossiping ways. You have to do what pleases God and not man. If you got saved for the right reasons, then you will grow off of milk, carnality, and come into the wisdom and the knowledge of Jesus Christ so that he can use you to help others to grow and be a help to others and not a hindrance to many.

The Corinthian church were divided due to having too much favoritism for one minister over the other: Peter, Paul, and Apollos; these were the three men whom the Corinthian church chose to focus on instead of the Word of God, which came out of the mouths of these men as God used them individually and collectively to bring the word of life. Some like this one and others like that one. Just as in today's society, this has and still will be an issue from one decade into the next. People like one minister over another because one particular message that may have brought them to the Lord, or another minister may have prayed the prayer of healing for a lost family member and they were healed and are now saved, or maybe it was the minister who held on the longest when someone was falling deeper into sin and that particular minister was highly favored to them for bringing them back into a closer relationship with the Lord. Whatever the situation may be, it happens and will continue to be like this because people are that way and go through their life picking and choosing not just a favorite minister but family member, coworker, boss, teacher etc. It's not right in relation to being saved, but it will take people recognizing that God uses whom he chooses, and you as an individual cannot be focused on looking to favor any man or woman; but your goal is to keep your eyes on Jesus and not emphasize one servant over another to cause division.

This is what the Corinthian church chose to do with their time instead of taking something positive from each minister. Instead they chose to be critical and judgmental through having favorite ministers, wanting to hear this one but not that one. This began to form all sorts of cliques, and if you aren't careful, you can to form an opinion too quickly of someone and miss what God is trying to say through them that might have helped you get out of your mess. Don't cause disruption by discussing who you think is more powerful, anointed, and can really rear back and give the congregation a word. Don't be a gossiper talking too much about this or that in a conversation that you don't start or get into with others. Be careful because your day may come and you may have to be the one talked about for the worst. You need to remember that a minister is a servant of the only God, and Paul tells us that they are instruments of God. They are not yours to worship, but God is to be worshiped and praised for using someone to help you in the time of need and to help you get right and stay right with God so that you too can be about your Father's business. This is another problem that the enemy uses in getting your attention away from loving God and walking in his characteristic.

You cannot please God in the flesh at the same time or hear from God when you are fleshy and carnal in your thinking and conversation. Warning: if you or someone you know is not spiritually mature, he or she is a babe in Christ Jesus. I don't care if they have been saved for years, decades, or even centuries, but watch what they say and be careful always and pray because the spirit of carnality is always looking and lurking for a body to dwell in. Remember, without a body, the spirit of the devil cannot operate in your thoughts to make you act out what he puts before your mind. Think like God's mind and do as God's Word tells you to, keeping yourself away from those who pretend to be something but are misusing the name of God for a show and a performance. Don't let people speak their dirty, foolish, and ignorant thoughts on you to use you as a prey by hindering you from getting from God the plan and purpose of your destiny.

But we have a new life that is hidden in Christ Jesus, and remember we will see him one day face-to-face when we leave these old mortal bodies. We shall be changed in a moment and in a twinkling of the eye changed from mortal into immortality. Hallelujah!

> Behold, I shew you a mystery, We shall not all sleep, but we shall all be changed. In a moment, in the twinkling of an eye, at the last triumph: for the trumpet shall sound, and the dead shall be raised incorruptible, and we shall be changed. For this corruptible must put on incorruption, and this mortal must put on immortality. 54. So when this corruptible shall have put on incorruptible shall have put on incorruption, and this mortal shall have put on immortality, then shall be brought to pass the saying that is written, Death is swallowed up in victory. O death, where is thy sting? O grave, where is thy victory?
>
> 1 Corinthians 15: 51–55 (kjv)

The Bible is a mystery that is revealed to those who are born again and have received the free gift of God's Spirit (Holy Spirit), but for the unbeliever and those who choose to live in unrighteousness, it will remain a mystery. If you want to live forever and receive this eternal life that is found in Jesus Christ, you must be born again.

But if the Spirit of him that raised up Jesus from the dead dwell in you, he that raised up Christ from the dead shall also quicken (revive) your mortal bodies by his Spirit that dwelleth in you. Therefore, brethren, we are debtors, not to the flesh, to live after the flesh. For if ye live after the flesh, ye shall die: but if ye through the Spirit do mortify (kill, destroy, self-denial or self control of your body) the deeds of the body, ye shall live. For as many as are led by the Spirit of God, they are the sons of God.

Romans 8:11–13 (kjv)

You only obtain eternal life through salvation, and then after salvation, you must daily mortify (kill), destroy your flesh to have control over your desires; it's up to you to choose to have self-control by denying ungodly and worldly pleasures that only destroy you. You can only have son ship by being led by the spirit (Holy Spirit) of God. Then you can be a son or daughter to the Lord of the universe, for he is the creator of all and all things. Don't think that you can conduct yourself any kind of way after you are born again and obtain son ship. The Scriptures say that as many as are led by the Spirit of God, they are the sons of God. You are not called into Christ to live after the flesh but after his spirit.

Remember, it is through the mind of God only that we can receive his power, and when you walk in his thoughts, follow after his ways, and live, breathe and move in his righteousness, then you can do the works of him that sent you. Remember, he is all powerful, all knowing, omnipresent, and omnipotent, and you can only obtain his power when you live according to his Word.

The Day of Judgment

Judgment of the Goats

Are you ready to meet the Lord of lords and the King of kings? The Son of Man is coming to judge and he is coming in his glory with his angels to be enthroned and to gather all nations; to separate the sheep from the goats. Right now Christ sits on the throne at the right hand of God. The throne of grace is where we come for help from God for he is making intersession for the saints according to his will.

> For we do not have a high priest who is unable to sympathize with our weaknesses, but one who in every respect has been tempted as we are, yet without sin. Let us then with confidence draw near to the throne of grace, that we may receive mercy and find grace to help in time of need.
>
> He. 4:15 15 esv

Christ throne of judgment is when he judges mankind for the life in which he lived upon the face of the earth. He will judge those who are dead and those who are alive. All of mankind, will come before his throne to be judged. (1 Pe. 4:5, 6)

> Then he will say to those on his left "Depart from me, you cursed, into the eternal fire prepared for the devil and his angels. For I was hungry and you gave me no food. I was thirsty and you gave me no drink, I was a stranger and you did not welcome me, naked and you did not clothed me, sick and in prison and you did not visit me. Then they also will answer, saying, "Lord, when did we see you hungry or thirsty or a stranger or naked or sick or in prison, and did not minister to you? Then he will answer them, saying, "Truly, I say to you, as you did not do it to one of the least of these, you did not do it to me." And these will go away into eternal punishment, but the righteous into eternal life.
>
> Matthew 25:41–46 (esv)

Have you ever heard someone speak of a twofold event? This means there is two parts to the occasion or event. On the Day of Judgment the word says that, Christ will say to the (goats), on the left hand, depart from me, you cursed, into the eternal fire prepared for the devil and his angels. These will be separated from God and cut off from him eternally. Those on the left hand will be sent into outer darkness. This sounds like a lot of misery and anguish. Those who rejected turned away and refused to receive Christ Jesus as their Lord and Savior will be punished and sent to a world of weeping, wailing, crying and gnashing of teeth. In St. Mark 9:46; this place is described like this: Where their worm dieth not, and the fire is not quenched. When they stand before him they will be known for not wanting to associate themselves with Christ, while they lived upon the face of the earth. These individuals did not choose to be called "brothers," or "sisters," and chose not to inherit the kingdom of God.

Therefore, Christ calls them, "cursed." For those who Christ calls, "cursed," will inherit the curse.

> For all who rely on works of the law are under a curse; for it is written, "Cursed be everyone who does not abide by all things written in the Book of the Law, and do them."
>
> Ga. 3:10 esv

When I am given the opportunity to share the free gift of salvation with someone and if that person is reluctant and it's evident that they don't want to hear of the truth of the gospel; I tell someone that is ignorant and refusing to hear the truth these words: I would rather by faith receive Christ as my Lord and Savior than to reject him and not have a chance to the eternal life in which God gives freely. I believe there is a better chance of receiving him alive than to reject him altogether and not have the opportunity once my life ends. Our life will one day be all over and once we take our last breath and it's too late to come back and repent after death has set in and the body has separated from the soul and the spirit goes back to the Lord that giveth it; it's all over and then our soul waits for the Day of Judgment.

> Then shall the dust return to the earth as it was: and the spirit shall return unto God who gave it.
>
> Ecc. 12:7 kjv

The book of Ec. 12:13 and 14 it's written:

> Let us hear the conclusion of the whole matter: Fear God, and keep his commandments: for this is the whole duty of man. For God shall bring every work into judgment, with every secret thing, whether it be good, or whether it be evil.
>
> If many would learn to fear the Lord and keep his commandments which is the whole duty of man while he or she is upon the face of the earth, then hell wouldn't have

to enlarge itself but; because of the iniquity of mankind the scripture lets us know that hell has enlarged itself.

Woe unto them that rise up early in the morning, that they may follow strong drink; that continue until night, till wine inflame them! And the harp, and the viol, the tabret, and pipe, and wine, are in their feasts: but they regard not the work of the Lord, neither consider the operation of his hands. Therefore my people are gone into captivity, because they have no knowledge: and their honourable men are famished, and their multitude dried up with thirst. Therefore hell hath enlarged herself, and opened her mouth without measure: and their glory, and their multitude, and their pomp, and he that rejoiceth, shall descend into it.

Is. 5: 11–14 (KJV)

Those who are goats live very selfish lives. They do not minister to anyone and live a life unto themselves. They refuse and will not help the hungry, thirsty, stranger, the naked, the sick and the prisoner. These are people who will not get involved in helping anyone nor do they try to meet the needs of those who are less fortunate. Goats don't seem to have a desire to help those who are just at the time down and out. A goat will ignore and not help the poor, broken and destitute because of their own greed to get wealth and they have selfish ways. A goat, has no concern or care other than themselves and lives a life of material gain, pleasure, have plenty of money and more than enough houses and land. A goat is one who just refuses to see the needs of God's people and will not open their eyes or ears to listen and see the needy.

On the Day of Judgment, the goats are judged to depart and go away from Christ to spend their eternity with the devil and his angels. Goats are those who should have done what they knew to do but, did not do it. And they will be condemned for what they should have done but refused to do it. Their sin is that they neglected to see the need in people and they left many suffering that they could have helped, but refused to help them.

Who are the Brethren?

> And he shall set the sheep on his right hand, but the goats on the left. Then shall the King say unto them on his right hand, Come, ye blessed of my Father, inherit the kingdom prepared for you from the foundation of the world: For I was an hungered, and ye gave me meat: I was thirsty, and ye gave me drink: I was a stranger, and ye took me in: Naked, and ye clothed me: I was in prison, and ye came unto me. Then shall the righteous answer him saying, Lord when saw we thee an hungered, and fed thee? Or thirsty, and gave thee drink? When saw we thee a stranger, and took thee in? or naked, and clothed thee? Or when saw we thee sick, or in prison, and came unto thee? And the King shall answer and say unto them, Verily I say unto you, Inasmuch as ye have done it unto one of the least of these my brethren, ye have done it unto me.

Matt. 25:33–40 (KJV)

Christ has always had an order for all things. He is very orderly with what he does and says. When he uses the word brethren, He is talking about, his disciples. The disciples in which Christ is describing in this text are his offspring, descendents. Therefore, let's look at the text and read it this way. So as much as you have done it to one of the least of those who are Christ offspring or descendents; you have clothed, fed, sheltered, gave a drink and visited the prisoner; who is the offspring or descendents of Christ.

Judgment before the Great White Throne

> And the devil that deceived them was cast into the lake of fire and brimstone, where the beast and the false prophet are, and shall be tormented day and night for ever and ever.

And I saw a great white throne, and him that sat on it, from whose face the earth and the heaven fled away; and there was found no place for them. And I saw the dead, small and great, stand before God; and the books were opened: and another book was opened, which is the book of life: and the dead were judged out of those things which were written in the books, according to their works. And the sea gave up the dead which were in it; and death and hell delivered up the dead which were in them: and they were judged every man according to their works. And death and hell were cast into the lake of fire. This is the second death. And whosoever was not found written in the book of life was cast into the lake of fire.

Re. 20:10–15 kjv

The fire of hell was prepared for the devil and his angels but, many goats who neglected and refused to help other's who where God's offspring and his descendents made a choice to be condemned and chose the eternal separation from God willingly.

To those who are born again, if you choose to not do what God tells you to do or designed you to do than that's when you are living a life of selfishness. You are held accountable to fear God and live by his commandments and if you confess him with your mouth yet, live a hypocritical life, you're a goat too and will go to hell just like the goats who are selfish. Why? You say you are born again yet, you choose to go in your own way and live a selfish and greedy life. If you have things you don't use and can't give them to the needy you are self-righteous and very greedy therefore, you have placed your will above God's and you are a goat dressed in sheep's clothing. Get right or get told by God on Judgment Day, depart from me you worker of iniquity.

The Substance Abusers and Such Like Things

Just like in the days of Isaiah, as is today, people are filled with addictions like; alcohol and all sorts of drugs, they arise early in the morning to party late at night. Drink and do drugs all day. Yes, we live in a time where people party hard and listen to all sorts of seductive music and live immoral lives, they call it today living it up! The "woe," God issues is a warning to watch out! Be careful! This text covers all substance abusers who habitually have a alcoholic condition or any sort of drug addiction. It's clear that heavy drinking was going on in the days of Isaiah. As we see here, the people where too busy, having a social good time that, they forgot about fearing the Lord and keeping his commandments. These people where warned by God that if they did not get right with God, they would be spewed out of his mouth and driven away from their home land, they would be led away into captivity and exiled, this was due to them not knowing God by rejecting him. As we see in verse 12; the latter part of the scripture says, "But they regard not the work of the Lord, neither consider the operation of his hands." We see this today and many live as though God does not exist and are blind to the fact of the word and its truth. People choose to reject the truth and go in their own sinful ways.

Even though God said that the land would not have a sufficient supply of food and water. The addict often denies himself or herself food, water and health because they have an addiction. The word tells us that those who choose to live this kind of lifestyle will suffer judgment and death. It's evident if someone has these kind of addictions that they are killing themselves and shortening their days upon the earth. Sin shortens the human life and our days vanish at a faster rate for the weight of sin. And whether someone is addicted to drugs, alcohol, sex, fornication, adultery and other sins of this sort as the scripture let's us know they will die the death of sin.

For the wages of sin is death; but the gift of God is eternal life through Jesus Christ our Lord.

Ro. 6:23 kjv

The word warns us to, "watch our selves" lest the day of the Lord come and our hearts are weighed down with excessive drinking and living it up, so to say. Turn with me to; Luke 21:34–36.

> But watch yourselves lest your hearts be weighed down with dissipation and drunkenness and cares of this life, and that day come upon you suddenly like a trap. For it will come upon all who dwell on the face of the whole earth. But stay awake at all times, praying that you may have strength to escape all these things that are going to take place and to stand before the Son of Man.
>
> Jn. 5:26, 27 and 6:53

When the word says, "to stay awake" that means to watch and pray being aware of the time and season that we are in.

Judgment is coming, and for those who are not ready, it is inevitable for all to get ready and stay ready by being alert to the signs of the time and wake up from your slumbering sleep. If you know you are living any kind of way, "Stop!" Don't live on this earth and think for one second that, you can live any kind of way; Judgement Day is coming and it cannot be avoided or escaped!

The Goats

Selfish people who refuse to help others are not going to make it into heaven. The bible describes the nature of a goat. The bible clearly explains what not to do that is sin and what to do that is righteousness. If you are not doing what he created you to do then, stop the non-sense and do what is right and you too can have eternal life.

> Pure religion and undefiled before God and the Father is this, To visit the fatherless and widows in their affliction, and to keep himself unspotted from the world.
>
> Ja 1:27 kjv

Jesus said unto him, If thou wilt be perfect, go and sell that thou hast, and give to the poor, and thou shalt have treasure in heaven: and come and follow me.

Mt 19:21 kjv

I was a stranger, and ye took me not in: naked, and ye clothed me not: sick, and in prison, and ye visited me not.

Mt. 25:43

But whoso hath this world's good, and seeth his brother have need, and shutteth up his bowels of compassion from him, how dwelleth the love of God in him?

I Jn. 3:17

Offences

If anyone offends a believer, God said it is better for that a millstone were hanged about his neck. Be careful not to offend or there is the wrath of God to come.

And whosoever shall offend one of these little ones that believe in me, it is better for him that a millstone were hanged about his neck, and he were cast into the sea.

Mk 9:42 kjv

Him that is weak in the faith receive ye, but not to doubtful disputations.

Ro. 14:1 kjv

Do not judge those who are doubtful in thought but help them. We then that are strong ought to bear the infirmities of the weak, and not to please ourselves. Let everyone of us please his neighbour for his good to edification for even Christ pleased not himself; but, as it is written, The reproaches of them that reproached thee fell on me. For whatsoever things were written afortime were written for our learning, that we through patience and comfort of the scriptures might have hope. Now the God of patience and consolation grant you to be likeminded one toward another according to Christ Jesus: That ye may with one mind and one mouth glorify God, even the Father of our Lord Jesus Christ.

Ro. 15:1–7 kjv

The Sheep on the Right

The second event of the Day of Judgment is when, God tells the sheep to go to the right and invites them to inherit the kingdom of everlasting life. To the Sheep, Christ Said, "Come."

When the Son of man shall come in his glory, and all the holy angels with him, then shall he sit upon the throne of his glory: And before him shall be gathered all nations: and he shall separate them one from another, as a shepherd divideth his sheep from the goats: and He shall set the sheep on his right hand, but the goats on the left. Then shall the King say unto them on his right hand, Come, ye blessed of my Father, inherit the kingdom prepared for you from the foundation of the world:

Matt. 25:31–34

There is No Escaping the Day of Judgment

There is not one person on the earth who can escape the Day of Judgment. Every one who has lived from one generation to the next generation will have had the chance to receive or reject God. One day we will die, and there is a place where we will be in heaven (unbeliever's day: see 1 Co. 6:9, 10). The saint will be gone, don't miss the first resurrection see: (Jn. 5:28, 29; Ac. 24:15; 1 Co. 15:23; 1 Th. 4:13, 14; 2 Tim. 2:8; Re. 20:5,6). Then on the day we are called before God to the judgment seat, God will show us the time and the place that we had the opportunity to hear the gospel. The judgment seat is the time when God will judge us individually (we all will answer to God for how we spent our time on this earth). Every person who understands right from wrong, good from evil, righteousness from unrighteousness becomes accountable for his or her own soul, for what they have done with the time that God gave them on this earth. Just think back to what is written on a tombstone for example: (John Doe 1934–2004). The space between the date we are born until the date we expire is the time we have to accept Christ Jesus as our Lord and Savior and to complete the work that all mankind has been given individually, to serve God according to his will for our life.

Those who are not mentally capable of having the faculties to make the right decisions for their life, God created them, and he will make the final decision for everyone's lives individually. He knows the hearts and minds of all mankind. Even children who are capable of picking up the Bible or learning the Word through research, the library, Internet will be judged. Remember, God is the last and final judge of those he has created. Some call this the age of accountability where one is responsible for his or her own sins. It depends on the situation, and only God truly can judge people and their motives for why they acted or behaved in the manner they did while they were upon the earth.

Paul wrote it in these words: "For we must all appear before the judgment seat of Christ that every one may receive the things done in his body, according to that he hath done, whether it be good or bad" (2 Corinthians 5:10, kjv).

No one is exempt from going to the judgment seat to be judged by the Lord of lords and King of kings. Those who have been born with a defect, handicapped, or born with an illness that causes them not to be able to function according to how God intended for them to function are not responsible for their sins. The judgment seat applies to all who understand clearly what is right and wrong. If you want to dare to differ with me, search the Scriptures for yourself, and maybe you can write another book and give your belief to what you think about the statement I just wrote. I have read at least one book or met at least one person I agreed to disagree with on a certain topic or point they made. Even though we mean well, it's more important to know the truth. Many mean well, but it's more important to know and understand what God has to say about all things. Just as I have spoken from my heart, don't judge me by one disagreement you may have, for I have spoken as I have been lead.

Just like we have those who we know truly have a disability, as humans we deal with them according to the knowledge that we have concerning them from a specialist or a doctor that is educated in that field. You must realize that there is an age of accountability. God knows this, for he is an all-knowing God. You will be responsible for your sins in this life, and then once you die, if you are unrighteous, then your spirit will go to Sheol (Hades)—a prison, holding place that the unrighteous go at the moment of death. Hell (Hades, Sheol) is a holding cell for unbelievers until their final day of judgment. (the unbeliever will experience torment in Hades; it is a place where unbelievers are conscious and suffer torment.) The scripture says, And in hell he (the rich man) lift up his eyes, being in torments, and seeth (study: Lu. 16:20-31). Note: those who did not make it on the day in which Jesus comes to reign with the saints and his angels upon the earth will not be reigning on earth for the thousand-year millennium. They will have to go through being on earth and receive or reject the mark of the beast. See: (Re. chapter 13, and chapter 14:8-20). Then at the Great White Throne: Re. 20:14; the scripture states that, hell (Hades, Sheol) is a place that holds the unrighteous condemned sinner, in Re. 20:13, sinners who died and went to hell (Hades, Sheol a place of torment, this is a place that is distinct from the lake of fire) at the second death (Re. 20:11-15). All sinners who died before the judgment and are in Hades, they are thrown into the lake of fire. (study: Matt. 23:33 also; 24:51, 2 Pe. 2: 4,9 also; 3:7, Ro. 2:8, 2 The. 1:9, He. 2:2, 3. You want to be ready when Jesus returns or you die, whichever may come first. You must be ready for the Lord return. I pray you will be.

In the book of 1 Peter 3:17–20 (kjv), the scripture says this:

> For it is better, if they will of God be so, that ye suffer for well doing, than for evil doing. For Christ also hath once suffered for sins, the just for the unjust, that he might bring us to God, being put to death in the flesh, but quickened by the Spirit: By which also he went and preached unto the spirits in prison; Which sometime were disobedient, when once the long suffering of God waited in the days of Noah, while the ark was a preparing, wherein few, that is, eight souls where saved by water.

As we see in the nineteenth verse, Jesus went and preached to the spirits in prison.

On the day you are in the judgment seat, you must realize now that your judgment is set once you take your last breath. Then when it's time, you have an appointment with God that no man can give an account to God for but you—it will be you and God. But God knows our heart and he knows the thoughts of our minds. This is why he is the only one who will judge all and pronounce where each one of us will spend eternity. Now, we have many people who pretend to be disabled and are not. They will be judged according to their ways and how they made the choice to pretend to be mentally or physically handicapped. God has a day of judgment for all, and he created man to glorify him in truth; therefore if someone chooses to reject God after they have known the truth and still choose to pretend to be mentally or physically handicapped, God is not slack concerning what he says he will do. God does not have sympathy for those who play with him and refuse to adhere to his Word. God's Word lets all know that the gospel must be preached in the entire world as a witness to all nations, and then shall the end come. If someone ignores, avoids, and wastes their time away doing nothing to prepare themselves for that great day, the truth still is the truth that everyone (the whole world) will be judged according to God's Word. This is why God's Spirit speaks to us daily because, he came to seek and to save that which was lost. "For the Son of man is come to seek and to save that which was lost" (Luke 19:10, kjv).

One thing about God is that God has patience with all to give everyone from the smallest to the greatest an opportunity to know him. From the educated to the uneducated, even if someone thinks what is being said is too elementary for them, God's will is for all to know him, and this is important in how the writer relates to the reader, making sure that words are used to reach all. I would that you pray and we end this chapter in a closing prayer that this book will wake those who are asleep to knowing the truth to wake up, get right, and serve the Lord with gladness.

Lord Jesus, I come to you to say thank you, thank you for those who have taken the time to read what was written in this book. Lord, I pray that something was said to change someone's mind and that they have found the truth in the scriptures that where used in this book. Let these words penetrate the hearts and minds of your people. Father, touch each letter, word, sentence, and example that it will illuminate the reader to be enlightened and quickened in there spirit. May the reader have a desire to change his or her ways into becoming more like you. Oh Lord, I ask that the sinner repent, the backslider come back to you and that the atheist will turn and be convinced that, you are God and there is no other God besides you. I pray that those who need to grow closer to you and understand what they are called to do on this earth, will surrender all to you and serve you with all their heart, mind, and soul. I come against the enemy that would try to cause confusion and every evil work. I speak deliverance and peace to your people and pray that the flesh will get no glory out of your life anymore. I come against the tactics and strategies of the world and the systematic teachings of false doctrine. These things I pray in the name of Jesus. Amen.

Bibliography

The Thompson Chain-Reference Study kjv Bible: Kirkbride, 1988.

The Holy Bible English Standard Version: Crossway, Bibles. Good News Publishers, 2001

Merriam-Webster's Collegiate Dictionary, Eleventh Edition, Encyclopedia Britannica Company, 2003

The Preacher's Outline & Sermon Bible, kjv: Volumes 1–13

Dictionary.com

listen|imagine|view|experience